THE WILLOW WAND

SIR DEREK BIRLEY IS ALSO THE AUTHOR OF A SOCIAL HISTORY OF ENGLISH
CRICKET, WHICH WON THE 1999 WILLIAM HILL AWARD FOR SPORTS BOOK OF
ſHE YEAR, AND THE CRICKET SOCIETY'S BOOK OF THE YEAR AWARD. HE ALSO
WROTE THE TRILOGY SPORT AND THE MAKING OF BRITAIN, WHICH WON THE
ıTISH SOCIETY OF SPORTS HISTORY'S ABERDARE LITERARY AWARD IN 1995. HE
ETIRED AS VICE-CHANCELLOR OF THE UNIVERSITY OF ULSTER IN 1991 AFTER A
DISTINGUISHED CAREER AS AN EDUCATIONAL ADMINISTRATOR,
AND NOW LIVES IN CORNWALL.

'eresy his book certainly is, from first page to last, but its enormous
st engths are the indefatigable research, the moderation of the language, the
frequent wit, and, above all, Birley's transparent love of the game'
– Ian Wooldridge

ıe appearance of a completely fresh and unpredictable cricket book is a
ſe event . . . Such a searching and well-researched examination of feudal,
tocratic, righteous, hypocritical – as well as non-critical – attitudes and
ons of the game's administrators, as could have been utterly scathing but
ır its undertones of affection, leavening of humour, and gossipy manner'
– John Arlott, *Wisden Cricket Monthly*

'Rips through the veil put up by orthodox cricket history . . . a veritable
tour de force' – *Time Out*

The Willow Wand

Some Cricket Myths Explored

Derek Birley

AURUM PRESS

This second revised edition first published in Great Britain 2000 by Aurum Press Ltd
25 Bedford Avenue, London WC1B 3AT

First published in the Wisden Cricket Library 1979
Reissued in a revised edition by Sportspages/Simon and Schuster 1989

A catalogue record for this book is available from the British Library.

ISBN 1 85410 729 1

1 3 5 7 9 10 8 6 4 2
2001 2003 2002 2000 2004

Design by Roger Hammond
Set in 11/14 Janson Text by M Rules
Printed and bound in Great Britain by
MPG Books Ltd, Bodmin

Thank God who made the British Isles
And taught me how to play,
I do not worship crocodiles,
Or bow the knee to clay!
Give me a willow wand and I
With hide and cork and twine
From century to century
Will gambol round my shrine!

Rudyard Kipling, Verses on Games, *1898*

CONTENTS

ACKNOWLEDGEMENTS

IT WOULD BE IMPOSSIBLE to thank individually all those with whom I have played, watched and argued about cricket over the years, but many friends and colleagues will recognise their contributions to this book. Even the most superficial glance will show the enormous debt I owe to scores of writers, ancient and modern – for their insight and idiosyncrasies, scholarship and polemics, humour and humanity. I have quoted freely from them. In particular I am grateful for permission to quote from material in which copyright is held. I have tried to indicate all sources, and in the notes and references section details are given of publishers, authors and dates of works from which quotations are taken or to which reference is made.

One book which is not listed I should like to mention here: *The Cricket Addict's Archive*, edited by Benny Green (Elm Tree Books, 1977). This admirable anthology lifted my flagging spirits at a critical time, introduced me to Marvin Cohen, reminded me of the Sun Clan tribe and confirmed a vague suspicion about H. M. Hyndman.

My grateful thanks are due to Brian Baggett, Librarian of Ulster Polytechnic, and his colleagues, for their patience and ingenuity in securing books and information from many sources.

Words are inadequate to convey my thanks to Mrs Sarah Faulkner, Sadie, for her devoted work in deciphering my scribbles, impenetrable to most. Initially knowing nothing of cricket she rapidly reached the stage of not wanting to know more, but her dedication was unshaken.

INTRODUCTION

CRICKET, OF JUVENILE AND rustic origin, had already become an organised adult game since by the time of the Civil Wars. It became fashionable after the Restoration under the sponsorship of powerful aristocratic patrons. Gentlemen played the game themselves, but they also hired the lower orders to play for them. Their purpose was gambling as well as sport, and huge sums of money were soon changing hands. Local entrepreneurs, notably inn-keepers, also made cricket into a commercially successful spectator sport.

By the later eighteenth century control of this fashionable and profitable new leisure activity was in the hands of a number of gentlemen's clubs. By the nineteenth century these had evolved into county organisations which, led by the Marylebone Cricket Club, subsequently dominated English cricket. Their influence spread throughout the British Empire and survived the transition to the Commonwealth. Though they became, over the years, increasingly dependent on income from the turnstiles, MCC and its associates still preserved many of the attitudes of the old patrons.

Then in 1977 a new patron arose, an Australian magnate who decided to stage his own brand of super-cricket. In a matter of months, following his failure to secure exclusive television rights for a Test series, Mr Kerry Packer had set up an organisation which lured some fifty of the world's best cricketers away from their traditional allegiances to play for fat salaries and spectacular prizes as a rival attraction to the official Tests between Australia and India.

The West Indians turned out – initially, at least – to be the best super-cricketers. At the farewell party marking the end of the first season of Packer cricket the manager of the victorious team presented his host with a voodoo doll. It had, he said, been useful in overcoming the West Indians' opponents; now Mr Packer might like to try it on his own enemies. Packer could certainly have found plenty of targets. Notable amongst them would have been the Australian Board of Control, who regarded him as a moral and social outcast, and the Test and County Cricket Board in England, who had lost not only their pride but also a lot of money in contesting, unsuccessfully, an action against them for attempting to ban the renegades from orthodox games.

Mr Packer seemed more likely to rely on dollars than on voodoo to overcome the opposition. He had poured millions of them into his new venture, introducing floodlighting, special pitches and all the paraphernalia of a television spectacular including fake crowd noises. Soon there were rumours of other groups being set up in England and elsewhere. It seemed only a matter of time before a world series would take place in which paid gladiators battled it out on their patrons' behalf. So this startling modern innovation threatened to turn the clock back to the eighteenth century when the Duke of Dorset and Sir Horace Mann bought up the best available talent, issued challenges and put forward teams to joust on their behalf.

The Packer onslaught was the biggest threat the cricket establishment had faced since the middle of the nineteenth century when several teams of professionals toured England as a rival attraction to the early, somewhat desultory, contests between county teams. These players wanted to make more money by breaking away from their dismal and precarious conditions of employment. This they had in common with the twentieth-century Packer men, but there was an interesting difference. Though William Clarke, the first leader of the most famous of these teams, was paymaster to his fellow-players, he was in no sense their patron. He was their captain and manager, a player amongst players. Kerry Packer, on the other hand, offered a new-style patronage, in which the patron himself did not take the field and in which he owned all the teams. But there were two other differences, which made the Packer threat seem all the greater. First it was international in scale; and second, between William Clarke's All-England XI in 1846 and Kerry Packer's 1977 electronic marvels, cricket had come to assume an importance to many people, first in England and then throughout the Commonwealth, that had little to do with skill with bat and ball.

In England, the emerging public schools, believing that cricket fostered qualities of manliness and leadership, proclaimed it to be more than a game, in fact an institution. Poets and parsons praised its ethical qualities. H. M. Hyndman, a personal convert of Karl Marx, started a revolutionary socialist party, so his friends suggested, because of his chagrin at not getting a cricket Blue at Cambridge. W. G. Grace burst on the scene to symbolise British character and British sporting prowess.

By the turn of the century cricket had come to assume profound political significance, especially for imperialists. An Indian prince declared it to be the finest flower of Empire, and in Australia cricket captains played a leading part in welding together the separate colonies into a nation. Of its social importance there was no doubt. In England peers of the realm and their social inferiors came to regard the distinction between gentlemen and players as a reflection of the natural order of things and a mark of cricket's superiority over other games. The myth of a golden age of leisured amateurism grew up.

And then, after the First World War, the dream-world began to crumble. At home the golden age gave way to unromantic but remarkably effective professionalism. In Australia the solidarity of Empire was rocked by staunch upholders of the gentlemanly code who used ruthless means to assert their supremacy over upstart colonials. The English county game began its slow descent into anachronism.

Yet there was still much rich dream material in the game. The Test matches survived bodyline and grew in importance. Winning them helped Australia in her struggle for maturity. Other parts of the Empire measured their stature by the extent to which they were recognised as Test match contenders. MCC was at Lord's and there was at least something right with the world.

At first it seemed that the Second World War was no more than a temporary interruption of play. At the darkest hour G. M. Trevelyan, the most respected liberal historian of the day, suggested that the fabric of British society had been preserved because of aristocratic involvement in cricket. After the War was over, despite the world's having changed for the worse again, the spiritual significance of cricket was reasserted with undiminished enthusiasm. A well-loved Australian Prime Minister described it as a fine art as well as a game. A great British Prime Minister, and a socialist at that, told of his childhood indoctrination with the belief that cricket was a religion and W.G. next to the Almighty.

For a few summers the public, starved of entertainment during the war years, showed their appreciation of cricket's return by crowding through the turnstiles. But it was not to last, and soon fanciful critics were solemnly linking the Welfare State and slow play as cause and effect. Despite the return of the Tories, by the 1960s English domestic cricket had gone into decline. The county pattern had lost much of its meaning, and the games had become largely inaccessible to those who had to work during the week.

So the authorities turned for support to commercial sponsors who introduced a growing range of mini-cricket matches with gimmicky rules. Televised cricket matches publicised the wares of cigarette manufacturers who were barred from conventional advertising. The counties had also (with one exception) imported a growing number of overseas stars who made the turnstiles click but impeded the prospects of young English players. In short, the establishment had chosen to sell its soul in order to preserve the outward trappings of the old way of life in which county cricket was supreme. Its honour was already besmirched by the time Mr Packer evoked cries of outraged virtue. Indeed, it could be said that in some ways MCC invented Kerry Packer. This book is, in part, about how this came about.

It is not, let us be clear, about the Packer business itself. Indeed the dreaded name will rarely appear, and the defector Greig will be a very minor character, cropping up late and two-dimensionally as a representative contemporary anti-hero. But the events of 1977 in which the façade of cricket was rudely torn down give point to the book's general theme, which is the gap between myth and reality in this most English of games. The cricket establishment has sought to preserve an eighteenth-century feudal dream.

Some cricket enthusiasts may be shocked at this irreverent notion, particularly as it is presented with an eye to its comic side rather than as evidence of the imminent collapse of civilisation. However, if it is not always reverential to the pundits, the book by no means seeks to devalue cricket itself. On the contrary, it has been written in deep affection for and appreciation of a great game that has survived despite the efforts of its leaders. If it is critical of the sacred cows that have been allowed to stray on to the pitch (and also of the side-shows that have been installed to distract attention from these privileged beasts) it is deeply respectful of the hallowed turf itself.

Indeed, it will argue that the absurd claims traditionally made for cricket have detracted from its true value as a game and that games are of the highest importance in human life. Cricket is not, as some of its adherents appear to believe, an ethical religion, still less a natural source of sportsmanlike winners of wars or builders of empires. But it offers, like other great games, opportunities for vicarious mastery of dangerous aspects of the human condition, an outlet for imagination and loyalty and a focus for the aspirations of industrialised man.

Cricket literature, though abundant, has many gaps. This book originated in the belief that there is room for a serious – though not solemn – comparison of the game's mythology with the reality. In the next phase of cricket's history the need for this kind of study seems likely to become more and more apparent. If first-class cricket survives the latest threats to its existence it will be time for revaluation of a living, flourishing activity of great value in the modern world. If not, then the moment will have arrived for the more melancholy but equally necessary process of re-assessing the significance of a monument to the past.

ONE

THE MYTHOLOGY OF CRICKET

'WE DON'T PLAY CRICKET for fun, you know.' It is uncertain who first uttered this traditional rebuke to frivolous young players, though nobody doubts that it was a Yorkshireman. The weight of opinion favours the magisterial Wilfred Rhodes, who is also reputed to have disapproved of the late cut on the grounds that 'it never were a business stroke'. Since Yorkshire had already been playing cricket for many years before Rhodes first turned out for them in 1898 it is possible that when he used these immortal words he was merely passing on what was already conventional wisdom, and that the originator was someone like Louis Hall, an obdurate batsman of earlier years.[1] What is certain is that by the time Wilfred Rhodes retired in 1930 there had been established a long line of implacable professionals for whom cricket was an intensely serious matter. Furthermore the tradition has continued unchanged to the present day when Geoffrey Boycott exudes the doctrine from every pore.

But despite this great tradition it would be a mistake to regard the saying, as some have done, as if it were simply a joke about Yorkshire.

It is, in fact, a commentary on the game itself. The illustrious Sussex amateur and classical scholar, C. B. Fry, described it as, amongst other things, 'a cult and a philosophy inexplicable to the profanum vulgus . . . the merchant-minded . . . and the unphysically intellectual'.[2] A Boston newspaper article in 1903, at the very height of cricket's golden age, began: "'Pa, what is eternity for?" "To see a cricket match played through."'[3] To play, or to watch, cricket for fun is like reading Freud for the jokes.

The literature of cricket is extensive and much of it is very solemn indeed. We should, perhaps, discount the poets on the grounds that they are, as a profession, inclined to exaggerate, whatever the subject. Certainly A. E. Housman's representation of cricket as one of the more unsuccessful ways of staving off misery can be discounted, because we know he always loads the dice against his heroes. This is clearly the case in the well-known verses from *A Shropshire Lad*:

> *Now in Maytime to the wicket*
> *Out I march with bat and pad:*
> *See the son of grief at cricket*
> *Trying to be glad.*

> *Try I will; no harm in trying:*
> *Wonder 'tis how little mirth*
> *Keeps the bones of man from lying*
> *On the bed of earth.*

For Housman's hero cricket is obviously a poor second to the nearest cemetery or the local abattoir as a source of enjoyment.

We get nearer the heart of the matter with Francis Thompson, who a few years later (in 1907) wrote the poem entitled 'At Lord's'.[4] A significant point about this poem is that it isn't set at Lord's. On the contrary, though it was evoked by an invitation to Thompson, towards the end of his troubled life, to watch Middlesex play Lancashire, it had the opposite effect to that intended – namely, to try to take him out of himself. When the time came he could not bear to go because he was overwhelmed by memories. In his youth when he should have been studying medicine he used to spend his afternoons at Old Trafford and the recollection was too much for him. In particular he remembered a game in 1878 when the 'Shire of the Graces' went north to play 'new-risen Lancashire', and he preferred to recollect old emotions in near-tranquillity rather than experience turbulent new ones. So he produced these lapidary verses:

> *It is little I repair to the matches of the Southron folk*
> *Though my own red roses there may blow;*
> *It is little I repair to the matches of the Southron folk*
> *Though the red roses crest the caps, I know.*
> *For the field is full of shades as I near the shadowy coast,*
> *And a ghostly batsman plays to the bowling of a ghost,*
> *And I look through my tears on a soundless, clapping host*
> *As the run-stealers flicker to and fro;*
> *To and fro;*
> *O my Hornby and my Barlow long ago!*

The rest of the poem shows a rather marked drop in literary quality. Indeed this particular stanza might not have found its way into so many anthologies if Thompson had retained his original last line: his first effort in celebration of these famous opening batsmen was 'O my Monkey and Stonewaller long ago!'

However, the point of the quotation is that for very many addicts cricket is not so much a game as institutionalised nostalgia. The myth of the golden age, as we shall see, has social implications, but for some it goes deeper. The true devotee has to suffer.

Old Trafford seems to have been a good place to do the suffering. Neville Cardus, for example, endured exquisite agony there a generation after Thompson, having to avert his eyes from his boyhood hero, Reggie Spooner, lest he lose his wicket. The moral of this is that the dedicated cricket follower is not necessarily a cricket *watcher*, let alone a player, and that 'fun' is far too jolly and unpretentious a word to describe what he or she seeks from it.

It is crystal clear that the addiction is by no means confined to Yorkshire. For example, Bernard Hollowood, a recent editor of *Punch* who was once a Staffordshire player, started his autobiography: 'I was brought up to believe that cricket is the most important activity in men's lives.'[5] Admittedly little Yorkshire boys may have had to recite a slightly longer creed. 'I was brought up to believe,' wrote 'A Country Vicar', 'that the finest county in England (not only in size) is Yorkshire; that cricket is the greatest game in the world; and that the cricketers who play it best come from Yorkshire.'[6] But the true believer needs no such excuse. The actor and playwright Herbert Farjeon confessed, without apparent shame: 'When I was a small boy I used to pray for Surrey.'[7] Nor in Farjeon's case did the addiction owe anything to parental influence. 'Our father contended,' he wrote, 'that we thought too much of cricket. It became, in fact, a vexed question in the house and we can remember moments which we would prefer not to live over again. We think our father to have been wrong, for cricket was the romance of our childhood, and childhood must have its romance. Lancelot or W.G. – What does it matter?'[8]

It is not merely an adolescent phenomenon, either. The addict does not always grow out of it. Many otherwise sane and balanced adults get a glazed look in their eyes when the subject comes up. There are even signals from beyond the grave. Marvin Cohen, rejoicing that cricket continues though he be dead, sends this joyous message. 'Goodbye cricket. I died loving you, playing you. You were my life, my allegory. You gracefully received my poetry. My poetry helped my soul survive its ordeal. I'm on the other side.'[9]

Another form of addiction is that of scholarly research. The most usual form this takes is investigation into the historical origins of the game. Much learned ink has been spilt, and thrown at each other, by dedicated archivists agonising about whether stool-ball or club-ball were early ancestors of the game, whether it sprang up first in Kent or Sussex (or, as one suggests, in Flanders), and most absorbing of all – to them – how the name 'cricket' arose. These studies are enjoyable and entirely harmless – though, until Rowland Bowen's remarkable work restored the balance in 1970, somewhat narrow in their scope and tending to dwell lovingly on public school and university cricket.[10] Associated with this gentlemanly orientation is an innocence which occasionally lands the researchers in difficulties. A great deal of speculation went on for years about the meaning of a toast drunk at Hambledon Club dinners – 'To the immortal memory of Madge'; E. V. Lucas in particular excluded any ladies from consideration on the grounds that a gathering of cricketers would have had its collective mind on higher things. Unfortunately for this theory some later researcher found that Madge was eighteenth-century slang meaning 'the private parts of a woman'.[11]

History apart, few aspects of the game have escaped prolonged and learned scrutiny by indefatigable students of the game. Bernard

Hollowood described in his autobiography how once, amazed at the extraordinary range and depth of the scholarly articles in *The Cricketer* magazine, he tried to break in with a contribution of his own: 'I called it "Sawdust" and allowed my pen to consider in mock-serious language the advantages and disadvantages of various timbers as sources of material. I sent it to Sir Pelham Warner and he published it, and to this day I believe that he accepted it as a genuine and constructive examination of a hitherto neglected item in the paraphernalia of the game. There may in fact be groundsmen operating today with my article as their Bible, groundsmen who talk seriously to their saw-mill suppliers of the virtues of elm sawdust, the reliability of ash and the absorbing quality of sycamore.'

Scientific research has its own special place in cricket scholarship. An early exponent was the idiosyncratic schoolmaster, Nicholas Wanostracht, otherwise known as Felix, who invented the catapulta (a bowling machine) and tubular leg-guards. His great work, *Felix on the Bat*, aimed at discovering 'whether this splendid game is or is not so connected with some of the beautiful laws of motion as to deserve the appellation of a science'. He was essentially an applied scientist: the study 'promises the probability of long and well-earned scores'. But he was also a realist who did not 'presume to reduce batting to a certainty: fortunately for the bowlers and for the interests of the game, this cannot be done.'[12]

Most scientific study, however, has concentrated on the ball. There has been endless – and inconclusive – research into the puzzling question of why and how a cricket ball swings in the air variably according to climatic and other factors. Another classic question which challenges basic scientific principle is whether a ball can gather pace off the pitch or whether this is just an optical illusion. Fortunately a solution has been offered, at least to all right-thinking cricketers' satisfaction, by Maurice Tate, the great medium-pace bowler who seemed to every batsman who faced him to make the ball accelerate after pitching. Jack Fingleton has described how Tate, an engaging character with a confidential manner and enormous feet, regarded the phenomenon:

'"You know, Jack," said Maurice, in a tremulous whisper, looking about as if on the verge of imparting a secret about the atom bomb, "I got pace off the pitch from these." And he motioned down towards his feet. "Maurice," I said, "Say nothing more."'[13]

In contrast to the scientific school of thought another aspect of cricket mythology presents it as an art. Neville Cardus made himself a corner in this. The circumstances are well enough known. After a storybook delivery from the slums to the superior journalism of the *Manchester Guardian* in its early Georgian heyday, Cardus was put on to cricket reporting as an aid to convalescence. He coped with the demands of this new role by drawing heavily on his childhood reverence for Old Trafford and its heroes, by presenting cricket as a literary and dramatic spectacle and subsequently by introducing parallels with his first love, classical music. As Cardus himself said, he helped create a cricket intelligentsia. In his first book[14] he propounds the view that great batsmen express 'their own private and immortal souls . . . using bats as great artists use fiddles, paint brushes, pianos.'

His subsequent writings, pressing the metaphor to the limits of sense, tapped a view of romanticism in cricket-lovers which, skilfully mixed with nostalgia, broad humour and occasional shrewd observation, convinced succeeding generations that cricket was, in addition to all its other admirable qualities, an art. Though usually entertaining, Cardus's books have too much of the baseless snobbery of the higher journalism. As Arthur Mailey put it, 'Neville Cardus would go crazy if he had to spend half an hour with a commercial traveller: I know because I introduced him to one a few years ago.'[15] Equally unfortunate, he has encouraged others, less skilful with words, to draw dubious conclusions from the fact that it is possible to describe cricket in aesthetic terms. Thus, in the 1950s a woman writer, introduced with high praise by Cardus, delivers herself of this: '. . . the mere piling up of runs and the falling of wickets is incidental. For cricket is an art in itself.' And 'A batsman who is dull and stolid, dour and ungainly, gives little to the game.'[16]

Arthur Mailey was less pretentious than Cardus aesthetically as well as socially. He demonstrates that what is usually meant in discussions of 'cricket as art' is skill: 'When rebuked by the manager of the 1930 Australian team for giving Ian Peebles advice during the Manchester Test, Mailey answered: "Please understand that slow bowling is an art, Mr Kelly, and art is international."' John Arlott ventures further into consideration of art proper: 'As a cottage sport profoundly played it became a cottage craft, and, just as much of the early cottage pottery is now recognised as primitive art, so the playing of the game of cricket has achieved not only a very high technical standard but also a poetic and epic standing.'[17] In a fuller discussion of the subject the highly individual C. L. R. James, West Indian political radical and cricket traditionalist, has argued that 'Cricket is first and foremost a dramatic spectacle. It belongs with the theatre, ballet, opera and dance.'[18]

There is, however, another school of thought, one that has been more influential, amongst those who are not content to accept cricket as just a good game. It tends to be less attractive because it feels the need to describe cricket in sententious, holier-than-thou terms as if it were a path to salvation. It usually projects the yearnings of people who pine for a vanished era.

There is a spectrum of these yearnings which at one end touches the innocent romance of Farjeon and 'A Country Vicar'. Slightly less innocent is the immediate post-war escapism of G. D. Martineau: 'Cricketers are incorrigible. The approach of the final battle for civilisation could not make them forget that the cricket season was also near.'[19] After his wartime sojourn in Australia Neville Cardus wrote of the dark days of 1939 and the noble member of Lord's who witnessed the removal for safe-keeping of the bust of W. G. Grace from the Long Room, declaring 'That means war.'[20] Nowadays, with the war long gone, and the finest hour with it, there are people for whom an idealised view of cricket and its past glories seems to be the last mental bastion against admission of defeat for a way of life.

1977 must have seemed to these troglodytes the year of the last straw. Was it not sufficient that for the first time for decades English touring teams would not bear the label of MCC? Alas, no. Even the rare triumph of winning back the Ashes was marred because a brash Australian tycoon had made a take-over bid for the Test matches, and the High Court, introducing harsh contemporary concepts of fair employment, had upheld his actions.

The shock this decision gave the cricket orthodoxy was painful to behold. It was no time for cricket-lovers to rejoice in the irony of it: they could not be seen to condone the piratical Packer. Still, it was ironical, for the cricket establishment has over the years thought itself a model of what the fair-minded British constitution was all about. The sententious part of cricket mythology can be directly related to a passage in one of the most influential works of the Victorian period, *Tom Brown's Schooldays* by Thomas Hughes. It all begins when a well-meaning master at Rugby School tries to pay cricket a compliment. Having seen it in action he describes it, fulsomely enough one would have thought, as 'a noble game.' '"Isn't it?"' replies Tom Brown. '"But it's more than a game, it's an institution."' This in itself was enough to spark the imagination of dozens of later writers. But Tom Brown's protégé had to go further. '"Yes,"' said Arthur, '"the birthright of British boys, old and young, as habeas corpus and trial by jury are of British men."' This adds to the 'more than a game' dimension the further perspectives of freedom within the law and patriotic self-congratulation.

Cricket-lovers do not like to be told new things, so it is only mildly surprising to find Cardus declaring nearly a century later, with the air of one producing a rabbit from a hat, 'It is far more than a game, this cricket'[21] and invoking, even more grandiloquently, the same talismans in support of his claim: 'If everything else in this nation of ours were lost but cricket – her constitution and the laws of England of Lord Halsbury – it would be possible to reconstruct from the theory and the practice of cricket all the eternal Englishness which has gone to the establishment of that Constitution and the laws aforesaid.'[22] Whether Cardus was directly indebted to 'Tom Brown' for this splendid piece of nonsense is not certain. One curious little point suggests that he may have got it at second-hand. 'Tom Brown' had referred to 'British' boys. In 1893 Andrew Lang, rather oddly for a Scotsman, substituted: 'Cricket ought to be to English boys what Habeas Corpus is to Englishmen, as Mr Hughes says in "Tom Brown".'[23] But this may be an accidental nuance in the midst of largely undifferentiated British chauvinism, in which English predominance is taken for granted.

Patriotic references began to appear in the middle of the nineteenth century. Early writings on the game had mostly been content to talk about the honest, sterling yeoman quality of the players. But by 1849 Fred Lillywhite, publicist and scribe to William Clarke's All-England XI, was proclaiming: 'Cricket by common consent has gained the appellation noble . . . and we may justly be proud if foreigners judge of our national habits and disposition in reference to an amusement of so excellent a character.' Two years later an encomiastic historian, the Reverend James Pycroft, put it less delicately: '. . . the game is essentially Anglo-Saxon. Foreigners have rarely, very rarely imitated us. The English settlers and residents everywhere play at cricket; but of no single club have we ever heard dieted either with frogs, sourkraut or maccaroni.'[24] And Cardus, eighty years after Pycroft, still felt able to feed this kind of prejudice (in his book entitled

Cricket) with witticisms such as: 'Where the English language is unspoken there can be no real cricket, which is to say that the Americans have never excelled at the game.'

Englishness is of course equated with virtue, and both relate closely to the love of tradition. Cardus reserves his most respectful tones for the community emblems of piety: 'in every English village a cricket field is as much part of the landscape as the old church.' Lillywhite's eulogy made a point of the fact that the game was 'untainted by vulgarity and cruelty' and claimed also that women could watch it 'without a blush or any painful sense of impropriety' and that there was no 'heart-burning or jealousy' as a result of winning or losing. By the end of the century Edward Cracroft Lefroy, the sonneteer, was writing: 'There is something idyllic about the pastime . . . The whole edifice of the Christian virtues could be raised on a basis of good cricket.'[25]

In 1920 a new chapter was added to the Badminton Library volume on cricket. It was called 'Playing the Game' and it began: 'It is fundamentally necessary that cricket should be free from malice and guile.' The corollary of this, it contended, 'was that "it's not cricket" has become a stigma, and its accepted meaning, "dishonest and lacking in integrity", illustrates the undoubted understanding that nothing can be tolerated in the game which bears the least sign of chicanery or sharp practice.'[26] The following year Lord Harris, one of the pillars of MCC, wrote: 'The psychology of the game is accurately condensed in these few words "It's not cricket."'[27] (That winter in Australia J. W. H. T. Douglas, the England captain, had threatened to report Arthur Mailey for illegally using resin to help him grip the ball. He was dissuaded when Mailey pointed out that Douglas's thumb-nail was worn down to the flesh from illegally lifting the seam to help the ball swing. Indeed, as we shall see, as long as there have been laws of cricket there have been law-breakers.)

Anyone tempted to think of the Badminton chapter as the last gasp of a troglodytic few should read a work published in 1960 by E. G. French of Willington, Devon, MCC, I Zingari and Free Foresters, dedicated exclusively to 'an analysis of the game's unwritten laws' and appropriately entitled *It's Not Cricket*. 'Of this unwritten code, cricketers are intensely proud,' he writes, 'and small wonder seeing that it sets a standard of conduct which serves as a guiding light not only in the realm of cricket but in every sphere of human endeavour.' He is contemptuous of other sports, from polo to football, which 'are notorious for conduct that would not for a moment be tolerated in cricket' and suggests that the curriculum of all schools should include 'lectures on cricket's proud traditions'.[28]

Some of the traditions are not in fact as proud as all that. The southern gentry who brought cricket from rustic obscurity in the eighteenth century were as interested in gambling as in healthy out-door exercise. Cricket has been played for money ever since. The first record of a match, at Coxheath, Kent, in 1646 includes a reference to betting. The opening county fixture between Kent and London in 1719 ended in a lawsuit because of the money involved.

Cricket has also been exploited as a spectator sport since those early days. In 1668 the landlord of the Ram Inn at Smithfield had to pay rates on his cricket field, suggesting that it was run for profit. By the time of the Yorkshire juggernaut in the years between the two World Wars, the game had become an industry, and subsequently it became a branch of show-business.

It is not only the professionals who have been interested in cricket as a money-making activity. The leading amateurs of the day, from Lord Frederick Beauclerk, who reckoned to make six hundred guineas a year from the game, through W. G. Grace to twentieth-century 'shamateurs', have always been able to cash in on the game just as much as, and often more than, the professionals. Indeed the distinction between gentlemen and players was never a matter of money, but rather of caste.

However, these truths were but prologues to the swelling act of the imperial theme. The spread of the game over vast stretches of the globe was widely regarded as a major contribution to the onward march of civilisation. Statesmen as well as sportsmen considered it a cornerstone of the Empire. How far the reality corresponds to the image is another matter. One problem is that a fair number of the mother country's representatives, whether their objective was to show the flag or to make money, seem to have taken the view that their mere presence should have been enough to compel respect. No doubt there were those in far-flung regions who were sustained in their task of subduing hostile environments by occasional glimpses of the vision, but Heaven knows what rebelliously-inclined colonists made of it.

One of the earliest tours was to Canada. It was organised by no less a personage than the Secretary of the MCC, R. A. Fitzgerald. His book about it – which is often hailed as a triumph of wit – describes how two gentlemen came to see him in the summer of 1871 to propose a tour, 'pointing out to the Secretary where Canada was and explaining who the Canadians were. The precaution was necessary,' Fitzgerald adds, 'as great ignorance prevailed in England at this time respecting its colony.'[29] On subsequent tours the blessings can hardly be claimed to have been more than mixed. In 1932–33, for instance, the bonds of Empire had to withstand the shock of bodyline bowling and the dubious tactics used by an ultra-imperialist, D. R. Jardine, to combat the otherwise invincible anarchism of the colonial D. G. Bradman.

Yet the flag has continued to wave. An Indian prince, K. S. Ranjitsinhji, had set the tone by dedicating his *Jubilee Book of Cricket* 'by her gracious permission, to Her Majesty, The Queen Empress' and offering cricket for her approval as one of the blessings of 'her happy occupation of the throne'.[30] Later he said: 'Cricket is certainly amongst the most powerful links which keep our Empire together. It is one of the greatest contributions which the British people have made to the cause of humanity.'[31] In 1921 Lord Harris claimed that 'Cricket has done more to consolidate the Empire than any other influence.' Even after the Second World War the emblematic Major C. H. B. Pridham was quoting with approval Ranji's description of the Empire as the world's greatest cricket team. Fearful of the imminent collapse of such a virtuous combination, Pridham suggests: 'We need more team-work, more patience and more unselfishness. To put the matter briefly we need more of the spirit of cricket.'[32]

Since then imperial responsibilities have perforce grown less every year, and Britain's preoccupation with her own social and economic troubles has left little time for thinking about other people's. However, the cricket authorities have persisted with the white man's burden, whilst ruefully grappling with the domestic implications of such alarming phenomena as the ballot box and the mass media (though not as yet the trades union movement). Yearning for the golden age has had to contend with the strident demands of new social patterns. The distinction between amateur and professional, not so much a convention as a reflection of the proper natural order of things, died hard. Only one relic of the old order remains, county cricket; and that has been protected against all threats with a fervour worthy of a crusade against the powers of darkness. Yet ironically, in their efforts to preserve it, the authorities have had to sup with the devil – show-business – and now themselves seem to be the next course on the menu.

Meanwhile, though, across the lost Empire cricket has come to have nationalist and racial significance for the under-privileged as well as the more favoured. This clashes fiercely with the game's feudal tradition. Thus we have the curious circumstance that C. L. R. James, a radical deeply committed to the cause of emerging West Indian black nationhood, and with an intellectual and emotional commitment to cricket as a source of national, racial and human pride, expresses as strongly and as eloquently as anyone the notion that the golden age has passed.

Returning to Britain after fifteen years in the United States James was profoundly shaken by the change he saw in cricket. He also detected a change in British society and, putting two and two together, made five. Imbued with the mistaken belief that cricket changes in response to changes in society, his assessment of the type of cricket being played in the 1950s led him to relate it to 'The Welfare State of Mind'. He deplored the rise of the 'long, slow, forward defensive stroke' and the abortive measures being taken to try to brighten up the first-class game. So did everyone else, not least the diehards who thought that cricket had never been worth much since the golden age of the amateur.

James was not, of course, arguing for the restoration of the former glory of amateurism. He believed that the root problem was the capitalistic, soul-destroying theory of the division of labour. 'The remedy,' he writes in *Beyond a Boundary*, 'is somehow to abolish not professionals but the specialist character of first-class cricket, whether professional or amateur . . . The cricketer needs to be returned to the community . . . He must do a job of work with his fellows so that cricket, essentially an artistic expression of life, becomes an artistic expression of his own individual life.'

The link between James's views and those of the extremely conservative people who also yearn for the golden age is his belief that 'Cricket is an integral part of British civilisation' and that 'Whatever road that civilisation takes, it will take cricket with it.' It is no surprise to learn that Mr James's West Indian schooldays taught him that cricket was ethically superior, and that 'playing the game' was the golden rule.

In any event, as Ronald Mason put it, the cricketer's addiction 'tends to make him a romantic. The game itself is too finely founded in visual beauty and felicity of conception, and too traditionally inseparable from the perennial national clichés of white-clad figures patterned on green grass and surrounded with historic community emblems, ever to be entirely dissociated from moods of nostalgia.'[33]

One way and another, then, it is clear that the Yorkshire professionals were by no means unusual in taking cricket seriously. The patronising attitude of those brought up in different social and economic circumstances towards 'we don't play this game for fun, you know' is based on the view that cricket reflects all that is best in life, that it is more than a game.

Now, for all their stern approach to cricket, Wilfred Rhodes and company were not disposed to festoon it with ethical and spiritual trimmings. Their belief that it was a game, a good one and one that should be played properly, but a game all the same, seems not only a more honest appraisal of the realities but a more perceptive appreciation of the significance of games in human life.

It is a view-point that has been heard very little over the years, in contrast with orthodox opinion which has been regarded as received doctrine for more than two centuries. The chapters that follow will try to restore the balance.

TWO

THE WARNER SPIRIT

THE UNCTUOUS PROSE OF P. F. Warner's Badminton volume on *Cricket* (1920) was entirely suited to the high moral tone that it suggested was an intrinsic part of the game. Warner himself was one of the most influential figures in the history of cricket, as player, writer and administrator. He was dedicated to the principles of sportsmanship and the unwritten code, and he was prepared in their defence to bury his head deep in the sand (though as we shall see he was quite good at protecting his rear).

John Shuter, the author of the chapter on 'Playing the Game', though less well-known, seems to have been an admirable stable-mate for Warner. His pleasure at being 'able to record that a deviation from this high code is seldom met with' has the authentic odour of sanctity. It was this same Shuter, the captain of Surrey, who against Nottinghamshire in 1887, when it was illegal to declare an innings closed before all the wickets had fallen, ordered four of his batsmen to get themselves out by hitting their own wickets or standing outside the crease so as to get themselves stumped. This provoked the comment from Gerald Brodribb, himself a believer in the high code, that this kind of thing 'does not do much credit to the game'.[1] The Trent Bridge crowd thought nothing of it and booed the fall of the Surrey wickets.

Part of the punditry of cricket is that it has laws, not mere rules like lesser games. The high code assumes unquestioned adherence to these laws, written and unwritten, to the letter and the spirit. History suggests, however, that many leading exponents have found even the basic legalities somewhat restrictive.

The discrepancy between theory and practice has often been increased by the extreme conservatism of the law-makers. For decades after 1835 a team falling a certain number of runs short of their opponents' first-innings total were required to follow-on whether the other team liked it or not. Often they did not like it because it could mean having to bat last on a worn pitch after fielding twice in succession. Yet MCC, though altering the margin of runs required for compulsory follow-on, declined to make it optional. Playing for Essex in 1897 the amateur F. G. Bull had the bright idea of preventing Lancashire falling short of the total needed by bowling wides to the boundary. The batsman, Arthur Mold, not to be balked, knocked down his own wicket. Even this did not bring a change of law. Nor did pressure from the Australians. However, when England failed to win the 1899 Old Trafford Test after Australia had been obliged to follow-on, MCC took a more objective view of things and legislation followed in 1900.

Such poignant conflicts between ethics and self-interest were by no means confined to the written code. 'I remember,' wrote 'A Country Vicar', 'when it was considered a sad want of etiquette – almost immoral – to pull a ball. When a bowler tossed one up, outside the off-stump and you . . . inadvertently allowed the bat handle to slip round in your hands in such a manner that your drive sped to the boundary past mid-on, you instantly ejaculated "Sorry" . . . For in those stately days it was considered that every off-ball must be hit to the off, every straight ball driven straight, and only the ball when pitched outside the leg stump could, with ordinary decency, be carted to the on-side.'[2]

'Had you committed such an ill-mannered offence of set purpose . . .' he adds, 'well, there! You would have been outside the pale of polite society – an outcast, a Goth, a vandal – no cricketer!' What are we to make, then, of C. B. Fry, the greatest run-maker of his generation and one of the pillars of the golden age? 'Being by nature a rebel,' he wrote of his early days, 'I used to heave a short ball round to the on boundary on slow wickets, even if it was straight. An advantage was that the opposing captain never by any chance put a fieldsman there; he expected you to drive to the off-side like a gentleman.'[3]

In fact, Dr E. M. Grace, thirty years Fry's senior, had already shown the way in the first-class game. His exploitation of the pull shot, though arousing chagrin in opponents, was remarkably effective, and in this – and in less agreeable ways, such as talking incessantly to upset opponents' concentration – his methods of playing the game reflected an amateur tradition that contrasted starkly with the theory expounded by Shuter and Warner. The tradition can be traced back at least as far as Lord Frederick Beauclerk, who first played for MCC in 1791, and it continued until the distinction between gentlemen and players was finally abolished in 1963. It was given much strength by the enthusiastic way it was taken up by E. M. Grace's younger brother, W.G.

A lesser man than P. F. Warner, who on his retirement from first-class cricket turned in 1921 to propagating the faith through books and articles and assiduous committee work, might have found it hard to reconcile unpleasant fact with pious fancy. For with him the unwritten code was far from being a matter of mere conventions: cricket was a noble way of life. Fortunately Warner enjoyed a rare talent for seeing only what he wanted to see. In 1926, when he had become the chairman of selectors, he wrote to A. W. Carr, the new captain of England: 'I know you will do well, as you have the right spirit . . . towards the game.' But Carr, though a product of Eton and Sherborne (and briefly, Oxford), did not subscribe to the Badminton Library view of life. In his autobiography he firmly rejected the notion that 'cricketers are clean-limbed noble Englishmen, on the verge of sprouting wings. No, no, a thousand times no!' he declared with feeling. Nor did he confuse Christian charity with his duty as a leader. As captain of Nottinghamshire he unequivocally supported the intimidatory bowling of Larwood and Voce to a packed leg-side field, and indeed was dismissed for doing so.

The spirit Warner so much admired in Carr included a special way of getting an extra yard of pace out of Larwood: 'I made it my business,' wrote Carr, 'to see that he took to beer.' The connection between fast bowling and beer, it seems fair to suggest, is a long and honourable one, but it is an aspect of the tradition to which little space is devoted in the Badminton book. Indeed the annals of cricket as a whole contain little direct, documented evidence on the point. What information there is, is anecdotal and therefore open to challenge. For what it is worth, however, we have the testimony of J. C. Laker, subsequently a most circumspect commentator for the BBC, who in the outspoken autobiography of his unregenerate years wrote of Ray Lindwall, one of the greatest fast bowlers: 'He was a great man at a party, and played his part [in 1948] in ensuring that no English brewery went out of business through lack of patronage.'

Laker's revelations have a wider interest in that the account they offer of his life as an international sportsman indicates the concern that was felt, well into the permissive era, lest demon drink erode the professional cricketer's soul. Of course, it had been a major problem for many years, not least in Laker's native Yorkshire. Before Lord Hawke took over the captaincy in 1883 things were in a sorry state. Hawke's predecessor, the professional Tom Emmett, was famous for his red nose, and he used to delight in telling the story of how once on the morning after a good party he had immersed his nose in the washbasin and 'it made the water fair phizz'.

Hawke's new team-mates, it was said, consisted of nine drunks and a chapel parson, and much of his Lordship's energy had to be directed towards redressing the balance. His memoirs record his gratitude for the support of Louis Hall, a teetotaller who was 'the first who ever played for Yorkshire', and later from 'Long John' Tunnicliffe, a lay-preacher whose maxim was that 'cricket and religion go together'. But it was his Lordship's painful duty to dismiss both Edmund Peate, the county's first great slow left-arm bowler, and Bobby Peel, his successor, for insobriety, before Wilfred Rhodes finally brought stability and respectability to the post.

Hawke's concern could doubtless be justified on purely pragmatic grounds, but it had distinct social overtones. To substantiate this claim with reference to the attitude of the cricket establishment generally towards the drinking habits of their employees over the years would require a separate study, based on somewhat specialised research. It may be worth digressing, however, to the extent of noting that stories of beery professionals letting the side down could be matched, if truth were told, by comparable illustrations of the debilitating effects of high living on their betters.

In this, as in other more serious respects that will be discussed later, the Great Cricketer himself is something of an embarrassment for those who have equated cricketing ability with saintliness. Major James Gilman, shortly before his death, recorded for *Wisden* his first experience of playing with W.G. The great man was out after lunch, when well set, for 71. 'This wasn't at all surprising,' Gilman recalled. 'The "Old Man" was very keen on the catering and we had a sumptuous lunch with hock and claret on the table. He had a real whack of the roast, followed by a big lump of cheese. He also tackled his whisky and seltzer which was always his drink.' On the other hand Sammy Woods, of Somerset and Australia, who knew W.G. well, reckoned it was impossible to get him drunk – 'his nut was too big.'[4]

A. W. Carr evidently believed in the restorative powers of alcohol for all ranks, and revealed in his autobiography, doubtless adding to Warner's disillusionment with him, that once when out of form he 'went to the Pavilion bar and drank off three double whiskies and soda almost before you could say "knife" and then went out and scored a double-century.' Carr's frankness was unusual and was clearly intended to shock. Others felt the need to justify their drinking on medical grounds. The golden-age amateur A. E. Stoddart added another layer of hypocrisy to his denial that he took payments for playing when he explained that he had not been given money to lead England in Australia in the 1890s but only 'discretion' in ordering champagne. 'With the weather we experienced there,' he wrote, 'this was almost a necessity, and the discretion was exercised by me freely but wisely in the best interests of our health and cricket.'

However, these amiable weaknesses are peripheral matters. The substantive point is that, on the field as well as off, cricketers have borne little resemblance to the paragons who populated the fancy of Warner and company. 'Playing the game' may evoke lofty notions but the reality is that sharp wits have contributed more to the game and its development than high ethical standards.

What it was like in the earliest days of bucolic innocence we can only speculate. Perhaps before there were laws there were no transgressors. And cricket needed no laws – written ones at least – until the gentry took it up and played for stakes. After that the numerous revisions tell the story of the authorities' efforts to counteract persistent and ingenious attempts by cricketers to take unfair advantage of their opponents.

In 1771 the Hambledon Club reacted strongly against one such bit

of enterprise, and their minutes record the decision 'In view of the performance of one White of Ryegate on September 23rd that
four-and-a-quarter inches shall be the breadth [of the bat] forthwith.'
Thomas White, known as 'Shock' to his friends, had acquired a bat
which, in John Nyren's words, 'being the width of the stumps, effec-
tually defended his wicket from the bowler'. One can see how
disconcerting this must have been for Hambledon, who had in any
case been having a lean spell, especially as 'these grand matches were
always made for £500 a side'. The laws were officially amended in
1774.[5]

The earliest codes of laws made no specific reference to leg-before-
wicket as a form of dismissal. One of the great early batsmen, 'Silver
Billy' Beldham, who played from 1787 to 1821, said that 'The law for
leg-before-wicket was not passed, nor much wanted, till one of our
best hitters was shabby enough to put his leg in the way and take
advantage of the bowlers.'[6] The first revision of the laws by the newly
formed Marylebone Cricket Club in 1788 had required a closer definition of 'standing unfair to strike', and clearly there were other
attempts at shabbiness – references to the batsman's 'legs' had to
become 'any part of his person'. However, until the 1880s l.b.w. was a
rare form of dismissal: it was not considered the thing to use pads
instead of bat. As cricket grew ever more competitive, though, the
practice became normal (and thoroughly tedious), and this law and its
evasion have been a major preoccupation for many years.

One of the curious, and unsatisfactory, features of the laws, which
can only encourage pad-play (as it is now called) is the award of leg-
byes for balls that bounce off the batsman's legs. By 1932 it had
become necessary to add a note to the laws saying that no runs could
be scored if the batsman deliberately kicked the ball, and this was later
strengthened by allowing leg-byes only if the batsman tried to hit the
ball or tried to avoid being hit by it.

Under the aegis of MCC the law was in no danger of getting ahead
of contemporary morality. From the outset the Club was reluctant to
introduce new legislation, partly out of conservatism but partly also, as
we shall see, through a touching faith in the philosophy of 'it's not
cricket' as administered by gentlemen. The most celebrated instance,
and the biggest failure, of this approach was when in 1933 in the aftermath of ugly international incidents over 'bodyline' bowling it was
decided that 'no alteration of the law was desirable . . . and to leave the

matter to the captains in complete confidence that they would not permit or countenance bowling of such type.' (The captains were, of course, the amateur leaders of the counties.) The events of the 1934 season, of which more later, showed this confidence to be misplaced, and legislation followed.

There were, however, exceptions to MCC's general slowness to legislate. By 1811 a penalty had to be imposed for bowling balls outside the batsman's reach. This followed hard upon a match the previous year in which the most famous professional of the day, William Lambert, pulled the game out of the fire by playing on the notoriously short temper of Lord Frederick Beauclerk and deliberately bowling wide after wide, then slipping in a straight one to bowl him. Lord Frederick was the first autocrat of the MCC, and it may be that this unhappy experience, which cost him a lot of money, had something to do with the speed of the amendment.

In the same year the privilege given to visiting teams of choosing where the wickets would be pitched, within a radius of thirty yards of a point picked by the home team, was removed. Nyren's comment that the choice normally fell to the side's leading bowler 'whose chief art was to select a situation that would suit his own bowling' explains why the change was made. A poem of 1773 about the team tells of Surrey's guile: 'Far from the usual place of play, They pitch'd the wickets for the day.' As it happens, the new arrangement of leaving the choice to the home team's groundsman has not entirely removed all occasion for dissatisfaction, though the need to toss a coin for choice of first innings has doubtless prevented worse abuse of the privilege.

Legislation and occasional reviews have been needed for the obstructing of fielders in the execution of their duties. Few players have actually been given out for this offence (though one T. Straw managed it twice, in 1899 and 1901) but this is partly because of lack of clarity about what was legal and what was not. England's most famous batsman of the day, Hutton, later Sir Leonard, was convicted of the offence as recently as 1951 in a Test match, and there have been many unpleasant incidents in which it has been a matter of doubt whether the obstruction was wilful or not.

Fieldsmen have also been known to kick balls deliberately over the boundary in order to prevent a good batsman, batting with a less good one, from scoring singles so as to keep the bowling at the end of an over. In 1938 Hutton, again displaying something less than knightly chivalry perhaps, not satisfied with scoring 364 runs himself in a total of over 900 and seeing the Australians, beset by injuries, struggle feebly in reply, kicked over the boundary a ball hit by W. A. Brown to prevent him taking a single off the last ball of an over and thus shielding a weaker batsman from the bowling. Unfortunately for Hutton, but just as well for the spirit of the game, the umpire awarded Brown five: the original single plus the four contributed by Hutton.

However, with the exception of pad-play and intimidatory bowling (neither of which does much for the aesthetic, let alone the moral, standards of cricket), the worst feature of the modern game is time-wasting. Before there were fixed hours of play and when games were played to a finish this was not a problem. Lambert's wides were not intended to avert defeat by keeping the ball out of reach until close of play. Nowadays it is a menace that no one seems able to control.

The first Test of 1905, according to C. B. Fry in his autobiography *Life Worth Living*, was 'the match in which Warwick Armstrong introduced his method of bowling wide outside the leg stump to a numerous leg-side field. He was rather angry with me for describing this as "negative bowling". But such it was.' (Fry's respect for the conventions seems to have increased since his own early days.) A feature of Armstrong's leadership of the victorious Australian team of 1921 was his exploitation of opportunities for delay at crucial moments, including the use of illegal trial balls. In 1953 the Cambridge and England bowler, Trevor Bailey, was brought on at a critical stage of the game when Australia looked like winning and England were in no position to, and he bowled wide down the leg-side in order to restrict the Australians' scoring chances. His success, which led eventually to England winning the series, was the source of great national rejoicing.

The long run-up to the wicket of most fast bowlers, though doubtless often rooted in psychological if not physiological necessity for the bowlers themselves, has been found of great and increasing value to captains seeking ways of consuming time. E. A. McDonald, one of Armstrong's men, had a long run, and in 1938 E. L. McCormick, under Bradman, needed over 30 paces. Since the last war, bringing on fast bowlers because of the time they take to deliver an over has become a recognised tactic. However, this is a somewhat specialised aspect of time-wasting and one at least as deeply-rooted in psychological intimidation of opponents as in time-consumption for its own sake. The great post-war West Indian sides, for example, though acclaimed for their 'dynamic attitude' to cricket, have indulged their fast bowlers – in deep-breathing exercises, restorative strolls back to a mark near the boundary, and so forth – more than any other international side.

Time-wasting takes many other forms. One of the most famous examples of what might be called comprehensive time-wasting occurred in 1967 when the reigning England captain – in a county game – staved off defeat by reducing the number of overs available to his opponents through protracted and frequent rituals of field-changing and passing the ball back slowly and hand-to-hand from wicket-keeper to bowler, who stood at his own wicket to receive the ball before beginning the slow walk to his mark. Brian Close's exploit caused such chagrin that he was deposed from the England captaincy.

Advocates of 'it's not cricket' could perhaps argue that this very deposition proves that high standards are required and generally prevail. Unfortunately the most it proves is that there were two schools of thought within the cricket establishment. Many of the most influential still hankered after the good old days when there was no question of professionals leading England. M. C. Cowdrey, of Tonbridge and Oxford, apart from his initials seemed in principle more acceptable. Close, with an incomplete (northern grammar school) education, was far too brash for their tastes. Others seemed concerned with victory, for prestige purposes, at almost any cost. Whatever the motivation the outcome was that, although the Executive Committee of the County Cricket Advisory Board censured Close and the MCC Committee took their decision in the light of this, the Chairman of the actual selectors, D. J. Insole, publicly stated that he and his colleagues would have chosen Close willy-nilly but had been outvoted by the full Committee.

Indeed it seems likely, as even E. W. Swanton, erstwhile cricket correspondent of the intensely conservative *Daily Telegraph* and himself a pillar of the cricket establishment thought, that Close would still have been chosen by the full Committee if he had apologised to them[7] – if, that is, he had, for the sake of being captain of England, observed the outward decencies necessary to preserve the myth of 'it's not cricket'. Instead this famous cricketer, who had been in the game at the highest level for nearly thirty years, said he would do the same again.

All this suggests that higher morality cannot reasonably be claimed for cricketers any more than for the rest of mankind, especially as the sort of tactics Close used were by no means uncommon. Otherwise it would scarcely have been necessary for the authorities to require from 1969 that in county matches the final hour of play should be extended, if need be, to allow for twenty overs to be bowled.

The Close episode was no more than a culmination, reached in the dramatic circumstances that the county championship hinged on the game in question and the England captaincy was also involved, of practices that had been going on for years. If things had grown worse it was not through some falling-off in moral standards arising from social decay, as some apparently thought, but because laws had not kept pace with changing social circumstances. One factor in this was the mistaken belief that there was some special quality in cricket, arising from its feudal social origins that made it unnecessary to make laws to prevent one side from trying to beat the other by any available means short of detectable and punishable cheating.

Arthur Carr had showed in 1929 how critical a few minutes could be in the county championship and how a gilded amateur, full of the spirit admired by P. F. Warner, could behave when it came to the crunch. By the end of the second day's play Hampshire needed one run to win against Nottinghamshire. 'They wanted to go on and finish it off that evening,' wrote Carr, 'but I would not agree. If it had happened to rain hard during the night and next day, play might have had to be abandoned and we should have saved the game.'[8]

An even more embarrassing incident took place between these same two teams as a result of time-wasting. Jack Newman, the Hampshire bowler, was being barracked by the Trent Bridge crowd for going slow. Newman lost his temper and flung the ball to the ground. His captain, the Hon. Lionel Tennyson, instructed him to pick it up and continue bowling. Newman refused and Tennyson ordered him off the field. Newman took his leave, but as he passed the stumps on his way off he took a kick at them and sent them flying.

Slow play is an inevitable, legitimate and – to all but the crudest seekers after sensation – sometimes desirable feature of cricket when batsmen are fighting to save a game against the odds. It is much harder to justify bowlers restricting the number of accessible balls in the time available, yet under the aegis of MCC batsmen have been blamed more than bowlers. There seems more than a suggestion of double standards in the explanation for this.

The authorities have been concerned for years about slow over-rates. But their exhortations and even fines have achieved little. People were highly critical about this slow play in the inter-war years. D. R. Jardine in 1933 complained: 'Ordinarily one reckons at least twenty overs to the hour, with normal scoring, but when two-thirds of the overs bowled from one end are maidens, the number of overs bowled in an hour should be considerably higher.'[9] No international matches for years have achieved anything like twenty overs an hour. To take a game at random, in the third England–Australia Test Match of 1975 Australia bowled only 83 overs in the course of the first day and 72 in five hours on the third, an average of 14 overs an hour. By the time of the tour of New Zealand in the winter of 1977–78 the authorities were trying to arrange for a guaranteed minimum over-rate to preserve even this low level.

The decline may partly be due to Parkinson's Law. Modern Test matches last longer, so the pace of play slows in proportion to the increased time allotted to it. But the number of overs bowled also varies according to the state of the game, and there is too often an element of trying to stave off the inevitable by slightly disreputable means.

The different standards applied to batsmen have to be seen in the context of the patronising and resentful attitude of many of the most influential cricket enthusiasts towards professional cricketers who began to supersede the amateurs after the First World War. Thus Sir John Squire wrote in 1930: 'That the first-class game is not so amusing as it was is generally admitted. It *stands to reason* [my italics] that cricket dominated by amateurs must be livelier than cricket in which professionals (though there are exceptions among these) set the tone.'[10] Squire's assumption is questionable, bearing in mind the predominance of amateur captaincy at the time. D. R. Jardine, for example, describing the 1932–33 Australian tour, writes: 'Sutcliffe was criticised for going slow during much of the second half of his innings. He was playing under instructions . . . the responsibility for those instructions were mine, and mine alone.' Apart from this, the social, as distinct from sporting, basis of Squire's view is clear: he blames the disappearance of the amateur on 're-distribution of wealth' (his inverted commas) and post-war 'public disapproval of whole-time cricketers'. It is part of the tradition of reverence for the golden age.

This tradition may well have influenced the behaviour and attitudes of the England selectors over the years. Admittedly, faced with the conflicting demands of winning (or not losing) games and of entertaining the crowds on whose support they depend, the selectors have often found themselves in a dilemma. Yet their attitudes and notions have frequently seemed to fall short of the Badminton code.

In the same season as the Close affair the selectors dropped Boycott for taking six hours to score 106 against India (despite, or perhaps because of, his adding 140 in 3½ hours next day), and the heaviest-scoring Test player of his day, Ken Barrington, had earlier been dropped for a similar offence. Desirable though these decisions might have been from the point of view of entertainment, in moral terms they resembled straining at a gnat whilst happily swallowing a camel. For the batting equivalent of poor over-rates is not slow scoring but delaying tactics, and these rarely incur punishment.

There are occasions when the fielding side wants to get in as many overs as possible – such as in the psychologically tense moments before the lunch interval or when, after a declaration, opening batsmen have to face, after a long day in the field, half an hour from fast bowlers who are fresh and who can let themselves go without having to conserve energy for long spells later on. Then sightscreen-moving, flies in the eye, pitch-patting, field-surveying and disturbances in the crowd assume greater importance and take longer. In 1953, as his book *Over to Me* records, Jim Laker had to join Trevor Bailey at the wicket on the last day of a Test when England was in danger of losing. The first objective was to play out time to lunch. 'At about 1.27 . . . Bailey beckoned to me. We met in the middle of the wicket. "It's a lovely day," remarked Trevor, looking up into a bright blue sky, "and we haven't a chance of an appeal against the light. But I can't say I feel like another over before lunch."' So Bailey appealed, and the Australians, knowing that by the time the umpires gathered to confer the clock would have moved on, resignedly walked in to the pavilion. Selectors are not given to dropping players for this sort of thing.

However, perhaps the clearest evidence of double standards on the part of the lawgivers relates to bowling, in the contrast between the treatment applied to two types of bowling of doubtful legality: on the one hand, faulty arm-action, and on the other, dangerous and intimi-datory bowling. In the first category the definition of a legal delivery has been entirely arbitrary and subject to curious swings of fashion, yet those who have fallen foul of current orthodoxy have been summarily dealt with, generally through harsh public retribution. In the second, when commonsense and civilised values make it perfectly clear what should or should not be permitted, the issue has been fudged, and moral factors have been brushed under the carpet.

The contemporary preoccupation in terms of arm-action has been with the bent elbow straightening to allow a snap of the wrist: this is called throwing and is illegal. In 1833, however, John Nyren's 'Protest against the modern innovation of throwing instead of bowling the balls' was directed against what we might call slinging the ball with a round-arm action with the hand lifted above the elbow. This was much less like 'throwing' than was the style of David Harris, whom Nyren eulogises: 'His mode of delivering the ball was very singular. He would bring it from under the arm by a twist, and nearly as high as the arm-pit, and with this action push it, as it were, from him.'[11]

Experimenters had a shot at round-arm and though rebuffed persisted until in 1816 a law was passed to stop this caddish practice. An account in the *Morning Herald* of a match in 1807 shows how arbitrary and illogical the objections were, and have subsequently been. 'The straight-armed bowling, introduced by John Willes, Esq.,' it said, 'proved a great obstacle against getting runs in comparison to what might have been got by straightforward bowling.' Like many another law of cricket that of 1816 was ambiguous and, as in many other subsequent instances, it was therefore not sufficient to sustain the required level of morality. John Willes appears to have felt no shame. But in 1822, by using his new bowling for Kent against MCC at Lord's, he went too far. The influential Beauclerk was playing for MCC. The umpire, a plebeian godson of one of the most powerful early sponsors of the game, Sir Horace Mann, no-balled the bowler. Like Jack Newman a century later Willes threw down the ball in chagrin, and, so it is said, 'jumped on his horse, and rode away out of Lord's and out of cricket history'.[12]

Willes's martyrdom seems to have drawn attention to the intrinsic unreasonableness of MCC's attitude. In any event some bowlers, including William Lillywhite, 'the Nonpareil', continued to use the straight arm. However, despite a demonstration of the advantages of the new style in experimental games in 1827, MCC declined to change, until in 1835 the authorities were obliged to legitimise what had become normal practice.

The wickedness of the new bowling was countenanced provided the hand at the end of the straight arm did not rise above the elbow. There seemed no particular reason for this restriction and in any case it was very difficult for umpires to decide whether a right-angled delivery was always strictly maintained. Innovators persisted, but again no changes were made. It was left to John Lillywhite, a batsman who had headed the national averages in 1856, to force the issue while standing as umpire in 1862 when an England XI were playing Surrey. He no-balled Edgar Willsher repeatedly, until Willsher, followed by most of his team, walked off the field. Lillywhite was replaced by a more complaisant umpire and the game continued next day, but within two years the law, again merely reflecting reality, was altered to allow raising the arm to any height.

Once this modification, which cricket historians refer to as a 'revolution', was made, new forms of wickedness were discovered. The very virtue descried in David Harris, thrusting the ball away with a jerk, became a vice when practised by the Lancashire bowlers, Nash, Watson, and, above all Crossland. Lord Harris, captain of Kent and a stern if selective moralist made it his special business to proscribe Crossland. (It was discovered that his residential qualification was suspect, something else Harris was fanatical about, and Crossland left the game in 1887.) The basic method of objection to these 'unfair actions' was not further legislation but refusal, notably by Kent, Middlesex and Nottinghamshire, to play Lancashire for continuing to employ these bowlers.

Umpires, for reasons worth later exploration, were not usually in a strong position to enforce the laws on 'throwing', even if these were clear and reflected the general will. James Phillips, an Australian who umpired for some time in England, was a notable and courageous exception – though he was castigated by C. B. Fry for getting above himself, for example by studying to be a civil engineer.[13] And Phillips required the support of the county captains. They held a meeting in 1900 to rid cricket of the 'throwing' scourge for all time, and bearing in mind the earlier hostility to Lancashire's men it seems an unfortunate coincidence that chief amongst the courageous and controversial decisions Phillips had made which this meeting endorsed was one against Mold, another Lancashire bowler. In the following year during the Lancashire v. Somerset match, Phillips no-balled Mold 16 times in 10 overs, and Mold left the game at the end of the season.

Gerald Brodribb, who in 1952 was able to write that since R. Whitehead (also of Lancashire) in 1908 no bowler in England had been no-balled for throwing, thought the 'answer' to the unfortunate circumstances of Mold's enforced retirement was that he should never have been allowed into the game in the first place. Events since then, in which, in a spiralling fast-bowling war, the clean copybook has been blotted, suggest that Brodribb's 'answer' begs a more fundamental question: why there should be such official hostility to peculiarities of bowler's actions when more serious offences are tolerated, and why it should be expressed indirectly through the umpiring system.

The issue is obscured by the subservient relationship of umpires to the establishment, and by the establishment's own ambivalent standards. They have preferred the gentlemanly way of doing things. Thus when Frank Chester, the most famous umpire in the world in the 1950s, said of Cuan McCarthy, the South African bowler, 'I'm convinced this man throws, Sir Pelham', Warner thought it wasn't quite the form to no-ball him: 'These people are our guests.' Chester was restrained, therefore, from intervening, though he spent the afternoon ostentatiously gazing into the middle distance whenever McCarthy was bowling.

On the scandalous occasion in 1960 when Griffin, another South African, was no-balled at Lord's in the Test match after taking a hat-trick it was not Frank Lee (who actually made the decisions) who came in for calumny but his outspoken and fearless partner Sid Buller, who had been making his views clear for some time and who rubbed it in by no-balling Griffin in the exhibition game that followed the Test. (Lee himself in the *Wisden* obituary of Buller professes astonishment but presumably it was because he himself had shown discretion in the matter that he had escaped obloquy.)

The gentlemanly approach was to the fore again in 1967 when the Advisory County Cricket Committee decided to defer introduction of an ICC ruling until 1969 to give back-sliders, notably H. J. Rhodes of Derbyshire, a chance to straighten their arms. This hypocrisy angered even the reverential editor of *Wisden*, who thundered: 'MCC has always held sacrosanct the edict that the umpire is sole judge, yet since J. S. Buller, who is considered the world's best umpire, gave his judgment in the middle the offending bowler has been whitewashed by a narrow majority in the Committee Room.'

Nevertheless the fact remains that much more heat has been engendered over the years in the Committee Rooms about this mote in fast bowlers' eyes than over the much more serious question of short-pitched, dangerous bumpers. Though there is much less ambiguity about what is or is not a danger to a batsman's personal safety, intimidatory fast bowling has only been checked effectively by placid pitches, and not even the most brutal transgressor has had more than a gentle rebuke from umpires. Indeed little has been done at all except during the aftermath of the bodyline tour, after much political pressure, when the fate of the Empire had been put to risk. There appear to be two main reasons for this. First, there is a connection between the public-school influence that has dominated cricket administration since Victorian times and the cult of virility that requires all red-blooded batsmen to present themselves as targets. Second, the prospect of mayhem attracts crowds.

We shall look at both these points in more detail later. Meanwhile it seems fair to suggest that the phrase 'not cricket', to be accurate, has to be defined with some care and in rather a relativistic and circular fashion – perhaps something like this: 'not the kind of thing which those who claim that cricket observes exceptionally high ethical standards happen to approve at any given moment'.

THREE

W.G. – TOO CLEVER TO CHEAT?

T HE PEOPLE MOST INCLINED to assert the moral superiority of cricket have tended to be those most convinced of the importance of preserving social hierarchies. So the conventions adduced to support claims of elevated ethical standards tend, on examination, to reveal a social basis. A gentlemanly code of honour has its points, but it is not to be compared with the sermon on the Mount, or even with the teachings of Micah the Morasthite. It displays a somewhat restrictive morality.

Even as social conventions, some aspects of the code seem more like wish-fulfilment than reflections of reality. One of the canons of 'playing the game' is that the umpire's decision is inviolable and always unquestioned. Anyone coming upon cricket for the first time in the winter of 1977–78 would need a large pinch of salt to swallow that. Listeners to the BBC radio commentaries from Pakistan could regularly hear the faultless accents of Henry Blofeld communicating scepticism about the standard of umpiring based on the expressions of doubt by various England players before they left the wicket.

Nor is this just modern decadence. In a county match in 1875 William Oscroft refused to leave when given run out, and only submitted after much debate and the lapse of half-an-hour. Lord Harris wrote of another county player: 'Jupp loved batting and was quite difficult to get to leave the wicket if there was a chance of the umpire deciding in his favour.' In one match on his local ground he was bowled first ball. 'He stooped, picked up and replaced the bails, and took his guard. "Aren't you going out, Juppy?" asked the opponents' captain. "No," said Jupp, "not at Dorking"; and he didn't.'[1]

But the code expects more than that the player shall leave the crease promptly without demur. He is required on occasions to own up to things the umpire may not have seen. In first-class cricket, for instance, he is supposed to 'walk' without waiting for the umpire's decision if he has edged the ball to the wicket-keeper. Now there is no doubt that 'walking' does occur (though probably more often when batsmen have just made a hundred than when the snick comes first ball after three successive ducks) but the custom owes as much to convenience and prudence as to virtue. It sometimes happens that a faint edge is neither seen nor heard by an umpire: if it is known by batsman and wicket-keeper to have happened, but the appeal is rejected and the batsman remains, bad feeling is created. In English county cricket since the teams play each other so regularly they find it convenient to operate a sort of knock-for-knock agreement. It seems likely that the convention had its origins in the predominance of amateur captains amongst whom the bonds of similar schooling, upbringing and class feelings made 'playing the game' important and whom history had set above the lowly umpire. Significantly the code is not associated with league cricket, where they tend, especially in the north, to think it foolish to try to do the umpire's job for him. Nor is it by any means so universally accepted in Australia where the special conditions of English county cricket do not exist.

This difference has frequently led to unpleasantness. There are those who solemnly maintain that the whole course of post-war Test cricket was altered because of failure to observe the code. On the 1946–47 tour of Australia Bradman, they say, should have 'walked' on the first morning of the first Test when caught in the slips.[2] Australia had lost two wickets cheaply while Bradman put together 28 not very sparkling runs, when, according to Bradman, 'came the most debated incident of the series. Voce bowled me a ball which was near enough to a yorker. I attempted to chop down on top of it in order to guide the ball wide of the slip fieldsmen. Instead it flew to Ikin at second slip. In my opinion the ball touched the bottom of my bat before hitting the ground and therefore it was not a catch.'[3] The fieldsmen thought it was. As one English writer put it: 'The batsman did not move and, after a pause, Ikin appealed, only to have it refused.' He went on: 'All those to whom I have spoken and who were there assure me the catch was a fair one and Bradman was out, but the umpires ruled otherwise.'[4] There were in fact other opinions, mostly Australian. But the England captain Hammond was incensed and at the end of the over said to Bradman: 'That's a damned fine way to start a Test series,' meaning that he should have 'walked'. But Bradman stayed, went on to make 187, and Australia won the series and held on to the Ashes until 1953.

Another Australian captain, Richie Benaud, explained the problem: 'It had always been drummed in to me that as soon as an appeal is made I must look at the umpire and if he says "out" or "not out" I must obey that decision instantly and without any display of emotion. Consequently when the business of "walking" came into vogue it proved a difficult assignment for me.' He goes on to describe an occasion when he moved without waiting for the umpire. 'For an instant I thought I had hit the ball and started to move to the pavilion . . . I was a couple of yards from the crease when I realised it had flicked my shirt – but there is no going back once you have started to move.'[5]

This was in 1960. F. S. Trueman appears to have encountered Benaud before he had taken to 'walking'. He tells us: 'At Lord's in 1956, I had Richie caught behind first ball, and he was given not out. He went on to score 97 . . . Some years later he told me the ball went off the edge of the bat, flicking his shirt and went to Godfrey Evans, but Richie, by immediately rubbing the arm where the ball had brushed his shirt, got the decision.'[6]

The television cameras reveal in close-up that 'walking' is by no means normal behaviour and that many players try to avoid errors on the part of the umpire: when suspected of having been caught off their gloves they may well rub their forearms vigorously. The England captain, Brearley, seemed likely to rub a hole in his shirt, near the shoulder, when in the fifth Test at Adelaide in 1978–79 he was given out caught at the wicket. Fred Trueman will also know that it is not only in Australia that cricketers are not used to 'walking'. There may be interesting variations in certain northern leagues. Young cricketers in Yorkshire are likely to be taught that it is very poor policy to let a fast bowler know that he has hurt you, even, or perhaps especially, if he has; but two exceptions may be allowed. If you are hit on the knuckles and there is an appeal you can rub your elbow, and if you are hit on the leg you can rub yourself high on the thigh.

In the second case the advice may also be to jump about a bit as well (as an aid to the umpire in reaching a correct decision about l.b.w.). It is interesting to note that, in contrast with the doctrine of 'walking', nobody seems to expect players to leave their feet in position after the ball has hit their pads. The difference between this and catches behind the wicket may be that with an l.b.w. decision only the umpire can see exactly what the position is. Another incident involving Bradman in the 1946–47 series has been amusingly described by the Australian writer, Ray Robinson. It happened in the third Test. 'That was the Test in which Wright felt sure he had Bradman when the batsman moved in front of the stumps and tried to force to the on a shortish ball which leapt through too quickly for him. The bowler turned to appeal for l.b.w., both hands raised supplicatingly, and Evans supported him with gloves eagerly aloft. Umpire Scott ruled against them. As if to provide circumstancial evidence of the correctness of the ruling, Bradman walked aside rubbing a place on his anatomy which was too high for the ball to have hit the wicket.'[7]

Differences in the code of honour stem from different social conventions. The difference between the theory of 'walking' and the more realistic Australian or league cricket view is largely that historically in England the amateur tradition set the gentlemen above the umpires. This began long before county cricket.

The earliest recorded legislation about cricket, dated 11 July 1727, is in the form of an agreement between the Duke of Richmond and a Mr Alan Brodrick, later Viscount Midleton. The agreement has some interesting features. The other players, apart from the principals, were referred to as gamesters. The 11th article provides for an umpire 'of each side'. It declares that 'if any of the Gamesters shall speak or give their opinion on any point of the Game, they are to be turned out and voided in the Match', adding, however: 'this not to extend to the Duke of Richmond and Mr Brodrick.' Indeed Article 12 states that these two shall determine disputes 'on their Honours', and that the umpires shall also 'be determined on any Difference between Them' by the great men.

This restriction of the code of honour to the gentlemen is understandable: it reflects the expectations of the social order of the day and also the financial responsibility for the contest. But it survived in a modified form for many years, and it led to an ambivalence in the relationship between the amateur captain and the umpires throughout much of the history of the first-class game.

The code of honour retained a special place in the scheme of things even when later legislation said the umpire was to be sole judge. The earliest true set of laws dating from 1744 declare that 'the umpire's determination shall be absolute', but add: 'and he shall not be changed for another umpire without ye consent of both sides.' Despite various revisions of the laws, this provision was still in force at the time of the notorious match in Nottingham in 1817 between 22 of Nottingham and England, at which both teams were said to have been 'sold'. At one point, we are told, 'Bentley was given run-out so unfairly that the umpire was changed.' In view of the money involved it seems likely that the powerful gentlemen sponsors would not leave decisions to their social inferiors.[8]

Now it could be argued that this unseemly skirmishing was part of cricket's age of scandal, the 'Dark Chapter' as the Rev. James Pycroft was to call it. But even until the turn of the century, right through the virtuous Victorian era, it appears to have been difficult to find umpires who would stand up to the gentry in the cause of impartiality. According to Joe Darling, a former Australian captain highly respected on both sides of the world, writing about his time in Test cricket (1894–1905): 'It was a well-known fact in England that some cricket umpires were reluctant to give Dr Grace and other prominent amateurs out.'[9] Lest Australian evidence be thought likely to be biased, there is the testimony of no less a person than Lord Harris describing an 'old county player standing in a match when C. J. Ottaway was playing'. He was taking quick runs and the fielders were shying at the stumps. Eventually one shot hit. The decision was 'not out' but at the end of the over this umpire came up to Ottaway and said *sotto voce*: 'You really must be more careful, Sir, you were clean out that time.'

Part of the trouble was that the amateur captains, following tradition, were set above the umpires in the English system and in county cricket were in effect their employers. Certainly captains felt able over the years to overrule umpires. Thus in 1922 a Somerset bowler appealed against the Oxford University captain, G. T. S. Stevens, for l.b.w. He apologised for what he believed a mistaken appeal, but by then the umpire had given Stevens out and refused to change his decision. Nevertheless Stevens continued to bat. More usually the captain's prerogative has been exercised on someone else's behalf. In 1935 Maurice Turnbull brought back A. D. Nourse after both umpires had given him out hit-wicket. In 1950 D. J. Insole recalled the Nottinghamshire captain after a doubtful slip-catch decision. In 1950–51 in a Test in New Zealand W. A. Hadlee insisted that Cyril Washbrook continue his innings after what he thought was a wrong l.b.w. decision, even though the umpire declined to change it.[10]

However, with W. G. Grace we have something more than the amateur overriding social inferiors. W.G. certainly did take advantage of his position but he also went a good deal further than that. Indeed W.G., the great father-figure of English cricket, provides one of the strongest arguments for suggesting that some of the claims for the high moral tone of cricket may have been overdone. In this respect Herbert Farjeon's father seems to have had a point in wishing his son would spend more time on Lancelot and less on Grace.

Lord Harris, despite his admiration for Grace, disapproved of his bowling methods which involved his covering ground rapidly to the left immediately after delivery. From this angle he evidently felt justified in appealing with the 'chance of the umpire making a mistake'. Harris, not entirely convincingly, explains that W.G. was so desperately keen to win that he 'was led, in his excitement, to be occasionally very rigid in demanding his full rights'. Less sympathetically Joe Darling recalls an unsavoury incident in a Test match in which S. P. Jones of Australia went out of his ground to pat down the pitch and Grace instructed the wicket-keeper to knock the bails off. 'Grace then appealed to Bob Thoms, one of the best and fairest umpires the world has ever known . . . Thoms . . . asked Grace if he wanted a decision and on Grace saying "Yes" replied: "It is not cricket, but I must give the batsman out."'

The case of W.G. is an embarrassing one for the supporters of 'it's not cricket'. If the greatest cricketer doesn't play 'cricket' then who does? 'The only painful exhibition I ever saw in amateur cricket,' wrote Frederick Gale in 1871 in his *Echoes From Old Cricket Fields*, 'was when Dr Grace tried to pitch a ball right up in the air so as to drop on the bails, leaving the batsman powerless. It was within the law of cricket, but that was all.' To those who consider cricket as a game there is nothing very surprising about a great exponent taking full advantage of the laws; but to those who think it 'more than a game' it takes some explaining. The early date suggests that Gale may have been referring to W.G.'s older brother E.M., who was much given to sharp practice. But there is no doubt that W.G. followed suit. Indeed his supporters have been hard put to prove that W.G. did not actually cheat. Cardus claims that he once asked an experienced Gloucestershire cricketer if it was true that W.G. cheated but that the man replied indignantly: 'Not he. The old man cheat? No Sir! He was too clever for that.'[11]

Certainly the Great Cricketer's apologists have never convincingly dispelled the suspicion that he did not play the game according to the Badminton canons: there is plenty of evidence of his guile, if not actual chicanery and sharp practice. As Darling said: 'We were all told not to trust the old man as he was out to win every time and was a great bluffer', adding that 'it was a pity such a great cricketer should adopt certain tactics.' A contemporary Australian newspaper account, with due colonial deference, put it this way in 1874: 'Now it may be confessed, if only in a shamefaced fashion, that in Australia we did not take kindly to "W.G." For so big a man he is surprisingly tenacious on very small points. We duly admired him at the wicket, but thought him too apt to wrangle in the spirit of a duo-decimo lawyer over small points of the game.'[12]

Since 1899 a ball lodged in the batsman's clothes has been considered 'dead', but before this, in 1878 for Gloucestershire against Surrey, W.G. ran six runs, three of them after the ball had stuck in his shirt from a throw-in. When he was eventually stopped he refused to remove the ball himself in case he was given out for handling it. On the other hand in 1893 he induced the batsman C. W. Wright to return the ball to him after a defensive shot and then appealed and got Wright out. When, in the 1978–79 series against Pakistan, the Australian batsman Hilditch was given out after a similar ball-tossing episode, the BBC reporter, Christopher Martin-Jenkins, declared it 'not cricket', associating it with the presence of Packer players in Pakistan's team. He did not mention W.G.

The great Victorian idol seems also to have offended against the moral code in questioning umpires' decisions publicly. In a friendly match, according to Darling, 'I was batting and Dr Grace appealed against me for a run-out. I knew that I had got home but it was fairly close and Bob Thoms gave me not out. Grace then turned and told Thoms it was a bad decision.' To appreciate the full significance of this we have to remember the normal relationship between the amateurs and the umpires. Darling adds: 'As Thoms was about the only umpire in England who was not afraid of Grace or anyone else, he told Grace to mind his own business, as he (Thoms) was the umpire. It was lucky for me in this match that the decision was with Thoms and not with the other umpire.'

Major Gilman in the *Wisden* article referred to earlier attributed W.G.'s reluctance to accept umpires' decisions to his feelings that the public had come to see him play, not the umpire. Gilman recalled an occasion when having made only two in the first innings the great man was given out l.b.w. by the same umpire in the second innings for 0. He stormed into the pavilion and 'there was,' as Gilman said, 'a rare old rumpus. Grace had one leg out of his flannels and kept saying "I won't be cheated out. I've a good mind to go home." We tried to calm him down, and a whisky and seltzer came to the rescue. But the real hero was the umpire who gave him out again.'

F. B. Wilson, in an article in *The Cricketer* in 1921, told of a less heroic official. 'I was allowed to bowl against W. G. Grace at the Crystal Palace once, and had him out! . . . He missed the ball entirely – so we thought – but hooked it round to short leg with his foot, and ran down the wicket shouting, "Out if I hadn't hit it, well bowled; out if I hadn't hit it". I had shouted, so had the wicket-keeper, and the umpire's hand was up. But he put it down again and signalled "a hit".' Under the laws of the time Grace was out even if he had hit it; by running after the ball had struck him he had played the ball twice for reasons other than guarding his wicket. But as Wilson commented, 'No umpire in the world would give him out under either count!' In 1891–92 an Australian umpire refused to stand in the second innings after Grace had made uncomplimentary remarks about him.

W.G., though the worst, was not the only offender amongst the gentlemen. F. S. Jackson, despite his aura of rectitude, was another England captain of whom Darling disapproved, describing him as one of whom the umpires were afraid and who did not scruple to take advantage of the relationship. On the 1897–98 tour the New South Wales Cricket Association complained to the golden amateur Stoddart about one of his team, Storer, who had said to the controversial umpire

Bannerman in the final Test: 'You're a cheat and you know it.' Stoddart declined to report the matter to headquarters. He himself came under a cloud on this tour, not, as previously, for his dubious amateur status but because of his criticisms of Australian sporting behaviour. Under the pseudonym 'Mid-On' a sorrowing Australian wrote in a letter to the *Melbourne Age*: 'It must always be regretted that the English captain on his departure from Australia this time will leave a very general impression that he is a better winner than a loser.'[13]

However, the case of W.G., with his demi-god status, is of special significance. Clement Attlee, Prime Minister, Socialist and founder of the Welfare State, told the Cricket Society 'that for him and his schoolfellows cricket was a religion and W.G. stood next to the Deity'.[14] C. L. R. James, despite his radicalism, approved of the Victorians for their forward-looking search for a culture of their own; it was, he says, 'symbolised for them in the work of three men, first in Thomas Arnold, the famous headmaster of Rugby, secondly in Thomas Hughes, the author of *Tom Brown's Schooldays*, and lastly in W. G. Grace.' He regards W.G. as a potent symbol with a personality 'sufficiently wide and strong to include a strong Victorian streak without being inhibited.'

How does James, the most intellectual and the most socially- and politically-conscious commentator on Grace, square his admiration for W.G. with his own lofty concept of cricket? The answer is: with difficulty. He has the same trouble that anyone has if they feel the need to reconcile the idea of cricket as an ethical religion with the reality. 'It would be idle to discount,' says James, 'the reputation he gained for trying to diddle umpires, and even on occasions disputing with them.' He is reduced to drawing a distinction between the sort of thing W.G. was reputed to go in for and real *cheating*. Yes, the great man when bowling may on occasion have persuaded a batsman to look up into the sun at a flight of non-existent birds and then slipped in a quick one in the hope that he might still be dazzled, but 'his face would have become grave and he would have plucked at his beard if a wicket turned out to be prepared in a way that was unfair to opponents.' (There is no evidence of this.) 'Everyone knows such men,' James goes on, 'whom you could trust with your life, your fortune and your sacred honour, but will peep at your cards when playing bridge at a penny a hundred.' Does everyone in fact know such men? And are they regularly entrusted with other people's fortunes? This is hagiology, not just hero-worship, but it is a reminder of how powerful and how widespread Victorian mythology became.

There were some sceptics, even at the time. One of the most delightful was E. W. Hornung. Hornung, who was Conan Doyle's brother-in-law, invented Raffles the Gentleman Cracksman as a counterweight to the virtuous detective, Sherlock Holmes, despite or perhaps even because of Doyle's expostulations that it was wrong to make a hero of a criminal. Nor is it an accident, having regard to Doyle's own typically English attitude to sportsmanship, that Hornung made this thoroughly disreputable fellow a cricketer. 'Cricket,' said Raffles, 'like everything else is a good enough sport until you discover a better. As a source of excitement it isn't in it with other things you wot of, Bunny, and the involuntary comparison becomes a bore. What's the satisfaction of taking a man's wicket when you want his spoons? Still, if you can bowl a bit your low cunning won't get rusty, and always looking for the weak spot's just the kind of mental exercise one wants. Yes, perhaps there's some affinity between the two things after all.'[15] If we have to choose (without going to the lengths of burgling silverware), Raffles's assessment of the benefits of cricket-playing seems more realistic than that of the Badminton book. It is, at the very least, a useful corrective to hypocrisy.

It was not only cynics who were sceptical of cricketers. Even staunch but unmuscular Christians sometimes took a poor view of them. The ascetic Rev. Mr Dodgson, Fellow of Christ Church, otherwise known as Lewis Carroll, was particularly scathing about the commandeering of the Parks at Oxford by cricketers. He was moved to write a long and vitriolic poem about it. All the innocent young children were being shut out:

> *Amidst thy bowers the tyrant's hand is seen,*
> *And rude pavilions sadden all thy green;*
> *One selfish pastime grasps the whole domain,*
> *And half a faction swallows up the plain;*
> *Adown thy glades, all sacrificed to cricket,*
> *The hollow-sounding bat now guards the wicket.*

Furthermore it was all for the sake of the well-to-do. It is an unlikely source for a denunciation of the élitist philosophy that, despite its claims, sustained cricket, but it is powerful stuff:

Funds even beyond the miser's wish abound,
And rich men flock from all the world around.
Yet count our gains. This wealth is but a name,
That leaves our useful products just the same.
Not so the loss. The man of wealth and pride
Takes up a space that many poor supplied;
Space for the game, and all its instruments,
Space for pavilions and for scorers' tents,
The ball, that raps his shins in padding cased,
Has worn the verdure to an arid waste.
His Park, where these exclusive sports are seen,
Indignant spurns the rustic from the green;
While through the plain, consigned to silence all
In barren splendour flits the russet ball.[16]

But these were rare dissentient voices. Cricket and the Victorian age were somehow made for each other. It may not yet have been the golden age but it must have been good to be alive if you were a muscular Christian and a gentleman.

FOUR

THE FEUDAL IDEAL

OW DID THIS GAME and its cult figures come to assume such importance to the Victorians? Before we can answer that we need to consider how it became an English national game in the first place. There is no shortage of information on this point, for the history of cricket has been fully and lovingly recorded. However, it is sometimes necessary to dig beneath the surface of the agreeable but lenitive accounts of the historians.

Cricket is not, as games go, very old. This in itself has been a disappointment for some, and a few have sought to overcome it by seeking out possible references to some remote ancestor-game in classical texts or by looking for leg-break bowlers on old tapestries. It must have been particularly disappointing for the public-school masters who wrote the best-known modern histories of cricket that there is no direct line of descent from classical times.

They found balls, but not bats. In the sixth book of Homer's *Odyssey* there is a famous misfield. Nausicaa, daughter of King Alcinous, was besporting herself on the sea-shore: she and her attendant maidens 'were playing with a ball, while Nausicaa of the white arms led them in their song' until 'when the princess passed the ball to one of her maids, she missed her and dropped it instead into the deep and eddying current'.[1] As well as such gentle activities with a musical accompaniment the Greeks also played sterner games. Harpaston, in which two sides struggled to win a ball, seems to have been an early version of those present-day affairs for villagers or schoolboys, a kind of mobile all-in wrestling with the ball as a prize to be fought for and then carried back to base. In another game, epikoinos, a ball placed at a centre point had to be thrown over the opponents' line, an early form of hurling. The Romans later on played with a blown-up ball. So even merely ordinary games, including football which was also played in ancient China, seem to have a longer history than cricket.

Nor does cricket appear to be descended from the earliest games that involved hitting a ball with a stick. By the seventh century the Persians were playing chugán, an ancestor of polo. It later came to be played on foot (evolving into hockey and similar games) and in this form came to Europe: in thirteenth-century France it was known as chicane. Various other bat-and-ball games emerged in medieval Europe, such as pall-mall, later revived in croquet and in a variant using holes in the ground instead of hoops.

The generic name for bat-and-ball games in France was 'crosse', and this included that type of game in which a ball was tossed for someone to try to hit, the pitcher's aim being either to get the ball past the striker or to hit a target behind him, the type to which cricket, like rounders and baseball, belongs. H. S. Altham, the most respected chronicler of cricket, coins a generic term 'club-ball' for these. He implies that they, and the specific variant 'stool-ball', which has obvious similarities to cricket, were English. (This, of course, is a more desirable condition than mere antiquity.) Altham is rather vague about it though, which is just as well, for it seems most likely that they came across the Channel from East to West.[2]

Worse still for the patriots, the first specific reference to a game actually called cricket, or something like it, cannot for certain be attributed to England. Even the possible references do not start until some time after the Norman Conquest. The royal Wardrobe accounts for 1299–1300 refer to money for Prince Edward, the 15-year-old son of Edward I, to play something called 'Creag'. This curious abbreviation of some unknown word stands out oddly from the Latin sentences and it may be Saxon or Celtic, but no one knows for certain what it means. Many staunch loyalists identify this as the beginnings of what goes on today at Lord's and The Oval.[3] Regrettably, however, the first definite reference to 'criquet', a much more intelligible word, is of its being played in 1478 near St Omer, in Flanders, then part of the Kingdom of Burgundy.[4]

There is little doubt that, wherever and whenever it started, it began as a children's game. The most reliable evidence of early cricket in England is from 1550 when it was being played by schoolboys at Guildford.[5] Nor is there much doubt that it was originally a game of the common people. The legend of shepherds using their crooks as bats, besporting themselves on sheep-cropped downland, is romantic but of dubious validity. When we first hear of adults playing the game, in fact, they tend to be in churchyards. These (which did not become graveyards until the early seventeenth century) were much in demand for games in general. Either way it was a plebeian pastime.

Since Sunday was the only free day for the lower orders, and after church was a good time for a game, people began to get into trouble in Puritan times for profaning the Sabbath.[6] Playing on weekdays does not appear to have been banned (except in Ireland by Cromwell) although games had never been popular with the authorities except as military training. The Tudors tried to forbid nearly everything but archery, but the prohibition seems to have been about as successful as the Volstead Act forbidding alcohol in twentieth-century America. People began to play new games that were not actually mentioned in the statutes; and cricket, perhaps because it was mainly for children, seems to have escaped inclusion on the forbidden list. This may have helped it to become popular with adults.

However it required another twist of political history and a some-what disreputable incentive to put cricket on the road to Victorian approval. One of the things about games that the authorities were inclined not to like was their connection with gambling, or gaming as it was called. In earlier, ecclesiastically dominated days, gaming had been thought not only a vice but in certain circumstances a crime. A statute of 1477 had laid down penalties of £10 or two years' jail for playing gambling games like 'cloish, ragle, half-bowle, quicke bord and handyn and handout'. But in the manor houses and elsewhere 'much money changed hands in "wagers at shootinge, wrestling, running and throwing the stone or barre"' throughout the sixteenth century.'[7]

Cricket would doubtless have remained an obscure plebeian country pastime but for the passion for gambling amongst the nobility and for the fact that from the time of the Civil War of 1642 many with Royalist sympathies found it prudent to be out of London, which was, along with Surrey and Essex, at once taken over by the Parliament side. (Few members of the House of Lords were Roundheads.) The period before the war had continued and developed the Elizabethan enthusiasm for great houses in the countryside, which by the time of Charles I had become the centre of great estates and domestic industry. It was to these havens that the Cavaliers repaired and it was there, it seems, that the younger set discovered cricket amongst the labouring classes. In 1646, as Charles was being surrendered to the Scots up at Newark, the first recorded formal game of cricket was being played at Coxheath in Kent. The players included men of social standing, and there was betting on the game.

The Puritans were against Sunday cricket, on general principle. A Rev. Mr Wilson had complained about the 'prophanity' of the inhabitants of Maidstone in this regard. Though it was never actually illegal there was not much heard of the game during the Commonwealth period of 1649–60, except for attempts at prosecution in England and Cromwell's calling in all the bats and balls in Dublin in 1656 for burning. After the Restoration in 1660, immorality and business began to flourish in partnership. By 1668 the Maidstone Justices were encouraging still more 'prophanity' by waiving excise duty on beer sold at a 'kriceting' and the proprietor of the Ram Inn, Smithfield, had to pay rates for a cricket field which very strongly suggests that it was a commercial enterprise.

The game retained its fashionable appeal, at least amongst the menfolk. In 1677 the Earl of Sussex borrowed three pounds from his steward 'to take to the cricket match' and his wife declared herself bored with the entertainment available in the country, including cricket. Presumably the three pounds was for a modest flutter. The first record of a bet was for a 'wagger' of 2s. 6d. on a match at Lewes in 1697 – a relatively small sum – but three years later the *Foreign Post* announced 'a great cricket match' of which it is reported 'they were eleven a side and played for fifty guineas apiece'. It soon became a metropolitan game. Cricket was being played in London by a team calling itself London at least as early as 1707. Twenty years later came the agreement between the Duke of Richmond and Mr Brodrick from which it is clear that the age of patronage, and the age of heavy betting and high stakes, was under way.[8]

From newspaper announcements it seems that stakes in the early eighteenth century were usually substantial and fairly often 200 guineas or more. By 1751 Old Etonians v. England was played for £1,500, and nearly £20,000 was at risk in side-bets. Enthusiasm for betting was not confined to the Old Boys. The school itself carried on a big trade well into the eighteenth century. In an account of the preparation for the 1813 Eton v. MCC match, M.F.H. recorded in *Bailey's Magazine* of 1864: 'It was the grand event of the half, conned over for weeks before it came off, and books were made for and against it; bets were hedged according to rule, and the scores of the favourites had their scale of odds with the precise regularity of Tattersall's.' Church parade provided a convenient occasion, apparently: 'The substantial business, the careful book-making of the Corner and Subscription Room, was carried on in eleven o'clock chapel in whole holidays.'

The size of the stakes may sometimes have been exaggerated for publicity purposes, but the betting was real enough and so were the crowds. Fighting brought an end to a match in 1731, and in the same year, when the first drawn game occurred, the crowd mobbed the Duke of Richmond and his team. In 1774 a match for a thousand guineas in Kent led to a great battle amongst the spectators and several people were injured.

But everything is relative. Gambling was the national passion. Riots were commonplace. There were serious riots in the Strand in 1749, started by sailors who accused a brothel-keeper of cheating them and put down by a detachment of soldiers. In 1780 Lord George Gordon stirred up a riot (on religious grounds) and let loose such a reign of terror that over four hundred people were killed in a week, many burned alive by the fires of their own supporters as they lay drunk on looted gin. And the game itself, though satisfying the contemporary requirement to be 'manly', was gentle indeed compared with some of the counter-attractions.

In 1728 César de Saussure was shocked to discover that the people of England amused themselves by, amongst other things, beating cockerels to death with clubs, and that on festival occasions they were accustomed to throw dead dogs and cats at each other. Cricket merely seemed to him baffling: all he knew was that 'they go into a large open field and knock a small ball about with a piece of wood.' Football, he thought, was appalling, with louts running about the streets breaking windows and threatening to knock you down, roaring with laughter (somewhat like certain supporters today). But English pleasures in general were 'very rude' – cruel and ferocious.

Sports which de Saussure didn't see included the annual bull-baiting festival in Liverpool and hunting a bull ceremoniously to death at Stamford. Cock-fighting, however, gave him a chance to see two creatures maim each other. Hunting and poaching, also much enjoyed, seem mild in. Comparison, and horse-racing, the fashionable sport, even more innocuous. Compared with satisfying blood-lust at a cock-fight or a prize-fight in which the contestants battered each other to insensibility, cricket seems harmless indeed.[9]

The claims that began to be made for cricket in Victorian times, then, stem partly from this relatively civilised standard. But they also had a good deal to do with the involvement of the upper classes. Cricket brought together the highest and the lowest in the land. In the eighteenth century it had this in common with racing and pugilism. The nobility came in for some criticism for so mingling by the more respectable, but in cricket the censure seems to have been aimed at neglect of more serious pursuits (and of course at the impropriety of larking about with the poorer classes) rather than at the game itself.

As an essay in *The Gentleman's Magazine* of September 1743 put it: 'The most wholesome exercise and the most innocent diversion may change its nature entirely if people, for the sake of gratifying their humour, keep unfit company.' The author thoroughly disapproved of 'Lords and gentlemen, clergymen and lawyers, associating themselves with butchers and cob(b)lers' as they did at cricket.

Satirical verses in 1778, attacking two of the most celebrated patrons of the day, the Earl of Tankerville and the Duke of Dorset, portrayed them confessing at their deaths that while letting the country go to rack and ruin

> *We Truants midst th' Artillery Ground were straying,*
> *With Shoe-blacks, Barber's Boys, at Cricket playing.*

The Victorian establishment was, of course, no more interested in democracy than this anonymous critic was. But by then mingling with the lower orders in this way was seen to be a valuable aid to social stability, and furthermore one that cost very little. There may have been socialising on the field of play, but off the field it went no further than the clubroom door.

Nevertheless it was a remarkable thing that gentlemen, including some of the highest rank, should not only consort with but actually compete against their social inferiors in public. Some sweeping claims have been made on the strength of it, notably the pronouncement of the distinguished historian G. M. Trevelyan: 'If the French noblesse had been capable of playing cricket with their peasants, their châteaux would never have been burnt.' This may or may not be literally true but it is worth remembering that when Voltaire first visited England in 1728 he assumed that the crowds in Greenwich Park on Sunday were superior folk, instead of, as they really were, ordinary people dressing up to imitate their betters. Things were different in France. Still, one cannot help feeling that Trevelyan's view may be somewhat sentimental. He paints an idyllic picture of it all: 'Squire, farmer, blacksmith and labourer, with their women and children come to see the fun, were at ease together and happy all the summer afternoon.'[10]

A more realistic aspect is suggested by a later historian, Derek Jarrett, in his book *England in the Age of Hogarth*; he reminds us that the old tradition was for the lord of the manor to lay on baked meats and plentiful supplies of ale on festival days, with all the implications of carnival and saturnalia. 'The Duke of Dorset, providing the locals with village cricket and discreet refreshments at Sevenoaks, was on an altogether safer and more economical wicket.' If we add the incentive of gambling and the fact that before too many years a younger son of the aristocracy was looking to cricket to augment his income the picture becomes clearer.

The British aristocracy, even more than that of other nations, has been characterised by a strong instinct and a well-developed talent for survival. Its noble families have saved themselves from extinction more than once over the years, by subordinating the doctrine of pure class to more utilitarian purposes, for example by judicious marriage into wealthy families of lower rank and by readiness to engage, if not directly in trade, in profit-making activities. Aristocratic involvement also helped establish the country's reputation for financial dependability and to make the phrase 'as safe as the Bank of England' mean something. By coming to terms with the industrial revolution the upper classes helped avert a social one; and they helped establish the concept of Empire which had a similar stabilising effect in Britain through the economic and psychological benefits it conferred. And of course they played a leading part in building traditions of stable government, at home and in the colonies, which worked well as long as the underlying social assumptions were unquestioned.

The aristocratic and squirearchic involvement in social and political developments ensured that the amateur tradition would remain strong. This has been a feature of British life, in government as well as in agriculture and industry, since modern society began to take shape. The Victorians built it into the system and made it into a philosophy, albeit one which required some agility in defining 'amateur' so that it did not mean that involvement carried no financial benefits. It was an up-dated version of the feudal system.

Cricket, as we shall see, followed similar lines, and its social structure, retaining feudalism in more than vestigial form right up to the present day, has been its most notable characteristic and one of the most cherished possessions of its administrators. Assisted, but not entirely caused, by the fact that games are, amongst other things, a form of escape from reality, the cricket world has preserved until late in the twentieth century an institutionalised post-Victorian version of Trevelyan's halcyon days.

The first real information about organised cricket comes with the beginnings of newspapers. There are accounts of a few games up to 1709, and then from 1717 there are regular references to at least one game every year. In London they took place on such grounds as White Conduit Fields, Islington, and the famous Artillery Ground at Finsbury. They were played for stakes and they were sponsored by patrons drawn from the 'principal noblemen and gentlemen of quality', of whom two of the best known were the Duke of Richmond and Sir William Gage. Patronage by the great men included not only putting up the money and gathering together teams from the locality (including 'gamesters' who were paid for playing) but actually employing star players on their estates. Thus the Duke of Richmond hired as his coachmen and gardeners men who were good cricketers.[11]

In these arrangements we can see the basis of the distinction between amateur and professional and the explanation of why in cricket the technical terms were 'gentlemen' and 'players'. We can also see the origin of the chief perpetuators of that system, the county cricket clubs. In 1728 de Saussure wrote of county matches often being played. They took place in London as well as in the rural counties. This, reflecting the nobility's pattern of dividing their lives between the country and the capital, explains why, unlike football, cricket's foremost competition was based on the county structure (and why the retention of that structure has been of such importance to the cricket authorities).

Amongst the chief associates of the nobility in staging cricket matches were the landlords of inns. Sometimes, like the landlord of the Ram at Smithfield, they provided the ground and charged admission. They doubtless made a handsome profit from selling beer at the matches. Quite often they arranged and advertised matches, and even sometimes employed professional cricketers themselves. Innkeepers also provided the meeting places and the food and drink for the gentlemen; in London the Star and Garter in Pall Mall (which was also used by the Jockey Club) was both the place where the earliest revision of the laws was carried out in 1744 and the base for the club whose home ground (in London) was White Conduit Fields. When this same Star and Garter/White Conduit Club moved in 1787 to a private ground, Thomas Lord's, in Dorset Square, Marylebone, it changed its name accordingly.

That the founder of what was to become first the legislative and then the administrative controlling body of cricket was a convivial club for gentlemen emphasises the point that, whatever may have happened on the field, social distinctions were preserved off it. The clubs, as distinct from the teams, had only gentlemen members.

This distinction between club and team, and its implications, can be seen clearly in the story of the meteoric rise and fall of the most famous cricket club of all, Hambledon. It was not a village club. It was founded some time in the 1760s by a group of London gentlemen (many of them old boys of Westminster School). They included the Rev. Charles Powlett, son of the Duke of Bolton, thought to be the initiator, the Earl of Winchilsea, the Hon. Charles Lennox (son of the Duke of Richmond), and a gentleman called Jervoise Clark Jervoise. No one knows why they chose to set up a club two miles outside the Hampshire village of Hambledon on Broad Halfpenny Down. They paid an annual subscription of three guineas, and they met for lunch, and also for meetings and matches, at the Bat and Ball Inn. The landlord was Richard Nyren, who was secretary of the club and manager of the various teams, under various titles, sponsored by the club. They usually played opponents gathered together by wealthy patrons such as Sir Horace Mann, the Earl of Tankerville and the Duke of Dorset.

The players, both for Hambledon and their opponents, were collected from a wide area, and the Hambledonians travelled to other centres. The Club itself appears to have played few if any games under its own name: many were in fact the early Hampshire county matches, some were under the colours of patrons such as Lord Winchilsea. (Occasionally the 'Gentlemen of the Hambledon Club' turned out on their own, and then the title of the Club was properly used for the team.) They often played against teams calling themselves 'England', but this was just another name for a team of professionals got together, and sometimes led, by a patron such as the Duke of Dorset. They played before big crowds: a contemporary newspaper suggests 15,000 to 20,000 for one match in 1772. And they played for big stakes. John Nyren, the son of Richard, said that 'these grand matches were always made for £500 a side.'

John Arlott, introducing Nyren's reminiscences, comments on the accounts recorded in the Club's minute-book for the period 1772 to 1796. 'They show,' he writes, 'the simple, near-feudal economics of the Club. Business meetings began with dinner which was advertised in London papers as well as in Winchester and Salisbury. Members' dinners cost two shillings – ten with wine – port was two shillings a bottle, sherry three.' According to calculations by F. S. Ashley-Cooper based on published reports between 1772 and 1781, the Club won £22,497 and lost £10,030, apart from side-bets. 'Against this spendthrift background,' Arlott continues, 'the players' pay was abject. For a one-day practice game – which for the Farnham players meant a return ride of fifty-four miles – they were paid "four shillings if winners and three shillings if losers". Before an away match the Club advanced one guinea for the whole team, presumably for their accommodation; when they returned, the account books show they were paid between seven and nine shillings a man for a three- or four-day match.'[12]

John Nyren's own account of the cricketers of his time provides revealing glimpses of relationships on the field. The gulf between gentlemen and players was as wide as the Amazon. Nyren tells how they all fell about laughing, for instance, when a 'plain-spoken little bumpkin', Lamborn by name, so far forgot himself as to shout out in broad Hampshire dialect, having narrowly missed the Duke of Dorset's leg stump: 'Ah, it was tedious near you, Sir.' The humour, which is based on shock, like a rather risqué story, is sharpened by the continuing tradition of the patrons employing many of the teams. These personal professionals included many of the star players. 'Lumpy Stevens, who could bowl any number of good length balls in succession, lived with Lord Tankerville,' Nyren tells us. Minshull, probably the best batsman in the 'England' sides who played against Hambledon, 'was a gardener to the Duke of Dorset', and Miller, another respected opposing batsman, was a gamekeeper 'either to Lord Tankerville or the Duke of Dorset, I forget which.'

John Nyren gives us a vivid and splendidly class-conscious picture of the honest yeoman Richard Nyren, his father. 'He could differ with a superior, without trenching on his dignity or losing his own.' As well as captain, secretary and innkeeper he was the go-between. It was Old Nyren, for instance, who negotiated the great honour bestowed on Noah Mann, batsman, fielder and fancy horseback rider, by one of cricket's foremost patrons Sir Horace, or Horatio, Mann. The two were apparently unrelated, but it seems 'Poor Noah was very ambitious that his new-born son should bear the Christian name . . . [of] . . . Sir Horace Mann.' Old Nyren, the link between the patricians and the plebeians, bore the petition to Sir Horace, who 'with a winning condenscension acceded to the worthy fellow's request'.

E. P. Thompson, in that work of sustained brilliance *The Making of the English Working Class*, makes the point that consciousness of an identity of interests amongst working people was still only fragmentary in 1780. It is hardly surprising that Nyren, born in 1764, should exhibit no such consciousness. But Thompson goes on to suggest that 1832 marks the end of an era. 'To step over the threshold from 1832 to 1833 is to step into a world in which the working-class presence can be felt in every county in England, and in most fields of life.'[13] In cricket the presence had scarcely been felt a century after that. There was no players' union until long after the Second World War and not until 1978 had it made the first hesitant steps towards achieving a minimum wage for all county cricketers.

The distinction between gentlemen and players, enshrined in the Duke of Richmond's agreement of 1727, was not formally abolished until 1963 and its influence remains. Throughout its long history this divide had little connection with economics. As everyone knows many amateurs were sham. It was in fact quite blatantly social, relying on an ingenuous acceptance of hierarchy like that of Nyren and his father before him and preserving an island of eighteenth-century feudalism scarcely touched by the world outside.

Furthermore the English cricket establishment, and in varying degrees their counterparts in the Empire, managed to continue this tradition long after the game had ceased to be financed by the great patrons. Such was the direct personal contribution of these patrons that in 1784 and 1785 when Sir Horace Mann and the Duke of Dorset had little time for cricket the games dwindled away until, after their brief absence, they returned refreshed. Yet the structure that replaced the early patrons was powerful enough to sustain to the present day a cadre of full-time cricketers playing the game for a living. There were two factors in this. One was that the county pattern harked back to times when the 'Country Party' had held the balance of power in Parliament. The other important link with the past was the Marylebone Cricket Club which came into being just as Hambledon began to decline, in 1787; neither development is surprising, for much the same people were involved in both.

The former Hambledonians who frequented the Star and Garter appear simply to have decided to make London their main headquarters. The White Conduit Club, in being from about 1782, consisted of 'Lord Winchilsea, Sir Horace Mann and all the leading patrons of the day',[14] and its successor, the MCC, included, apart from Winchilsea and Mann, the fourth Duke of Richmond, the Earl of Tankerville and the Duke of Dorset.

Until then Dorset had been the main influence on the game. Now the Earl of Winchilsea became the key figure. He was the direct link between Hambledon, White Conduit and MCC. It was he who suggested to Thomas Lord, trying to restore the family fortunes, that he should acquire a ground for the Star and Garter fancy, and who put him in the way, through the Portland family, of acquiring the first one, in Marylebone. And it was he who introduced to Lord's ground, and cricket, a powerful new influence.

Lord Frederick Beauclerk, whom Winchilsea discovered playing cricket for Cambridge University, achieved great fame as a player and later as what might loosely be described as an administrator. His background could scarcely have been more appropriate for believers in the high moral and social tone of cricket. He was born, in 1773, to a grandson of Charles II and Nell Gwynn. In 1787 his father succeeded to the title of Duke of St Albans. Beauclerk himself became a Doctor of Divinity and eventually Vicar of St Albans.

Nor was there any doubt about his ability as a player. Lord William Lennox, son of the Duke of Richmond, described Beauclerk as the first gentleman cricketer of his day, 'for although he could not equal David Harris in bowling, surpass Tom Walker in batting or Hammond in wicket-keeping, he united in his own person all those three great points in the game.' When Winchilsea first encountered him in 1791 he was chiefly thought of as a bowler. 'His bowling, though extremely slow, was very effective; knowing exactly where to pitch the ball, he so delivered it as to cause a quick and abrupt rise.'[15] He studied his opponents carefully and set his fields with care. Pycroft, writing in 1851, regarded him chiefly as a batsman 'formed on the style of Beldham, whom in brilliancy of hitting he nearly resembled'. (Others thought him rather slow, but a good hitter when he chose, especially on the offside.) Pycroft suggested that his very successful bowling had in the end been defeated by 'men running in to him'. He was quite clear, however, that Beauclerk was the only amateur in the later eighteenth century with any claim to play in an All-England XI.

For thirty-five years he was the dominant figure on the field of play – 'the greatest name in cricket', says Pycroft. He scored eight centuries at Lord's and had a highest score of 170. But beyond this he was renowned as 'a general', and many of the numerous anecdotes about him hinge upon his authoritarian approach. This seems to have stemmed only in part from his prowess as a cricketer. The early chronicle *Scores and Biographies* states flatly that 'From his good play, rank and influence he became a sort of autocrat at Lord's where his name in a match was legion.'[16] Like W.G. afterwards, he appeared to impress upon the umpires that he was a special case.

Another thing he had in common with W.G. was an ambivalent attitude to money. Lord Frederick declared in 1838 his great pleasure in cricket 'unalloyed by love of lucre', but he candidly admitted that he reckoned to make six hundred a year out of the game. This was chiefly through betting, and there have been rumours that, though later on he was to play a leading part in eliminating the practice of selling matches, Lord Frederick was himself tainted, by association at least. These rumours may have been unfounded (as Warner said, 'Like all dictators, Lord Frederick had his enemies'[17]) but the general impression is of something less than the noble ideal.

Beauclerk may not have been the first or last cleric to have a vile temper, and it is entertaining to think of him bowling to the immovable Tom Walker, flinging down his white beaver hat and calling him 'a confounded old beast'. But it is rather less amusing that this man of God should also have a reputation for sharp practice. As the current doggerel had it:

> *My Lord he comes next and will make you all stare*
> *With his little tricks a long way from fair.*[18]

That he was also hypocritical completes the picture. He was known when batting with a rival to be reluctant to run for the other fellow's hits. Yet he could speak sententiously of the absence of 'mean jealousies' in cricket.

For the later apologists who sought to invest cricket with elevated moral values it is doubly unfortunate that Beauclerk's petulant autocracy continued after his playing days were over. For twenty more years he held sway at Lord's, demonstrating as plainly as anything could that cricket's values were actually social. The feudal basis of the game continued under Beauclerk's aegis, even though in financial terms he had taken resources out of cricket rather than put them in. Furthermore, his autocratic judgements appear to have become completely arbitrary. Lord Harris, a successor to Beauclerk with at least some resemblances to him, was joint author of a book about Lord's and the MCC which included this vivid sketch: 'Lord Frederick might be seen within the entrance gate of the Old Pavilion generally smoking a cigar and attended by a snapping little white pup' (His Lordship was the only member allowed to take a dog on the ground), and he was to be found 'peremptorily ordering off the ground any spectator who was unfortunate enough to incur his displeasure'.[19]

By his death in 1850 Beauclerk's double-standards had been absorbed into cricket mythology. The Victorian talent was to translate his kind of haphazard exercise of authority into an organised, rational and spiritually justified model of the British way of life. Before long public-school boys, including future prime ministers, bishops and colonial administrators, were being brought up on cricket. It built up the character and taught leadership and 'playing the game', including the great game of war. It also helped to strengthen the belief in 'gentlemen and players' as a way of life. This, embedded in the consciousness of future leaders and unchallenged except by dangerous radicals from outside the magic circle, was not only thought inevitable and right, but the secret of British success.

FIVE

TWO NATIONS

B Y 1851, THE YEAR after Beauclerk's death, the first history of cricket appeared, entitled *The Cricket Field*. Its author, the Rev. James Pycroft, a more godly cleric than Lord Frederick, was intensely conscious of the game's moral and social potentialities. 'It is no small praise of cricket that it occupies the place of less innocent sports. Drinking, gambling, cudgel-playing insensibly disappear before a manly recreation, which draws the labourer from the dark haunts of vice and misery to the open common where

> *The squire or parson o' the parish,*
> *Or the attorney*

may raise him, without lowering themselves, by taking an interest if not a part in his sports . . . in the free and open air and light of Heaven.'

The gambling had died hard and at least one 'parson o' the parish', Beauclerk, had not done much to kill it off. But less innocent sports were no doubt worse, and cricket had more to commend it. Its ethical superiority, Pycroft thought, was an expression of racial superiority: 'The game of cricket, philosophically considered, is a standing "panegyric" on the English character: none but an orderly and sensible race of people would so amuse themselves . . . It calls into requisition all the cardinal virtues . . . the cricketer must be sober and temperate. Fortitude, patience and self-denial, the various bumps of order, obedience and good humour with an unruffled temper, are indispensable.'

The equation of Englishness and virtue was already well established by the time of Pycroft: 'Cricket is the pride and privilege of the Englishman alone,' wrote John Mitford in *The Gentleman's Magazine* in 1833. 'Into this, his noble and favourite amusement no other people ever pretended to penetrate.'

Pycroft, though he accepts the game as an amusement, charges it, and thus its reflection of the national character, with a moral force that stamps it as 'more than a game'. His assumption of English superiority appears to be entirely serious, though his xenophobia is cloaked in skittish references to frogs, macaroni, sauerkraut and, for the Irish, hard liquor ('The fact is very striking that it follows the course of ale rather than whiskey'). It was a rich vein of humour for later writers, such as Charles Box, who purports to find it incredible that 'the phlegmatic Dutchman, with his capacious round stern' could play the game successfully. 'The effete inhabitants of cloudless Italy, Spain and Portugal,' he suggests, 'would sooner face a solid square of British infantry than an approaching ball from the sinewy arms of a first-class bowler. Instead of the bat, their backs would be turned for the purpose of stopping it.'[1]

The various threads of Pycroft's eulogy were woven together more self-consciously into the later Victorian fabric. We have already encountered Andrew Lang, quoting Tom Brown with approval and substituting the more accurate 'English' for 'British' in the process. By 1893 his claims for cricket are couched in terms at once more playful and more knowing than Pycroft: 'Cricket is simply the most catholic and diffused, the most innocent, kindly and manly of popular pleasures, while it has been the delight of statesmen and the relaxation of learning. There was an old Covenanting minister of the straitest sect, who had so high an opinion of curling that he said if he were to die in the afternoon, he could imagine no better way than curling of passing the morning. Surely we may say as much for cricket. Heaven (as the

Bishop said of the strawberry) might doubtless have devised a better diversion, but as certainly no better has been invented than that which grew up on the village greens of England.'[2]

However, innocence is still the keynote, and though there is more emphasis on pleasure there is still a confident assertion of virtue, with a clergyman to assure us that all is well and, indeed, a bishop for good measure. He and the statesmen and scholars provide appropriate social tone, and the village greens of England furnish the final touch. Though the piety diminished with time as the Victorian synthesis gradually fell apart, these have been the basic ingredients of the cricket myth ever since, with, of course, imperial flourishes when circumstances allowed.

One other thread runs through cricket literature from the beginning to the present day – manliness. 'Hail Cricket! glorious, manly British game,' wrote James Love in his heroic poem celebrating Kent v. England in 1744; and in 1780 a contemporary report objected to sharp practice by a wicket-keeper, one Yalden, on the grounds that it was inconsistent with the character of an Englishman to use such methods in 'so manly a game'. In 1849 Fred Lillywhite used the word 'manly' to describe the game in his *Young Cricketer's Guide*, and so did Pycroft, and later on Lang. In the early days the association of courage with cricketers was chiefly a chauvinistic association – it was part of being an Englishman. This reached a high point with the pleasantries of Charles Box recorded above. But the social overtones, always in the background, gradually became more pronounced, and this coincided with the advance of the public schools. The *Quarterly Review* of October 1857 pointed out that English public-school education, where Christianity was muscular, in contrast to French or German counterparts, offered games which developed 'pluck, blood and bottom'. Tom Brown of Rugby exuded the manliness becoming to an English country gentleman. (As we shall note, rurality was also important to the cricket myth.)

A century later Neville Cardus, articulating the self-consciousness about class that grew in Victorian and Edwardian times, exploited the romantic imagery of England, village greens, dreaming spires and so forth, together with the feudal vision of gallant amateurs with old-style professional assistance of a bucolic kind, and, significantly, he extolled the virtues of the ruthless but gentlemanly Jardine in his sponsorship of bodyline bowling, derided the contemporary cricketer for padding himself out with protective clothing, and generally showed how easy it was to play fast bowling from the pavilion.

The bodyline era was a far cry from Lang's 'innocent and kindly' description and a sad commentary on Pycroft's 'panegyric'. Things have not improved since. It would be hard, for instance, to reconcile these elevated claims for cricket with the realities of the violent and often foul-mouthed Test series in Australia in 1974–75. Dennis Amiss and John Edrich got broken hands in the first Test. Luckhurst's knuckle was damaged and David Lloyd suffered 'a cruel blow' to the pit of the stomach in the second. Lloyd also had a finger broken and Titmus was 'almost maimed' in the third. Underwood was hit in the ribs, Willis had a beamer fired at him, Fletcher had to head an unplayable ball to cover-point, John Edrich broke his ribs while taking evasive action. Lillee and Thomson on the rampage were certainly not kindly, and it is hard to stretch the definition of innocence to fit them.

If England did less damage it was solely because they lacked the fire-power to retaliate. Against weaker opposition they were to blame for the worst episode of the whole tour when New Zealand's Ewen Chatfield, a number eleven batsman, was facing Peter Lever of England at Auckland. Lever 'dug the ball in'. It reared. Chatfield, behind the line of it, was helpless. It touched his glove and struck him on the temple. He staggered from the wicket and fell moaning, legs twitching, face turning purple. For three or four seconds his heart stopped. He swallowed his tongue. He survived miraculously, but as Lever himself said: 'What I can't forget is that the ball was a deliberate short one. Not deliberately at his head, but still deliberate.'[3]

Despite the anguish and the publicity things appear to have grown even worse since the Chatfield episode. In the summer of 1978 the idyllic English game was peopled at the highest level by batsmen wearing huge helmets complete with visors. Indeed, the fashion caught on with close-to-the-wicket fieldsmen. During the second Test of 1978 the England bowler, Ian Botham, hit the New Zealander Geoff Howarth such a blow on the back of the head that he had to retire for X-ray. When he returned the following day Willis bowled three bouncers at him in his first over. Howarth wore no helmet, but Botham, fielding at short-leg, did.

Cricket mythology requires us to believe in progression from rustic innocence to a golden age, followed by a decline. This decline is thought to reflect latter-day lack of moral fibre, itself an aspect of social collapse. On violence the diehards tend to be ambivalent, as well they might be, for the late twentieth-century position is the result of commercialism being overlaid on top of the gentlemanly but primitive code that is at the heart of cricket. National fervour has added another dimension, and there has been a history of violent retaliation ever since international cricket began. It can all be traced back to the early chest-beating in the name of Anglo-Saxon superiority. So far from reflecting social changes in the world outside, as many commentators on the game have tended to suggest either in sorrow or more recently in quasi-sociological detachment, English cricket at the highest level has reflected the yearnings of its leaders for the feudal ideal. In their little world, at least, they have sought to preserve the ancient values, in stylised format, in which the English gentleman, country-bred, his trusty yeoman at his side, exhibits virtues redolent of manhood, honest and chivalrous, untrammelled by the peevish and doctrinaire products of envious foreign minds.

The connecting link between the actual feudal world and the dream version is, of course, the Marylebone Cricket Club. In association with the counties MCC evolved leaders who were able to translate Pycroft's early Victorian vision, in which God had it all worked out and expressed Himself through a natural hierarchy, into sterner institutional terms. Lord Frederick Beauclerk showed that it was possible, in this way, to operate on the basis of 'do as I say, not what I do'. But it was left to his successor Lord Harris to invest the doctrine with full moral force, to make Tom Brown's constitutional hint a reality and, in due course, to satisfy imperial longings. Characteristically, too, Harris worked from a powerful county base, in Kent.

Harris took hair on the Anglo-Saxon chest for granted – particularly the gentlemanly Anglo-Saxon chest. If cricket had not existed one feels that Lord Harris would have found it necessary to invent it, as an outlet for his moral, social and political values. Conversely, so much does he epitomise the game at its high point, if Harris had not existed cricket would have needed to invent him. The amalgamation of Englishness, nobility and virility was never more complete.

'Noblesse oblige', as expressed by Lord Harris, is a formidable doctrine indeed. In his autobiography *A Few Short Runs*, he tells of an injury to Lord Wenlock, an old schoolfellow at Eton, who had a very serious accident while playing cricket one day. 'The ball hit him in the mouth, driving his lips through his teeth, and in writing him a letter of sympathy I could not help adding that I should advise him in future not to put his head where his bat ought to be.' Eton may have been particularly ferocious: history records that it was there that Lord Holland's fingers were deformed for life because 'it had amused his fagmaster . . . to make him toast bread in his bare hands.'[4] But the brutality and the hierarchical system and the prospect of revenge on someone else were common to the traditions of many schools. There was a riot at Harrow in 1771 because the governors refused to appoint as headmaster a man who, although so fond of flogging that he would offer to whip boys in advance and to excuse their next fault, was highly popular with the pupils. Setting aside hints of sadism, masochism and other deviations, it was generally believed that anyone who wanted to restrict flogging was effeminate.

It was part of a virility cult that also had its expression in the emergence in the eighteenth century of the gentlemen's clubs. Hogarth, the great portrayer of the age and archetype of the freeborn Englishman, was a founder member of the Sublime Society of Beefsteaks who expressed a belief in a powerful connection between eating bull's meat and acquiring its characteristic virtues. Women were thought best suited to certain limited functions according to their station in life. 'It was,' writes Derek Jarrett, 'in the segregated world of men's clubs, men's conversations and drinking sessions, men's political associations, that the average eighteenth century male expected to find emotional fulfilment.'[5] No doubt this was true of the Star and Garter and of MCC.

The inheritance, consciously differentiated on class lines, was an integral part of cricket's golden age. The gentlemen expected the players to lay their lives on the line for the honour of the side, even in relatively unimportant matches, and were critical if they failed to do so. C. B. Fry strongly condemns the prudential behaviour of the two leading professionals of the day in the first match of the Australian tour of 1896. With the dangerous Ernest Jones making the ball fly on a very nasty wicket they had evidently decided to save themselves for the Test matches. 'When Arthur Shrewsbury got to that end,' Fry writes in *Life Worth Living*, 'having watched the first two balls, he deliberately tipped the next into the hands of second slip, and before the catch was held had folded his bat under his right arm-pit and marched off. Then the 6 feet 3 inches of William Gunn walked delicately to the wicket. His first ball from Jones whizzed past where his head had just been. William withdrew from the line of the next ball and deliberately tipped it into the slips and he too had pouched his bat and was stepping off to the pavilion before the catch was surely caught.'

Their plans came unstuck: the selectors shared Fry's scorn and dropped them from the next Test. What it amounted to was that amateurs expected professionals to be always available, and had no sympathy with any problems this might cause. (The amateurs could choose when to turn out – that was their prerogative.) The pattern was to be repeated many times over the years, including, as we shall see, in 1948 when Hutton was dropped for flinching. It is the mentality that led to the branding of Australians as 'squealers' in 1932–33. It is as much a part of English cricket as the conventions that proclaimed the amateur tradition itself.

Lord Harris thought these conventions were perfectly natural. In 1909 he wrote to *The Times* pointing out how much better the arrangements were for dividing amateurs from professionals in cricket compared with football. The world of Association football 'was rent in twain over it' whereas in cricket it was viewed with 'calm indifference'. He tells us cheerfully that the difference between the two categories is not a mere matter of money: 'The real distinction is not whether A receives £5 or £2 for playing in a match, nor whether B receives £200 and his expenses . . . for representing England in a tour; but does he make his livelihood out of playing the game, is it his daily occupation in its season, does he engage himself day in and day out to play it from May 1 to August 31? If he does then he is a professional and he knows he is a professional.'

What this admirably lucid statement does not state, of course, is why, apart from snobbery, the distinction had to be preserved. Harris was the Beauclerk of his day, a man no one dared contradict. On this point, though, it seems that no one wanted to contradict. No one who mattered, that is. His Lordship believed that the professionals – knowing they were professionals – shared his 'calm indifference'. (It is hard to know what revolutionary alternatives were open to them, totally dependent as they were, in a highly precarious trade, on the whims of the gentlemen.) Indeed his exposition tells us that the professional 'recognises as convenient, and bows to those social regulations which distinguish the amateur from the professional at cricket'.

In practice, Harris tells us, these distinctions amount to 'little more than this, that the rule of the ground should be observed'. It is true that these rules vary, but they 'are accepted without demur'. For instance, amateurs may 'approach the wicket from a different gate in the pavilion from that used by the professionals'. (He neglects to mention that they also had separate dressing-rooms.) On the field distinctions are minimal: all wear the same uniform. (No doubt Harlequin caps were thought trifling variations.) Certain other ground rules Lord Harris passes off lightly – the practice of amateurs being called 'Mr' and the professionals by their surnames – and he says nothing at all of the curious convention that amateurs could have initials before their surname whilst the professionals' initials had to come after.

Things had changed little from the time Harris first wrote this until 1921, when, presumably as an article of faith, he reprinted it in his autobiography. His Lordship's exposition of sweet reason excited no comment in the second issue of P. F. Warner's reverential magazine *The Cricketer* where the book was enthusiastically, not to say sycophantically, reviewed. But this was hardly surprising since the conventions were rigorously upheld by the new organ even to the extent of according the visiting Australians the courtesy title to which their conformity with Lord Harris's dictum entitled them. The third issue included this indigestible paragraph about F. S. Jackson's historic over in the Nottingham Test of 1905: 'Mr Noble and Mr Hill looked set for the day when Colonel Jackson went on to bowl. Off his first ball Mr Noble was caught at the wicket by Lilley; the fourth bowled Mr Hill, and the sixth saw Mr Darling taken high up at slip by Mr Bosanquet.'

Warner's cricketing life had been based on Lord's where proper standards were to be expected. Elsewhere the vulgar herd was beginning to crowd in, led by a few daring radicals, traitors to their class. A visitor to The Oval reported in 1924 that 'On Monday we had several bad shocks to our sense of the solemnities of cricket. For example, we saw Fender, the Surrey Captain, lead the "gentlemen" members of his team to the professionals' quarters and bring his team out into the field in a body, just for all the world as though they were all flesh and blood. It was a painful sight, and many of us closed our eyes rather than look upon it. We felt that Bolshevism had invaded our sanctuary at last.'[6]

The Ovalites had been warned about the risks they were running by Lord Harris himself two years earlier. Surrey had continued to allow Mr A. Jeacocke, a leading amateur of 1922, to play for them though his residential qualification had lapsed. Harris, known for his relentless pursuit of misdemeanours of this kind, was replying to criticism of excessive zeal in the case of Jeacocke and also of the emergent Walter Hammond. In *The Cricketer* for 19 August he first of all pronounced magisterially on Jeacocke and Hammond, and then went on under the startling heading EFFECTS OF BOLSHEVISM: 'So much as regards the particular cases. Now a word as regards the general question. Bolshevism is rampant, and seeks to abolish all laws and rules, and this year cricket has not escaped its attack.'

Fortunately British society managed to sustain a few of the more important laws and rules against the onslaught, at least during the remaining ten years of Harris's lifetime. Bolshevism, even in Surrey, allowed the gentlemen to retain their separate dressing-rooms. And when all other distinctions were gone the etiquette of initials helped keep up appearances, rather like dressing for dinner in the middle of the jungle. Freddie Titmus, who made his début for Middlesex in 1949, recalled in a television programme how important these nuances were still thought in some quarters. His progress to the wicket on that important and nervous occasion was accompanied by a loud-speaker announcement correcting an error on the score-card: 'F. J. Titmus should, of course, read Titmus, F. J.' This announcement may have been in response to complaints from Major C. H. B. Pridham, who in the same year made the melancholy comment: 'The gradual elimination of amateurs from first-class cricket is a sign of the times in which we live. The latest tendency in that direction has been the abolition of all distinction between their names on score-cards and in cricket reports. It is therefore becoming impossible for the ordinary spectator to distinguish between them.'[7] Pridham's was one of the silliest but by no means one of the last laments of this kind. When the tradition was all but at an end F. R. Brown, the manager, told the 1958–59 tourists to Australia that the professionals could not call his assistant 'Desmond': it had to be 'Mr Eagar'.[8]

Lord Harris and his successors had managed to rationalise what would never have done for Pycroft, who complained in 1851 that cricket in London was 'nearly all professional: even the gentlemen make a profession of it'. At least Pycroft did not want it both ways. His was a pre-Victorian outlook. To him the precedence of birth was a law of nature: 'Society has its ranks and classes. Distinctions are there, not artificial but natural even as the very strata of the earth itself.' Victorian morality allowed gilt on the gingerbread.

By 1851, in fact, the world had already begun to change. Six years earlier Disraeli had published his novel *Sybil* with the sub-title 'The Two Nations', and it ended with the oppressed poor rising up against exploitation in a symbolic act of violence. The new masters of society, the industrialists and capitalists, were coming into their inheritance. It would be straying too far from base to plot the course of social and economic change, against a background of bitter struggle, in the long years of peace that followed Waterloo. But in the real world outside cricket the results of industrial advance included urbanisation, a more complex stratification of class, based on skill and earning power, the specialised division of labour, the co-operative movement and the trades unions.

In its dream-world, cricket, by contrast, managed to avoid such harsh intrusions. The industrial revolution, in the orthodox tradition of cricket literature, is no more than an unpleasant nuisance chewing at the edges of true values. Some commentators may indeed philosophically allow the advantage to cricket of the coming of the railways. (Ironically the railways helped to secure the preservation of eighteenth-century values in cricket by making the county games more accessible.) But the purists would have preferred to be without the benefits of modernity. In 1871 John Bowyer, then aged 81, told Frederick Gale: 'Just because money and railways help clubs to get more good players together than would be done in my day, and because the papers are so full of the matches, people think they have better talent now than ever was.'[9] The rural myth has remained central to the notion of cricket as part of the true English way of life. Nearly a century later G. D. Martineau was claiming, with some distortion of the facts: 'If cricket still preserves its high ethical standards it is because they were set by countrymen before the centre of authority moved to London.'[10] It was not only the ethical but the social standards that had been set in this way.

The decades before and after Pycroft's great work can be seen in retrospect to have been a turning point. There were moments when sordid realities might well have forced themselves into the reckoning. For some thirty years after Victoria's accession to the throne in 1837 there was in fact no firmly established pattern of cricket. The powerful alliance of MCC and the counties had not yet taken over, and the 'gentlemen and players' distinction, like the game itself, still had an air of innocence about it.

The most famous player of the age was the first career professional, Fuller Pilch, the Kent batsman who played from 1820 to 1855 and was paid a salary to manage a tavern as well as play. At that period amateur status seems not to have been highly significant. It did not mean being a patron, it was no substitute for incompetence on the field and it carried no great power, especially as MCC, drifting aimlessly in legislative matters, had little prestige. The Gentlemen and Players matches which had started in 1806 were not thought very important, and the Gentlemen had only fitful success. Single-wicket cricket was still popular, and the two leading amateurs Alfred Mynn and Felix played in a famous match in 1846. The exact nature of their amateur status is not clear. Mynn appears not to have had any other means of livelihood, and occasionally found himself imprisoned for debt. Felix had inherited a small private school, so perhaps may have kept the wolf from the door without cricket. However, both at one time played in the touring All-England XI, which was a professional organisation.

The All-England XI, founded in 1846, represented a brief attempt by professionals to break away from their humble status as employees. William Clarke had played as a professional in the Nottinghamshire eleven, one of the early county teams that engaged in sporadic competition, and in his middle age he saw an opportunity to make a little money out of publicising and popularising the game. The result was a circus, taking on all comers up and down the country, which injected new life into cricket. Before long there were two touring sides, arising from a dispute about rates of pay, and eventually three. Most of the great players of the day played in these teams, and for thirty years, before the somewhat artificial nature of the competition lessened the interest, this was the most popular kind of cricket to the paying public.

It seems to have been the need for genuine and organised competition that finally supplanted the touring teams. So the county teams, many of whom had had an intermittent existence, finally came into their own. The press began to have an influence by publicising scores and averages, thus building up interest in support of individuals and teams on a more regular basis. W.G. did the rest.

Applied to the wider world outside cricket Disraeli's description of Britain as two nations seems in retrospect, though just, an oversimplification. It fitted cricket like a glove (more snugly with the passage of time because the preservation of privilege became more selfconscious and less justifiable). The emergence of the modern game was also the occasion for a formal restatement of the philosophy of gentlemen and players.

At one end of the spectrum there was the Factory Act of 1847, which by limiting to ten the daily hours of women and youths in textile factories also compelled a limit for the men since they could not carry on alone, and which led to similar reforms in other industries. Once the concept of free-time was accepted, Saturday afternoon off, with profound implications for the development of sport, soon became established. At the other end there were the educational reforms pioneered in the 1830s by Thomas Arnold of Rugby. The country's growth in power and wealth demanded new-style leaders at home and overseas. Characteristically this demand was chiefly met, not by improving the state schools, but by the public schools which expanded rapidly. In the process Arnold's own educational ideas were modified by his imitators in response to the basically philistine ethos of the emergent middle classes: the emphasis on character-building and clean-living was accepted, but intellectual prowess tended to be valued less and organised games a good deal more than they had been by Arnold.

By the 1860s sport was to assume a fresh importance to both nations. The rootless new working class needed a folk-hero and they had at last a little leisure to cultivate one. The emergence of modern cricket coincided with the emergence of W. G. Grace, a man of heroic proportions. W.G. was also the epitome of the public schools' new model product: he was a strong character, energetic, whole-hearted, purposeful, healthy, physically adept, not oppressively intellectual, philistine – an ideal leader. So the two nations came together in admiration for W.G. The working classes used their newfound freedom to turn out in their thousands to see him play; and the middle classes brought up their children in his image.

W.G. is the single most influential figure in the history of cricket. Ranjitsinhji described him as 'not only the finest player, born or unborn, but the maker of modern batting. He turned the old one-stringed instrument into a many-chorded lyre.'[11] But his importance was social as well as technical. The conventions of cricket emerged in the eighteenth century and hardened into articles of faith in the nineteenth. And W.G. was one of the main reasons why this happened.

As a folk-hero Grace was a triumphant success and no doubt his psychological value to the populace at large was enormous. (As we shall see, sixty years later Australia was to need and get a national hero, too). His social influence may have been less satisfactory. True, he cannot be held responsible for the humbug with which the Victorians wished to invest their national game. But neither can he be dissociated from it. W.G.'s approach to the rules we have already noted. His amateur status, as we shall see, was dubious even according to the Harris principles.

Not that W.G. was alone in this. Joe Darling thought nothing of the Harris doctrine. He says bluntly: 'The only difference was that most of these "supposed" amateurs got twice as much pay as the "professionals",' and he gives not only W.G., but Stoddart, MacLaren, A. O. Jones and Jessop as examples.[12] And at least one professional ventured beyond 'calm indifference'. A. E. Knight's stately prose was fairly strong stuff for 1906: 'Many an "amateur" so termed, playing in county cricket is more heavily remunerated than an accredited "professional" player.'[13]

Cricket not only had two nations but double-standards to go with them. Joe Darling says: 'The poor old "pro" got his money as wages whilst the supposed amateur got his as expenses.' And what for the 'pro' was a handsome wage measured by his outside earning capacity was for an amateur seen as an inadequate and partial recompense for giving up his time and the prospect of more lucrative pursuits. (This was also the justification, presumably, for the amateurs staying at the best hotels for the Scarborough Festival whilst the professionals pigged it in boarding houses.)[14]

As in the matter of his conduct on the field, W.G. is an embarrassment to his supporters when it comes to money matters. Whether he actually cheated or whether again he was too clever for that, is a moot point. In the nature of things it is unlikely that there would be much hard evidence, but he certainly came under suspicion more than once. His name is mentioned in connection with the strike of players in 1896, when Lohmann, Abel, Richardson, Hayward and William Gunn demanded £20 for the Oval Test match, not £10 as at Lord's and Manchester; part of the complaint seems to have been that W.G. was receiving too much as expenses. The Surrey secretary reported that Grace was being paid £10 and the matter was dropped.[15] (Stoddart, more sensitive than Grace, withdrew just before the start because of sharp criticism of him in the newspapers for taking backhanders.) Negotiations broke down for W.G. to take a team to Australia in 1872–73 when he demanded £1,500 plus expenses. He went the following year when presumably his demands were met.[16] He seems to have felt no obligation to be correspondingly generous to the professionals he took, who felt he drove a hard bargain. They got second-class passage (itself a source of annoyance), £150 and £20 pocket-money. His lack of generosity led to some refusals and the team was not as strong as it could have been.

According to the minute-books, W.G. got £45 in expenses from Gloucestershire in 1874 apart from anything accruing from Gentlemen v. Players, Test matches, and so on. It seems likely that his earnings equalled what any professionals got, but this may be fair enough bearing in mind the likely loss of income from his medical practice. Later on we hear of him drawing sums like £36 to pay an assistant while he is away playing for his county. Again fair enough. His first testimonial in 1879 brought in £1,458, a marble clock and two bronze ornaments, which, though not excessive, was not bad for a 31 year-old amateur.

However, it was on the overseas tours that the great amateur cashed in on his fame. W.G. received £3,000 for his second trip to Australia in 1891, plus all his expenses including the cost of a locum. According to Joe Darling the expenses of his wife and daughter who went with him were also paid. One can understand Australian cynicism, especially as the year before W.G. had said sententiously: 'There is another thing I am afraid of: that is, that cricket will be made too much of a business like football.'[17] Four years later the second testimonial netted £9,073 8s. 3d. which was a very handsome amount indeed in those days.

It was perhaps no more than he deserved, and it was freely given by a lot of people who admired him and felt proud of what he had done. National monuments tend to be expensive to keep up, but they have their uses. The question only arises in the context of the great significance invested by the Victorians and their successors in the notion of amateurism and 'noblesse oblige'. What difference, other than an arbitrary social one, was there between Oscroft, one of W.G.'s first Australian tour members, and his captain? Oscroft told A. W. Pullin: 'I went out to Australia to make as much money as I could.' One of his devices was to take out cricket gear 'four times as much as all the rest of the team put together' and sell it to the colonials. W.G.'s motives were very similar. In 1898, near the end of his long career, he left Gloucestershire because the county did not see how he could combine the post of Gloucester captain with that of manager of London County, a post which paid £600 a year and generous expenses.[18]

The 1860s and 70s were the great heyday of organised sport. In 1863, when the 15-year-old W.G. was playing in his first big match, the Football Association was formed. The aim was to establish rules that would include the adherents of William Webb Ellis, of Rugby, who had picked up the ball and run with it. The attempt failed and the official Rugby Union followed in 1871. The first open golf championship had taken place in 1860 and the game really arrived as a middle-class pastime when the first major English club, the Royal North Devon, was formed in 1864. Athletics championships were held in 1866. Lawn tennis was invented in 1873 and the Hockey Association was formed in 1886.

All these ventures were characterised to a greater or lesser degree by the influence of the new public-school traditions. The new generation of young adults leaving the schools played a full part in organising these sports, and they left their mark on the structure of the competitions and institutions that developed them. In cricket, however, the historic relationship of the gentry with the lower orders, and the already established traditions of the MCC, gave added social significance to the contribution the public schools were to make to the administration of the game as a national institution.

Football is an interesting contrast. Though it was of more ancient origin than cricket, football had no pedigree. Tsu-chu (or kick-ball) may have been played on the Emperor's birthday in second- and third-century China, but the English nobility had not taken up football and feudalised it as they had with cricket. Shrove Tuesday games at Derby with Roman legionaries had conferred no social status on the players on either side. Indeed by the fourteenth century the mêlées with which the game was associated were clearly recognised as anti-social. There is no indication that the gentry took it up in exile or at the Restoration, for gambling or any other purpose. King James I thought it was 'rough and violent'. True, there were some early public-school headmasters who thought it potentially valuable. For instance, Richard Mulcaster, headmaster of Merchant Taylors' School, saw it as an aid to the bowels; indeed it 'strengtheneth and brawneth the whole body'. But nobody gambled on it, apparently. Joseph Strutt in his *Sports and*

Pastimes of the People of England in 1801 gave football at least as much prominence as cricket, but he added significantly that 'Cricket of late years is become exceedingly fashionable, being much countenanced by the nobility and gentlemen of fortune, who frequently join in the diversion.' Indeed Strutt appeared to think football in decline: 'formerly much in vogue among the common people . . . of late years [it] seems to have fallen into disrepute and is but little practised.'

Crude forms of football had been played at Rugby before Dr Arnold arrived there. Soon, under the influence of the new movement, it was made over into a body-and-character-building activity of a sufficiently respectable kind to be played amongst ten or a dozen public schools. After Webb Ellis's legendary innovation in 1823, handling and dribbling codes developed at the various schools, depending to some extent on tradition and to some extent on circumstances. For example, at Harrow the boys seem to have had to play uphill, whereas at Rugby they could boot the ball about more readily in the Close. (Eton made the best of their Wall.)

Various sets of rules or local agreements appeared, so that by the time of the great Victorian institutionalisation of games for adults it was a question in football of codifying a sport that was well-known up and down the country, with Sheffield a flourishing northern outpost. Unlike cricket, however, there were at that stage no professionals. This continued long after football had become an attraction for the crowds.

The Factory Acts transformed the situation. In the 1870s and 80s, mill and factory and colliery welfare clubs began to flourish and amongst their star players were Scots who had sought and found work in the industrial boom towns of Darwen, Accrington, Preston and Blackburn. Like the early cricketers a century before, their sporting talents secured them jobs. But the practice was not approved by many clubs, especially in the south. The secretary of the Football Association, Charles W. Alcock, proposed to legalise professionalism within strict limits, such as forbidding teams with professional players to compete for the FA Cup. His plans were rejected; meanwhile the amateur sides were being outclassed by the illegal professionals.

Alcock happened also to be the secretary of Surrey County Cricket Club, and if he had had his way perhaps soccer would have developed on lines that would have suited Lord Harris. As it was, his proposals for the payment and registration of paid footballers, accepted resignedly by the FA, were very closely modelled on the system in force for cricketers: that is, they were very restrictive and, *inter alia*, forbade professionals to serve on any committees. However by 1888 the leading professional clubs had formed the Football League and from then on a working-class ethos began to emerge.

By 1900 the early middle-class origins of the Association were less in evidence in the major competitions. First in the north and then the south amateur tradition gave way to harsh reality. The professionals were poorly paid and had no security, but at least their code was relatively free of hypocrisy. The Rugby code, too, soon divided into amateur and professional. As with soccer the north began the agitation for change. The works and miners' clubs sought approval for broken-time payment. The Rugby Union, heavily influenced by their secretary, no less a figure than Rowland Hill, resisted and the inevitable happened: in 1895 twenty-one clubs formed the Northern Union, which later became the Rugby League. The professional game soon flourished and became an international affair, though in England it has never spread far beyond the boundaries of Lancashire and Yorkshire. The Rugby Union, going its own way, would appear to have achieved more successfully the ideals of amateur sport (whilst offering opportunities for playing and watching at a high level) than cricket.

An important factor in this, of course, is the length of time taken to play football compared with cricket. Very few people cannot spare the time for football. It is only recently that the cricket authorities have begun to favour one-day games, and then only of a curious kind – over-limit cricket – which distorts the essential nature of the game. Furthermore this has been done not as part of a reform of the structure but as an attempt to prop up the county game, frozen in a six-days-a-week pattern, and to provide more finance for a cadre of full-time players. Few people have the time to watch county cricket, and the income from county membership fees is not sufficient to pay players enough for gate receipts not to matter. At the same time the number of people who can afford to play cricket for fun on a full-time basis has dwindled almost to zero.

The schisms in football, painful though they may have been, and socially motivated, allowed a freer response to changing community needs than the artificial preservation of the old order in cricket. By the First World War soccer had become the English game. It did so without anyone needing to acclaim its ethical superiority and without undue hypocrisy about amateurism. Furthermore it coped much better than cricket with another aspect of the two-nations division: the antagonism between north and south.

Despite the historical association of professionalism with the north in football this has left no permanent mark on the structure of Association football, and only the island of Rugby League in the handling code. The north is by no means the poor relation in any kind of football. It is quite different in cricket. Traditionally 'the Northern Leagues' are thought to be inferior to the kind of cricket played in the south. League cricket, with its star professionals playing in otherwise amateur clubs (accepting that expenses and perhaps even broken time may be paid to the amateur players), has always been much stronger in the north and in industrial areas like Staffordshire and Birmingham than in the south. Southern enthusiasts of the more traditional sort have regarded these competitions as somehow 'not quite cricket' and have believed them deficient in the kind of superior sportsmanship of true cricket.

It is not just a matter of professionalism. Even the purely amateur leagues are thought to breed a too competitive attitude. Anyone who has played in southern club cricket, and in the north, will know that the differences are often much exaggerated and that sportsmanship is fairly well distributed geographically. Nevertheless, cricket mythology requires the northerner to be a different breed from his southern counterpart. This applies to county and Test cricket also, and the differences are not just regarded as natural variants but tend to be considered as deviations from an ideal standard.

As late as 1977 E. W. Swanton felt able to include in a book of memoirs a chapter called 'A Northern Journey'. This is not as you might suppose an account of cricket in Greenland, but observations on what it is like in those foreign parts beyond Watford. It contains a patronising account of his late arrival for a wartime match at Southport, which is scarcely an industrial slum, where the natives called out such things as 'Eh oop, laad, tha's late, tha' knows' and 'let me carry tha' bag.' 'The North' is all the same to Swanton – accents, social standing, smoky chimneys – and all quite different from the leisured and gracious south. Elsewhere, writing of Raymond Illingworth for whom 'Cricket was *the* way forward, from manual employment . . . to a broader and more prosperous life', Swanton says: 'We Southerners can only strive to imagine what the goal of a blue cap with a rose of whichever colour as its crest has meant down the cricket ages . . . to generations . . . brought up in the hard industrial North.'[19]

Such remarks imply a charitable if unspoken acceptance of the otherwise somewhat regrettable fact that Yorkshiremen don't play cricket for fun. For them, and their slightly less obtrusive counterparts across the Pennines, cricket is the only escape from degradation in coal-field or mill-town. Indeed, had Swanton's book been written a century earlier Raymond Illingworth's great-grandparents would doubtless have been grateful for such a liberal perspective, and when they made their way to Sheffield or wherever and paid their hard-earned shillings to see W.G. hitting Tom Emmett out of the ground, they might have been fortified in their secret longing for their progeny to achieve what they could not do and escape the dark satanic mills.

SIX

IMPERIALISM AND THE GREAT GAME

MOST VICTIMS OF THE industrial revolution had to endure as best they could. For the intrepid, however, there was another possibility. The annual rate of emigration doubled the previous record when it became 60,000 in 1830: by 1842 it was 130,000, and in 1847–49, the worst years of famine in Ireland and bad years elsewhere, the average was over a quarter of a million.

The main destinations were North America and Australia. In Canada the explosive situation between British and French settlers was only one of several hazards. After a serious rebellion in 1837 a new Governor, Lord Durham, began gradually to introduce policies that encouraged settlement – partly to help outnumber the French – but there can have been few social attractions to persons of repute. This must have applied even more to Australia: it was only in 1840 that the 130,000 white settlers persuaded the mother country to stop dumping criminals there. In 1851 the discovery of gold at Ballarat provided a powerful magnet for some but doubtless did little to improve the colonies' outlandish image.

Cricket, like the Empire itself, spread somewhat haphazardly and not always for the noblest motives. The very earliest settlers had taken the game with them: cricket was being played regularly in Sydney in 1808, for instance, and the Melbourne Club dates from 1838, but of course it could scarcely be compared with the real thing. The commercial possibilities of this situation became apparent in England and in 1861 two promoters induced H. H. Stephenson, the Surrey professional, to take a team out to Australia that winter. They made over £11,000 on the deal. Two years later George Parr, who had succeeded William Clarke as manager of the All-England XI, took out a team of professionals. (There was one 'amateur', E. M. Grace, but like his brother he was known to take fees.) The rapacious behaviour of Parr's men, avid for every penny they could make by selling equipment and buying up cheap gold and jewellery, soliciting gifts and hogging themselves at official functions, lessened the Australians' enthusiasm for this kind of tour. There was a long interval before the next.

The possibility of attracting an amateur side was seriously debated. The colonists' attitude to amateurs was ambivalent. The Melbourne Club arranged a series of Gentlemen v. Players matches in the 1860s, and though the experiment failed and indeed attracted some criticism it showed that at least there were some with aspirations towards the better things of life. On the other hand, there were doubts about whether the standards of the kind of amateur who might be willing to come would be high enough. Conversely there were grave doubts about whether they could afford to secure the services of the better ones: W.G. in particular was an expensive proposition.

Canada had the great advantage of being much nearer to England. The first major overseas tour of all, by George Parr in 1859, was to North America, and the Kent professional Edgar Willsher took a team there in 1868. But the settlers seem to have been less interested than the Australians in standards of play. It was Canadian *gentlemen* who approached R. A. Fitzgerald, explaining where the colony was, in 1872. Now, although Fitzgerald was, as Lord Harris put it, 'the presiding genius' at Lord's and 'a power in the land, as the secretary of MCC should always be', the tour he so gallantly arranged was not an official one.[1] The Canadians had agreed to defray all expenses, but he had the greatest difficulty in raising an amateur eleven. He describes his relief as they embarked, complete with umpire, and clearly felt a warm missionary glow: 'The twelve apostles of cricket were committed to their work.'[2]

Regrettably, apart from a few enthusiasts, North Americans seem always to have regarded the game with modified rapture, a circumstance that has clearly irked the pundits, who have retaliated by providing facetious and unflattering explanations. They should perhaps count their blessings. The United States in 1873 produced, without really trying, one of the greatest bowlers the world has ever seen, J. B. King of Philadelphia. But the Monroe doctrine pointed in the direction of baseball. And in Canada, culturally as well as racially confused, cricket never became a national sport, despite Fitzgerald's gesture.

In Australia it was a very different story, though the difficulty of finding missionaries was just as great. It was 1873–74 before W.G.'s price could be met. As well as his professionals he took his younger brother, Fred, and his new wife on a honeymoon trip with profits. Apart from the mercenaries there seems to have been no great desire to carry the flag. In March 1877 an Australian XI won a game that has retrospectively been celebrated as the first Test match, but in fact scarcely an eyebrow was raised in St John's Wood. Indeed in 1878–79 a projected amateur tour nearly fell through for lack of volunteers. When 'The Messrs. Walker – V.E., R.D. and I.D. – who had undertaken to get up the team were prevented by domestic bereavement from going themselves' the task fell to Lord Harris, who was reduced to requisitioning the Yorkshire professionals, Tom Emmett and George Ulyett. (The compensation was that they were able to do most of the bowling chores.)

Few in England can have been surprised to learn that one of the features of this tour was a full-scale riot. The first Australian team to visit England in 1868 had been a troupe of performing aborigines, who threw boomerangs as well as cricket balls. When D. W. Gregory's more orthodox tourists of 1878 arrived in Nottingham for their first match someone had shouted: 'Why, they ain't black.' (This, Lord Harris tells us, 'was heard and resented by the team.') According to H. S. Altham, the president of the Cambridge University Club also thought Gregory's team would be black. The public were not particularly interested in the visit whatever their colour, and only when a strong MCC team, dismissed for 33 and 19, was beaten by nine wickets did anyone take the visitors seriously.

They did little to endear themselves to their hosts. For one thing they had the temerity to criticise the English umpiring, and there was a series of incidents, fully reported in the Australian press. In addition they had chosen as a member of their side one W. E. Midwinter who was born in Gloucestershire and had played for that county in 1877. This caused ill-feeling, and the climax came when the Australians chose Midwinter for a game at Lord's. W.G. was leading Gloucestershire at The Oval at the same time and he decided that Midwinter should play for them. So he drove round to Lord's in a cab and plucked him from the Australians' midst, using some very abusive language in the process, for which he later had to apologise.

Back in Australia the following winter, the pugnacious Gregory, captaining New South Wales against Lord Harris's XI, refused to play because of his objections to the English umpire. There was much betting on the game and the dissensions eventually erupted into violence, with crowds swarming on to the field and threatening the English team. (It was an occasion that left its mark on the mind of D. R. Jardine, convincing him of the paranoid nature of Australians.) Lord Harris, gallantly defended by his team and notably by 'Monkey' Hornby, seems to have recovered his poise quickly enough to write up an account of the incident and send it to the press.

Undoubtedly this rough colonial jostling diminished English enthusiasm for encounters with Australians. This may be why when another touring team came in 1880 nobody seemed to know about their trip until a week or two before they arrived. Lord Harris tells us: 'They asked no one's goodwill in the matter, and it was felt that it was a discourteous way of bursting in on our arrangements; and the result was they played scarcely any counties, and were not generally recognised.' This was quite understandable, he suggests: 'We had to make some protest against too frequent visits.'

It says much for Harris's forbearance that it was he who, late in the season, was prevailed upon to offer a sort of olive branch by getting together a scratch side to meet these gauche fellows. Thus casually was the first Test match arranged in England. Conciliatory gestures of this kind were to become of increasing importance politically, as Harris was to realise as an administrator in India. But in 1880 the motivation seems to have been more to do with 'noblesse oblige', as if some appallingly vulgar relations from a branch of the family one would prefer to disown had arrived unannounced at tea-time. The new

Australian captain, W. L. Murdoch, was after all more of a gentleman than the coarse-fibred Gregory. Cricket had not yet come to realise its imperial obligations.

In fact in 1880 the Empire was not yet a fully articulated political concept. True, the Tories under Disraeli had attacked the Liberals for wishing to dissolve it; they had made much of proclaiming Queen Victoria Empress of India in 1877 and various other flag-waving gestures. But, in power, the realities of government kept them clear of incurring additional responsibilities and unnecessary risks for the sake of far-flung possessions.

Things soon began to change. The 'historical hodge-podge of accident, trade, strategy and conquest'[3] became a positive political affirmation under Joseph Chamberlain, Lord Rosebery and younger Tories such as Balfour and Curzon. Britain's status as a world power was seen as depending on some organised response to the growing threat of European competition. In retrospect imperialism has the apparent simplicity of all great ideas: it was a splendid opportunity to combine self-interest with benevolent paternalism. For the cricket authorities it was a golden opportunity to enact the feudal ideal on a worldwide scale.

Not that this was immediately and consciously proclaimed. It was nearly half a century after Parr's first trip before MCC acknowledged its duty to the Empire by organising an official Australian tour, and even then it was a reactive gesture. There had been growing concern about the professional ventures. In 1881–82 Shaw, Shrewsbury and Lillywhite had organised a tour which had been marred by 'disquieting rumours as to the conduct of certain members of the side, and a persistent report that two of them had actually contracted to "sell" the last innings' of a game against Victoria on which there was heavy betting. After a thoroughly sporting interlude in 1882–83 in which the Hon. Ivo Bligh and his largely amateur team recaptured the Ashes, the professionals took over again. Shaw and company went out again in 1884–85 when good cricket was 'largely vitiated by a series of unsavoury disputes'. Worst of all, after Shaw and Shrewsbury had toured successfully in 1886–87 Shrewsbury took a team out the following winter as a business venture, only to find that Lord Hawke, at the invitation of the Melbourne Club, also had a team out there.

It was clearly time to relieve the professionals of the burden. Lord Sheffield, whom H. S. Altham describes as 'the Maecenas of cricketers', persuaded W.G. – for a consideration – to show the flag in 1891–92 and from then on it was 'amateurs' all the way, with A. E. Stoddart taking two tours in 1894–95 and 1897–98, until in 1901–2 the imperious A. C. MacLaren, accepting an invitation the MCC had declined, got into great difficulties in raising a team.

Bowlers were his chief problem. According to MacLaren, who had invited Hirst and Rhodes of Yorkshire, their county committee had not allowed any of their professionals to go. Whether there was more to it than that is hard to say. Lord Hawke and MacLaren appear to have disagreed profoundly. Also for whatever reason none of the leading amateurs found themselves free to make the trip, and in the end MacLaren had to resort to inviting the crossgrained Barnes from the Lancashire League. It was clear that this haphazard and unseemly approach was no longer appropriate: beating the Australians had begun to be too important to leave things to chance. So from 1903–4 the premier club assumed the imperial burden.

By then the world and the Empire were very different propositions from the days of the first tours. MacLaren's trip took place as the Boer War was reaching its final stages. In 1870 when competitive county cricket began to flourish British foreign trade was greater than that of Germany, France and Italy combined and four times that of the United States. Afterwards, despite growing prosperity in absolute terms, Britain seemed to be falling back in the race. The economy was relying too much on invisible exports and the like: British technology on which her livelihood seemed chiefly to depend was not keeping pace with America or Germany. France had doubled her colonial possessions between 1815 and 1870. A land-grab had developed with all the European powers competing. Markets; raw materials; reception areas for immigrants; Christianity; exploration – all played their part in making Africa and Asia skirmishing grounds for rival imperialistic ambitions.

For Britain Germany was gradually emerging as the chief economic and political threat, one so great that it led eventually to an alliance with France. Cricket's golden age was a period of ferment, a time darkened by the shadow of war. Yet the prospect did not seem entirely dark to many: it was a time of jingoism. With Joseph Chamberlain, the dominant figure of Lord Salisbury's government from 1895 to 1902, as Colonial Secretary, and Cecil Rhodes dreaming of an English Africa from the Cape to the Zambesi, imperial expansion was a central political issue. The one substantial literary figure to appeal to the man in the street, Rudyard Kipling, was the apostle not only of imperialism but of the disciplined yet brutal moral code needed to sustain it. Jingoism, which could withstand against world opinion the charge of bullying two small states in southern Africa and recover from the humiliating setbacks of the Boer War, was also able to translate the assertion of Britain's God-given right to rule, complemented by economic self-interest, into a great cause which would if necessary have to be defended.

The public schools, expanding rapidly after 1840, became increasingly conscious of their role as the prime source of leadership for the imperial cause and also, almost as a corollary, in preparing young men for their destiny as defenders of their heritage. Archie MacLaren's attitudes, on the field and off, were unusual only in being slightly less predictable, slightly more imperious, than most. Otherwise he was a not untypical product. When the First World War eventually came he wrote of the Kaiser as 'a crowned madman' and 'a hog in armour'.[4] It was all part of the code of sportsmanship that distinguished British imperialism from rival brands.

The classical expression of the link between cricket and war is that of Sir Henry Newbolt's 'Vitaï Lampada', a gem of the golden age:

> There's a breathless hush in the Close tonight,
> Ten to make and the match to win,
> A bumping pitch and a blinding light,
> An hour to play and the last man in,
> And it's not for the sake of a ribboned coat,
> Or the selfish hope of a season's fame,
> But his Captain's hand on his shoulder smote
> 'Play up! play up and play the game!'

This famous opening stanza is in itself remarkable as an illustration of the noble motives cricket is supposed to inspire. But the second reveals the game's true purpose in the eyes of the Almighty:

> The sand of the desert is sodden red,
> Red with the wreck of a square that broke.
> The Gatling's jammed and the Colonel dead,
> And the regiment blind with dust and smoke.

The river of death has brimmed his banks,
And England's far and Honour a name,
But the voice of a schoolboy rallies the ranks,
'Play up! play up! and play the game!' [5]

And when the golden age had spent itself in the mud of Flanders, the victory proved the value of the code. Sir Theodore Cook, the Editor of *The Field*, published in 1927 his *Character and Sportsmanship*, a 300-page exposition of Newbolt's theme. For Sir Theodore sportsmanship is the best guarantee of success in 'the great game' of war, which is why the British always win. Great men like Lord Harris had helped inculcate the true belief 'that after Lord's they would be able to keep up their wicket under conditions even more responsible and on a pitch considerably more dangerous.'

Admitting that his words may be unacceptable or unintelligible to some, Sir Theodore explains that he is writing in code: 'the code . . . which is common to every true subject of the British Crown; the arguments which are native to the English because they are drawn from the most deep-seated instincts of the English race – the instincts of sportsmanship and fair play.' He assures us, however, that he does not believe the 'code of honour . . . is solely to be found in the public schools and universities', though 'the constant cry for elevating the masses can never effect what is expected of it while it is accompanied by neglect of these admirable institutions.' The chief purpose of this type of education, he tells us, 'is the formation of an élite, not for its own sake, not for its own glory, but for the advancement and benefit of society at large.' (The élite, we may take it, would be unlikely to extend to all sections of the Empire. Sir Theodore at one stage writes approvingly: 'he could handle niggers.')

It is not a matter of intellectual superiority but of leadership by 'men whose character and hearts have flourished in the sunshine of the fair play they are always ready to extend to others'. And it is not just a matter of training. 'No theories will ever destroy the fundamental fact of nature that some people are born to govern and others to work.' Indeed, Sir Theodore goes on, 'it is almost tempting to try and discover whether the sporting instinct that brought us safe through the Great War was not the offspring of a far older racial characteristic which had been in the English fibre ever since England was a nation that could hold her own abroad.'[6]

Sir Theodore may have expressed himself colourfully, but he undoubtedly expressed widely held beliefs: (i) that the British are superior to everyone else, because they play fair, but (ii) they can only demonstrate their superiority to the rest of the world – by defeating it and keeping it in order – if the gentlemen lead the players into action. These beliefs have served the cricket establishment as a philosophy over the years. They make up the dream-world it has defended against the harsh realities, in cricket and in social and political affairs.

By the time Britain was facing a second World War C. B. Fry was writing in *Life Worth Living*: 'It is not true that breeding, environment, and the atmosphere of the home count for nothing. Of those at a good public school at least 40% are capable of making first-rate officers . . . compared with no more than 10–12% . . . from the council schools and the environment of wage-earning homes.' And a decade after it G. D. Martineau offered a revealing comparison: 'Professionals are as much the backbone of English first-class cricket as non-commissioned officers are the backbone of the British army.'

Martineau's image is part of a loving exposition of the early days of cricket through which the yearning for the old feudal order shines bright: 'There was, then, a clear, natural division between the patron, often a member of the nobility, who organised teams and matches and the man who was "kept to play cricket", that is to say between Gentleman and Player.' This 'natural' division is all-important. 'First-class cricket at its best has depended for more than two centuries on a nicely-adjusted balance between these two elements.'[7] 'Nicely-adjusted', a splendidly question-begging phrase, suggests a divine hand at the controls.

The conventional view is that the balance was at its natural, nicely-adjusted best during the golden age when the amateur code of chivalry was fully-developed, before the rot set in after the First World War. Orthodox opinion from Ranjitsinhji on has also held that cricket was one of the greatest gifts Britain gave the Empire, embodying as it did all the ingredients of her own special code of honour. The facts are somewhat different.

No one could deny that the amateur tradition produced some examples of chivalry, but it also produced the reverse. There was, for instance, the behaviour on a historic occasion of the deplorable Beauclerk. Edward Budd, a contemporary amateur, recounts how 'Lord Frederick, with Howard, made a p.p. [play or pay] match with

Osbaldeston and Lambert. On the day named, I went to Lord Frederick representing my friend who was too ill to stand, and asked him to put off the match. "No, play or pay," said his Lordship, quite inexorable.' Worse was to come: 'Mr Osbaldeston, feeling much too ill to play on the morning fixed for the match . . . continued to walk up to the wicket in order to be able to claim a substitute in fielding but this was overruled.'[8] And if we write off this first leading amateur as an unfortunate exception we can scarcely do so for the greatest of all, W.G.

W.G.'s 'duo-decimo lawyer' tactics were doubly unfortunate when he employed them in international cricket, and the evidence is that other great amateurs passed on some bad habits, even in the golden age. Indeed much of the chivalry in the Test matches at the turn of the century seems to have come from the Australians. C. B. Fry describes an incident in the first Test in 1905: 'Towards the end of the Australian second innings when they were well in the soup, the light became very poor. Charles McLeod, when his partner got out, ran to the pavilion and signalled. The big brown moustache of Joe Darling emerged. There was a consultation at the gate. Joe Darling surveyed the quarters of the sky as a farmer would, then shook his head, slowly indeed, but not without emphasis, turned his broad back, and went in. McLeod had wanted to know whether to appeal against the light. The light was bad. If Joe Darling had allowed the appeal I think it certain that the umpires would have stopped play, and Australia would have drawn the match. Joe Darling was a sportsman of the best. We had by that time morally won the game, and Joe Darling was not the man to slide out over a side-issue.'

On the other hand in the first Test of the 1897–98 series this same McLeod, who was deaf, failed to hear the umpire call 'no-ball' when the ball hit his stumps, left his ground and the Englishmen ran him out. In the fourth Test the great MacLaren, to much derision, claimed that a fly in his eye had caused his dismissal, and Ranjitsinhji was quoted as follows: 'When I say we had no luck I would instance Briggs' downfall to a very poor ball, while it was ill-fortune for him that a man should have been standing on the precise spot where it fell.'[9] Neither of these claims went down too well with the press or the public in Australia.

There is a suspicion in all this that the representatives of the mother country thought it not entirely necessary always to behave well towards colonials and that they felt it was an inversion of the natural order of things if they did not win. This at least is how it looked to many down under. For some it was confirmation of what they had long believed: for others it was the sad culmination of years of mounting disappointment. In the 1850s Australia had been not only already 'cricket mad' – the first priority of every new township seemed to be a race-course and a cricket ground – but utterly deferential towards England and starry-eyed about her standards in cricket as in graver matters. Even the early discovery that the tourists were not invincible but were intensely materialistic did not shake the beliefs of the faithful. There were some very red faces amongst sycophantic contributors to the press when W.G. himself eventually came and proved to be merely mortal, but the argument was still very much a family affair.

The inferiority feelings that beset Australians, at least until the 1890s, seemed to have little to do with the colonial relationship itself. The feelings of being a Victorian or Tasmanian only slowly became stronger than the feeling of being an Antipodean Englishman. The mother country was regarded exactly as the phrase suggests. Their chief anxieties were whether convict origins might somehow taint the blood and whether the hot climate might somehow shrivel it up, thus debasing the pure Anglo-Saxon stock. Cricket between the Australian colonies tested the relative quality of the various categories of settler; and, of course, prowess against England herself was the ultimate test. So, after setbacks in the 1880s, the convincing victories of the 1890s brought considerable feelings of relief. It was hardly surprising if this exhilaration sometimes spilled over into a cocksureness that added salt to the English wounds. By the 1890s these wounds were deep enough to hurt.

On W.G.'s 1891–92 tour and the two led by A. E. Stoddart in 1894–95 and 1897–98 it was no longer simply a question of whether eleven cricketers beat another eleven. Even back home the Test matches were treated increasingly seriously and the defeats grew harder to bear. In 1897 Queen Victoria was, according to Australian sources, sent cabled reports on the progress of the games.[10] By the time this tour was over, Ranji's and MacLaren's excuses and Stoddart's criticism of the barrackers – whose 'loud-voiced satire and banter' grew in volume and vehemence as Australian superiority became more obvious – appeared to have implications that went beyond skill at games. Was it possible that the 'Hinglish', as they were coming to be known in some circles, were not very good sports?

It seems clear that, if the barrackers were anything to go by, distinctly hostile and anti-British attitudes were gaining ground. The emergent nationalism was fed by social resentments that had sometimes found expression even in the 1860s when admiration for 'old England' was virtually unbounded. The social distinctions associated with English cricket, though they had their advocates, were not in keeping with the assumptions of this land of opportunity. When in 1860 *Bell's* boasted of the rich variety of social classes the Victorian gold field had brought to cricket, the echo of Pycroft was there, but the hope for the future was of a genuine social mix, not the preservation of the 'natural' hierarchical order of things on the English pattern. Sceptical expatriates were amongst the sternest critics of what they had left behind. In 1871 a former Cambridge Blue assured readers of the *Australasian* that neither 'spotless flannels, gorgeous stripes and caps' nor an array of fancy Christian names were any guarantee of good play. There were a few local professionals to add to the English imports, such as the famous William Caffyn who had set up as a coach in Melbourne after the 1863–64 tour, but the word did not carry the same connotations as it did at home. Full-time professionals were always a tiny minority of first-class cricketers and the conventions applauded by Lord Harris were never adopted.

Nationalistic attitudes began to surface in cricket once it could be seen that fears about the impurity of the stock were groundless. The argument of the doubters that the earliest successes were the result of expatriate skill was overthrown as local boys began to make good. Only one of the Australian tourists who defeated a strong MCC XI in England in 1878 was not native born, and he, Charles Bannerman, had gone to Australia as a child. The *Illustrated Sydney News*, whilst acknowledging that the colonists were 'from the old stock', suggested that it might have been 'improved by grafting on Australian soil'. And, conversely, there can be no doubt of the central significance of cricket in creating an Australian identity. By the late 1870s anxious social critics were complaining that the constant references to sport as indicators of national stature were 'out of all proportion'. Cricket was also a powerful unifying force: the sweet taste of victory over England did much to subdue inter-colonial rivalries, even that between New South Wales and Victoria. (According to Dr W. Mandle, Sydney was a dangerous place for certain opponents in the 1860s. ('There's a Victorian cricketer, 'eave arf a brick at him,' the locals shouted.)

In 1874 the Australians called themselves simply a 'combined team' but this became 'an Australian XI' in 1877. The Governor of New South Wales, welcoming these tourists home, even anticipated events by referring to them as 'the federal team of Australian cricketers'. A coat of arms of uncertain origin was used by the 1884 tourists. By the 1890s cricket was widely quoted as a notable example of what could be achieved through inter-colonial co-operation. In 1898, still three years before Federation, the *Bulletin* wrote of the defeat of Stoddart's team: 'This ruthless rout of English cricket will do – and has done – more to enhance the cause of Australian nationality than could ever be achieved by miles of erudite essays and impassioned appeal.'

Significantly, as this feeling of national identity grew so did criticism of the 'Hinglish' with their 'everlasting snobbery'. In the English magazine *Cricket* in 1899 the visiting Australians' manager expressed the view that one of the reasons for his team's success was their more democratic views on captaincy and their rejection of the whole debilitating philosophy of gentlemen and players. By contrast, frequent references by Englishmen to Australian commercialism, excessive keenness, rough manners and other indications of low breeding suggest an increasing irritation at the challenge to standards, social as well as cricketing, by the colonials.

For a time during the early part of the present century, when the pendulum swung some way back towards England in the Tests and the cult of the golden age held sway, attitudes relaxed. There was the consolation that other parts of the Empire were still under tutelage – parts, furthermore, such as South Africa, West Indies and India, where the caste system ensured that gentlemanly conduct still prevailed. Indeed the Antipodes could not be entirely written off even after the Great War. In 1921 the first issue of P. F. Warner's magazine *The Cricketer*, a monument to the high code, recorded with pleasure the statement of the New Zealand Prime Minister, the Rt. Hon. W. F. Massey, that 'cricket had perhaps done more than any other game in the formation of national character.' The slight qualification, 'perhaps', which was presumably included with an eye to the voting strength of rugby players, was more than offset by his peroration; he concluded with an exhortation to 'Play up, play up and play the game!' It did not matter whether the game was cricket or the game of life. 'In his estimate of the value which attaches to international tours,' Warner adds, 'Mr Massey is in complete agreement with the late Mr Joseph Chamberlain.'

But 1921 was also the year of Warwick Armstrong's altogether too successful tour. It had been bad enough to be defeated in every Test the previous winter in Australia, but to be thrashed on English wickets was too much to bear. Armstrong and his men confirmed the worst suspicions of many at Lord's that Australians were 'too keen to win'. They were ungentlemanly in a number of ways, including being diffi-cult over hours of play, a matter which was to upset one rising young amateur, Douglas Jardine, in particular. In fact they were a threat to the amateur tradition, which was already under siege. The desire for revenge, the re-establishment of the 'natural' order of things, grew strong.

Unfortunately, when it came in 1926 it was short-lived. Armstrong was followed by an even greater bogeyman, Don Bradman. A neutral observer, and particularly one insensitive enough to regard cricket as simply a game, might well conclude from all this that the code the English gave the Empire had no higher ethical basis than tit-for-tat. Such heresy has never been acceptable to the cricket establishment, who took to heart Joe Chamberlain's injunction to think imperially, for it undermines the social values they have sought to preserve. This may explain why they have tended to attribute the growing fierce-ness of Test match cricket to colonial boorishness or excessive professionalism.

Bradman was a godsend to the diehards – a great batsman, they allowed, but typical of the age, and of Australians, far too hard and ruthless. Even his friends saw little chivalry in him, as a batsman or a captain. A fellow-Australian, Ray Robinson, wrote of his batting: 'You might say a batsman gifted with so much had no need always to push his barrow so hard that it could run over the toes of others. To expect a man to go against the dictates of his nature would be like telling a river not to run' – and of his captaincy: 'He was no believer in other-cheekmanship. Adverse events left him implacable in vengeance, inexorable in pressing for every advantage existing law permitted. He was relentless, striving for crushing victories to weaken every resist-ance for the series.'[11]

But some very unlikely people drew certain improbable conclu-sions from this. A. W. Carr, not exactly the soul of chivalry himself (indeed sacked as a county captain for lack of it), complained in 1935, after England had fractured the code almost beyond repair in the bodyline tour, that Australians did not seem to realise that cricket was 'a game not a mixture of war and all-in-wrestling', endorsing Lord Castlerosse's smug pronouncement: 'Here in England we do not know the bitterness which these games engender . . . These Test matches are not carried out as games but with all the ferocity of war.'[12]

From where Bradman stood it all looked very different. He said he had learned his relentless captaincy at the hands of the happy and charming English amateur A. P. F. Chapman. 'In my first Test match,' Bradman said, 'England, though leading by nearly 400, went in again and left us over 700 to attempt in our last innings with two men out of action.'[13] If this indeed was what induced Bradman's later attitude to Test match cricket, that decision was one of the worst moves England ever made. Australia had won Test matches before the Bradman era, but when he arrived it began to look as though they might never lose one again.

As in captaincy, so in batting. In the first week of Bradman's first tour of England in 1930 he scored 421 runs for once out. He would have had more but for rain, and despite the wet weather he scored a thousand by the end of May. He made 974 runs in the Test matches, including 334 at Leeds, 309 of them in a day. But this was a response to an equally crushing total of 905 runs by Hammond in the 1928–29 series when Bradman was a boy of 20. Thereafter it was tit-for-tat. Quite apart from team considerations there was intense rivalry between the two great men: it emerged again in 1938 when Hammond, by then England's captain and an amateur, batted on at The Oval to a total of 903 for seven before declaring. Bradman, humiliated and frustrated as he was carried off the field lame, vowed his revenge and took it in 1946–47 and again in 1948.

The mythology, which does not acknowledge tit-for-tat, sees in this a decline from the ethical standards of the golden age. C. L. R. James held this view: 'The ethics, the morals, the personal impulses and desires of cricketers were quite different from those who had played the game in the decades that had preceded.' He believed that 'modern society took a turn downwards in 1929' and that the notion of '"it isn't cricket" was one of its casualties.' There are more convincing explanations.

For one thing the orthodox view assumes that cricket is 'more than a game'. It requires us to believe in the high moral tone of W. G. Grace. Is it not conceivable that W.G. or those who immediately followed him, given the placid pitches of later years, would themselves have built up huge scores before venturing to declare? (In 1886 Hampstead batted all day for 813 leaving no time for their opponents to bat: the dashing A. E. Stoddart made 485.) Conditions apart, any game will generate rivalries. Hammond versus Bradman, and Jardine and Larwood versus Bradman, whatever else they were, were clashes between strong personalities.

But even if we seek deeper causes there seem better explanations for the growth of ruthlessness in the interwar years than decline from the golden age. Britain was having to face the beginning of the end of colonialism. Cricket was an integral part of the creation of the Empire, as well as an emblem charged with emotion, redolent of the highest social values, imbued with overtones of personal and political potency. This potency mattered greatly in Australia, too. Cricket was a focus for national pride at this stage as it had been in the previous century. There was a national cricket team before there was a nation: and cricket was highly influential in the move towards federation of the separate colonies. The captaincy of the team acquired a political significance and a social status that lasted until recent years. Cricket heroes have had a special place in Australian legend, so it was in no way surprising to find the greatest one of all at the centre of things in the interwar years.

The federal Commonwealth of Australia, having replaced the separate colonies in 1901, had gradually gained more and more independence. At the time of the First World War Britain had not felt the necessity to consult the Dominions before declaring war on their behalf. Australia, having played a notable part in the victory, was ready by the 1920s for further advance. The country was at the horrible stage, rather like an adolescent, when extremes of self-confidence alternated with extremes of self-doubt. So Bradman was much more than a cricketer. As Philip Lindsay recalled: 'Any name was needed to revive our shrinking egos . . . had there been a god of the game to whom we could have prayed, that lad's name would have risen from almost every home in Australia, freighted with a country's hopes.'[14] Bradman was a powerful symbol and his emergence in 1928–29 was a landmark in Australian history.

In England on the other hand the phenomenon was understandably received with less enthusiasm. It had taken the old country until 1926 to win back the Ashes after the depredations of the War, and now here was another threat. By the 1930 tour of England the menace was clear. MCC's choice of captain for the next series in Australia reflected this. They chose a strong man. Perhaps it was an accident, though if so it was a strange coincidence. D. R. Jardine was not only an archetypal amateur but also an archetypal imperialist. His attitude to the manly cricketing virtues and the public-school code would have done credit to Lord Harris himself, and his manner was cold, stern and unbending.

Jack Fingleton, in a telling comment, described how the Australians saw him. 'Had Jardine come to Australia in [the] eighteenth century and been cloaked in authority he would have strutted the stage with the early governors.'[15] In the bodyline tour the code of sportsmanship and its imperial obligations fell foul of the circumstances that (i) a game is not an ethical religion but a contest, and (ii) the colonials were not forever fixed in postures of docile admiration. The traditional view of cricket after the First World War is that it represented a decline from the standards of the golden age and its dashing amateurs. With regard to bodyline there is a strong argument for suggesting that the decline was the *result* of the golden age.

The morality of cricket, as that of any game must be, is much nearer that of the Old Testament than the New. In the golden age its god was Kipling's and Sir Theodore Cook's and Newbolt's – the god of the far-flung battle line, undoubtedly an upper-class Englishman.

SEVEN

BODYLINE AND THE PREMIER CLUB

WE DO NOT KNOW if the selectors of the MCC team to tour Australia in the winter of 1932–33 were imbued with the spirit of Kipling. There is no evidence that they had dark Old Testament thoughts as they chose Douglas Jardine as captain. Without a doubt, though, they worked on the basis of choosing the captain first (more for his qualities of leadership than for his playing ability) and on the assumption that he should be an amateur. This was but one of many ways in which the England and Australian traditions were poles apart; the Australian method was to pick the best team and then appoint a captain from among them.

But then the Australians had never been regarded as gentlemen. They had never understood the code. In a funny but revealing passage Cardus describes how A. C. MacLaren dealt with his opponents' vulgar behaviour.

> Joe Darling had placed three men near MacLaren's legs in a close semi-circle. MacLaren addressed himself to Darling: 'Joe,' he said,

'What's the meaning of this?'

'What's the meaning of what, Archie?'

'Why,' said MacLaren, indicating with a sweep of his bat the crouching leg-side fieldsmen, 'Why, what are these people doing here, Joe?'

'That's my field for you, Archie,' replied Darling.

MacLaren waved his bat at them again. 'Joe,' he said, 'Take them away.'

. . . Darling declined to change his field, so Ernest Jones bowled and the match at last began. MacLaren drove Jones twice or thrice for straight fours, then Darling removed a man from the leg-trap and sent him to the deep, behind the bowler.

'Thank you, Joe,' said MacLaren. 'Now we may proceed with the match like gentlemen.'[1]

The differences in social attitudes of the two countries were deep-rooted. In 1926 Joe Darling had written in his memoirs: 'I note there is a lot of discussion in England about the amateurs and professionals using the same dressing-room', recalling that in his day the professionals had not been allowed to sit at the same table as the amateurs, and that when an amateur and a professional opened the innings together for their country the professional had to be ready at the gate but dare not go on to the playing area ahead of his gentleman partner. 'I have heard some English captains speak to their professionals like dogs,' says Darling starkly.

Between the wars, as the Bolshevistic goings-on at The Oval remind us (with Fender scandalising the traditionalists by calling round at the professionals' dressing-room to lead them on to the field), the gulf between the amateur and professional was still as wide, in the minds of many, as in Hambledon days. Sharing a dressing-room would have been a gracious concession comparable to that of Sir Horace Mann allowing his name to be bestowed on Noah Mann's offspring.

When Joe Darling talks of English amateur captains speaking to their professionals like dogs this had nothing to do with chauvinistic rivalries: it is genuine sympathy for the downtrodden. His description of the double-standard, financially and in other respects, was a plain statement of the realities behind the myth of the golden age. Darling was convinced that the amateurs got a better deal from the umpires than they were entitled to. He describes incidents in 1895 in which a leading amateur (unnamed but from internal evidence almost certainly the model of propriety Sir Stanley Jackson) pulls rank on his county colleague, the professional J. T. Brown. 'I can well remember a certain English amateur . . . "rounding" on that fine little English professional, J. T. Brown, when we were playing Yorkshire at Bradford. This amateur called Brown for an impossible run, and Brown said "No, Sir." Brown was told that he had to run whenever he was called, and a little while later he called Brown again, and they ran, and the amateur was run out. All our team were pleased that Brown was not run out. At Manchester, when these same two batsmen were playing for All-England, the same thing occurred again only this time poor old "Johnny" Brown had to go.'

The difference between the English and the Australian attitudes from Darling's day to Bradman's is well illustrated by the cynosure C. B. Fry. In his autobiography Fry recalls with particular disdain how Sir Rufus Isaacs had said to him, intending a compliment: 'I wish I were as distinguished in my profession as you are in yours.' Fry took exception to this: 'Sir Rufus prided himself on his diplomatic gifts but that is the one and only time I have been called a professional cricketer.' On the other hand, Jack Fingleton records in *Cricket Crisis* the resentment Australians felt at an article by Fry in 1938 which said: 'In all this Australian team there are barely one or two who would be accepted as public school men . . . and while I am writing this, Curator – has just bowled another maiden over.'

After the First World War when the English amateurs had begun to feel threatened by the forces of outer darkness hostility to Australians had grown. In D. W. Gregory's day it had been easy to dismiss them as people who might not actually be aborigines but were of that order of being. In Joe Darling's time the amateurs were still secure enough to be tolerant of their opponents' social shortcomings. The inhospitable post-war world and the steamroller tactics of Warwick Armstrong's 1921 tourists – which seemed part of this unpleasant new era – began to set the teeth on edge of the new generation of amateurs. With the world of privilege shrinking they were highly sensitive to any assault on its values.

Despite the extraordinary rapacity of some leading English players and promoters, amateur as well as professional, there had always been a tendency to consider the Australians as commercially-minded: the 1882 tourists, for example, were thought to 'have seriously and perceptibly aggravated the symptoms of a commercial spirit in cricket'. By the 1930s A. W. Carr was denouncing the scandal that although cricket was 'more or less purely and simply a matter of £ s. d.' with the Australians, yet they were 'made a great fuss of and given privileges which are denied to our own professionals.' They were in effect a threat to the caste system, not only because, although they took money for playing, they were given amateur status in England, but because unlike their English counterparts who did the same they were socially unacceptable. 'I know plenty of professionals whom I would delight to have as guests in my own home,' wrote Carr in *Cricket With The Lid Off*, 'but I am afraid I cannot say the same thing about most of the Australians whom I have met.'

All of these tensions and resentments, added to the Bradman phenomenon and the uneasy transition from colonialism, made the choice of Jardine as captain something less than a triumph of diplomacy. Jardine's first experience of Australians had seared his soul, when he had been cheated of a century for Oxford University in 1921 because Warwick Armstrong's tourists insisted on curtailing the game so that they could rest before the Test match. When he went on the 1928–29 tour, Jack Fingleton suggests, 'Jardine's flannels had barely emerged from their first laundering before he made up his mind that he liked neither Australia nor the average Australian.' 'To take the most charitable view of the position,' Jardine wrote in 1933, 'the behaviour of Australian crowds at its best, when judged by the standards accepted by the rest of the world, is not naturally good.' His tone is that of a schoolmaster discussing an unresponsive pupil. He is sure Australians will 'resent reproof': 'Unlike most Englishmen, the Australian, while impatient of criticism from without, is not given to criticizing either himself or his country.'

He despised the sheer vulgar effrontery of their barrackers: 'Here was Democracy arrogating to itself the right to demand its full pound of flesh for which it had paid the magnificent sum of a shilling or two at the gate.' They even barracked umpires, and 'No sane sportsman can suggest that is anything but dastardly.' Jardine reminds us of the long history of crowd disturbance in Australia, including 1879 when Lord Harris had had to be rescued from the mob by naval officers and 'Monkey' Hornby seized a fellow by the throat, took him to the pavilion and pitched him through the committee-room window. (Lord Harris behaved 'awfully well'.) There had been a deplorable demonstration in 1903–4 when umpire Crockett gave out Clem Hill, 'who showed by his manner that he was greatly surprised at the decision'; there was yelling and hissing until close of play and 'even such hardened Test match players as Hirst and Rhodes were quite upset.'

Jardine thought it significant that he had never heard Australian crowds barrack their own team: yet, disgracefully, when he was hit by a fast bowler there was a roar from the crowd followed by sustained applause. Jack Fingleton on the other hand reckoned that Jardine was God's gift to barrackers: as he progressed, in Harlequin cap and silk scarf, in stately fashion to the wicket someone shouted 'Where's your butler to carry your bat for you?' He was a poor mixer, the typically aloof Englishman, who had declined to shake hands with an effusive stranger on a country railway station and who could not understand the ingenuous Australian habit of boasting. Jardine had also, Fingleton tells us, 'struck immediate press trouble at Perth in 1932. He would not play ball with them in announcing his team for publication purposes.' These things troubled Jardine little. 'I had long since ceased to care what the Australian press said about me, nor did I pay any heed to what individuals frequently said behind my back.'[2]

In fact Jardine's mind was set on one purpose: nothing else mattered but taking the Ashes from these colonials and stopping that fellow Bradman. This, and his disdain for them all, explains how so upright a gentleman, pillar of public school, Oxford and MCC cricket, the epitome of all it represented, should break the code and, in the process, rock the foundations of the Empire. Yet it would be wrong to suggest, as some have done, that it was all Jardine's doing. At the time few people in England saw it as a fall from grace. Most were too pleased about winning the Ashes to worry about how it had been done. The cricket establishment itself, though including several who privately deprecated Jardine's lack of humour and stern unbending attitudes, did nothing to deter him and put on a cloak of righteous indignation when challenged.

One man who was somewhat fortunate to come out of it with reputation unscathed and indeed feeling free to make self-righteous noises was P. F. Warner. As chairman of the selectors he must have known something of what was afoot: certainly he knew of Jardine's attitude. As joint manager he was in a position to see everything that went on. In one capacity or another he could, one feels, have done something to try to stop it. But Warner had a talent for reconciling the irreconcilable. He had had much practice, having been for years a Test selector and also a daily newspaper cricket correspondent: two ostensibly conflicting roles that he prided himself on never confusing.

Bodyline must have driven him to the point of schizophrenia. In the *Morning Post* of 22 August 1932 Warner had written of a Yorkshire game: 'Bowes must alter his tactics. Bowes bowled with five men on the on-side and sent down several very short-pitched balls which repeatedly bounced heart high and more. Now that is not bowling: indeed it is not cricket.' Magisterial, authoritative and plain: this was 'not cricket' and it must stop. Yet he did nothing to restrain Jardine in Australia. Whilst people were being battered on the field he seems to have restricted his activities to trying to offer soothing balm afterwards. He was puzzled and hurt when Woodfull, the injured Australian captain, did not want to chat happily to him about it when he visited the Australian dressing-room with Lionel Palairet, his co-manager. 'Our reception was freezing,' writes Warner. 'We said how sorry we were and Woodfull replied: "I don't want to see you, Mr Warner. There are two teams out there. One is trying to play cricket and the other is not".'[3] According to Ray Robinson, Woodfull also added: 'The game is too good to be spoilt. It is time some people got out of the game. Good afternoon.'[4]

Admittedly Jardine must have been a difficult man to control. In his stiff-necked way he managed to exude righteousness and also to conceal the harsh realities from the world – and perhaps also from himself. Thus he insisted on calling bodyline 'leg-theory' and claiming that it had a long and honourable history. It may be that he had that peculiar talent of the British upper set for subterfuge portrayed by Anthony Cave-Brown in his history of espionage.[5] Certainly his account of how bodyline came to be introduced is far from straightforward.

At one point he claims that it was invoked as a logical way of exploiting a discovery made in the second match of the tour: 'To our surprise we found an almost totally unsuspected weakness on the leg stump in the play of several leading players. This had been particularly apparent in the case of Bradman.' But, as Bradman pointed out, this was disingenuous to say the least. Jardine had also written: 'Though I did not take part in The Oval Test match of 1930 I have been told that Bradman's innings, impressive though it was in the number of runs scored, was far from convincing on the leg-stump.'[6]

Jardine was not the only one to offer several accounts. Indeed there have been so many explanations that the truth is hard to get at. There is no doubt that Jardine himself must take most of the blame, but the version preferred by Australians, of innocent professionals manipulated by wicked amateurs, though understandable, can scarcely be entirely correct. Larwood cannot have been just the quiet, gentle chrysanthemum-growing innocent that history seems currently to make of him. Indeed it was only after the tide of opinion had turned against bodyline that Larwood himself was disposed to let others take the credit for the innovation.

In 1935 A. W. Carr, his county captain, wrote: 'Until I began to write this book I always believed that leg-theory bowling started, where Larwood was concerned, for Notts in 1931.' Presumably Carr didn't read other people's books. Larwood had committed himself to print two years before. 'Fast leg-theory bowling,' he had written, 'was born in the Test match at Kennington Oval in August 1930. A spot of rain had fallen. The ball was "popping". My great friend the late Archie Jackson stood up to me, getting pinked once or twice in the process and he never flinched. With Bradman it was different. It was because of that difference that I determined then and there, that if I was again honoured with an invitation to go to Australia I would not forget that difference.'[7]

This seems more convincing than Carr's 1935 revelation that by then Larwood was claiming to have bowled two overs of leg-theory to Alan Kippax on the 1928–29 tour and that Jardine had taken a catch at long leg. (Jardine explained that there was an orthodox offside field, so it hardly amounted to bodyline.) The significant point about Larwood's 1933 version is that it states explicitly what the two accounts by Jardine imply – that Bradman was the target and that they thought they had discovered a chink in his armour, his instinct for self-preservation.

Bradman himself thought it was even more sinister. On the 1932 tour, he wrote, he had only been at the wicket a few minutes in the match in question, so Jardine could hardly have had time to spot weaknesses. At The Oval in 1930 the press reports had spoken of his lion-hearted display; he made a lot of runs; and in any case he was given out caught behind off Larwood when he did not hit the ball. (In Bradman fashion he is careful to make it clear that he does not complain of this: he just wants to clarify matters.) What Bradman is at pains to establish is that, from the moment he had been appointed captain for the tour, Jardine had been scheming his downfall through intimidatory bowling on the line of the body to a packed leg-side field.

Bradman reminds us that F. R. Foster, an early and non-lethal leg-theory specialist, had admitted, in order to purge himself of the guilt of allowing his knowledge to be used in this unscrupulous way, that he had been in conclave with Jardine at his 'flat in the St James'. And Bradman adds Walter Hammond's statement, on his return to England (having been hit on the chin himself, turning against body-line), that the plot had been hatched even before the Foster visits – 'in the grill-room of the Piccadilly Hotel, London'.

There is a delicious suggestion in Bradman's book that these meeting places prove that dissolute and wicked upper-class forces were at work. However he was undoubtedly correct in his facts. A. W. Carr admits to taking Larwood and Voce shortly after their selection to meet Jardine at the Piccadilly Hotel grill-room, where, although it took them some time to warm up to talk to 'their not exactly hail-fellow-well-met captain-to-be . . . they did eventually get going.' And, says Carr, what they discussed was 'subsequently developed on the ship on the journey out' – so by the time they got to Australia Jardine, Larwood 'and others of the team knew what the fast bowling campaign was to be in the Tests.'

Bradman is a hard man to agree with: he is too assiduous in proving himself right. He carefully makes no claim to be infallible, but he is always at pains to show, often with reluctance and out of regard only for the truth, that he is right on the occasions and in the way that it matters. But, though he may be too good to be true, there can be little doubt that he was intended to be a victim on this occasion. Jardine was out for his blood and had been for some time. Whether Warner was one of the inner circle who knew what was afoot before the Tests began is impossible to discover. He was an expert at letting other people hold wet babies. A. W. Carr was in the best possible position to know that. Indeed a point in favour of Warner's innocence is that Carr, who obviously detested Warner by then, would not have hesitated to implicate him if he could.

Warner's slipperiness went back, as far as Carr was concerned, to 1926. Having chosen Carr as England captain and having expressed great faith in him, Warner kept on interfering – behind the scenes and surreptitiously. Carr is quite plain about it: in the first Test 'P. F. Warner told me to declare the innings closed.' He goes on to say: 'I never really had a free hand. I was constantly being advised to do this or that.'

The crisis came in the third Test. The weather had been wet, and Carr was tempted to put the Australians in to bat. He took advice, listened to the groundsman who thought it a good idea, 'and certainly Warner was determined in that opinion.' As every schoolboy knows the plan went wrong. It all depended on two or three early wickets. Warren Bardsley was out quickly. In came Macartney. Poor Carr set a trap for him and then dropped the easy catch that popped into his hands. Macartney went on to grind them into the dust. Lunch was not a happy experience and, as Carr says, 'To add to my miseries P. F. Warner sat at a table a few places away with a face like nothing on earth.'

Though England drew the match, Carr was pilloried in the press. A. C. MacLaren hinted darkly at too many cooks spoiling the broth. E. H. D. Sewell thought Carr should not take all the blame, and the *Daily Express* said the public wanted to know whether 'the captain of England was exercising his unfettered judgement or was carrying out a policy dictated by the Selection Committee.' But the chairman of the selectors kept his counsel. Only he and Carr knew the truth, and only he and Carr knew that before that Test match Carr, out of form, had suggested that he should stand down, that Warner had telegraphed an affectionate 'Nonsense' followed by a long letter telling Carr he was 'the best captain we have had for ages and you are worth 100 runs an innings.' (If that were so, asks Carr ruefully, 'I wonder why I got the sack'.)

A more significant question, so far as Warner is concerned, is how Carr was sacked. He had missed the fourth Test through illness, and the twelfth man Chapman came in, not as captain, but as a player. Then when Carr showed up at The Oval to pick the team for the final Test he 'very soon sensed that something was not quite right.' Warner put it to him that he was not fit or in any real form and suggested 'for the sake of England' that he should stand down. Carr, taken aback, told them he was perfectly fit, but to save embarrassment left the meeting. He was out and Chapman was in. The excuse that he was unfit satisfied no one, but this was Warner's way. He wrote Carr a long and weepy letter: 'I believe I feel it almost as much as you do; in fact, I can think of nothing else,' and urged him to 'take it in the grand manner and don't be hurt and angry with me.' He offered him the consolation that 'you giving up your place will give you an even greater hold, if such is possible, on the affections of the cricket world.'[8]

Carr's account of his experience is interesting because it shows the peculiar values of MCC and their belief in the innate gift of captaincy (as the *Daily Express* asked, 'What was wrong with Hobbs or Rhodes?'). It also tells us a lot about Warner. First, it seems that he was capable of exerting pressure on England captains. Second, he seems to have been something of a fair-weather friend to Carr. Third, there is a whiff of hypocrisy in his calls for patriotic sacrifice.

In the bodyline affair Warner may not have been technically culpable, but in view of his expressed opposition to Bowes's tactics before the tour it seems strange that he apparently made no effort to curb Jardine. This was certainly easier said than done. The following winter in India, playing against the Viceroy's XI, Jardine's opponents had the pitch rolled for more than the statutory limits before play began. Jardine insisted on an apology from the official concerned in front of the Viceroy. It caused a great row but Jardine was adamant: 'I wouldn't have gone on to the field without it,' he said, 'even if the King of England had been playing against me.'[9] On the other hand Jardine had tremendous reverence for MCC and it seems inconceivable that if asked to cool things down a little he would not have done so.

The fact is that MCC in so far as they knew anything about what was going on approved of it (there was very meagre press coverage of the tour and some of the accounts were ill-informed). Indeed they were outraged when the Australians complained. It was absurd that MCC, who had practically a monopoly of sportsmanship, should be accused by these fellows . . . who did they think they were anyway? Lot of nonsense, what on earth's the bat for? Hook him, that's what to do when a fast bowler pitches short. The Long Room had its share of choleric non-combatants who thought Woodfull and Bradman were yellow. But that apart, what was the world coming to when the Australian Board of Control could, during the third Test at Adelaide, send a cable to the citadel, Warner's power-base and Jardine's source of inspiration, the MCC, complaining that 'Bodyline bowling has assumed such proportions as to menace the best interests of the game,' and adding the fateful words 'In our opinion it is unsportsmanlike.'

Jardine's belief in the 'Premier Club', as he called it, was absolute. Despite his contempt for Australian opinion of himself he was not prepared to let them 'stigmatise MCC as unsportsmanlike'. (The Board of Control ought to have realised 'that it was as unthinkable as it was impossible that an English team should take the field with such an accusation hanging unretracted over them,' he wrote afterwards.) This moral indignation was shared at Lord's. Whatever private reports Warner or his co-manager Palairet had submitted to them, they must have believed that Jardine was right. MCC's reply started off 'We, Marylebone Cricket Club, deplore your cable' and offered to cancel the rest of the tour if the situation was really as bad as the Australians made out. The implication was that it wasn't: and this seemed to be confirmed when the Australian Board backed down. (Whatever was happening, whatever the players thought, there was big money at stake, so cancellation was unthinkable.)

In England the nation united behind the Old Testament and MCC. Clearly the Australians were squealers. There seems to have been no difference of opinion on this issue between the authorities and the mass of the population – who, untroubled by notions of 'not cricket', were quite clear that in the end games were there to be won by any means within the law.

It is the Warners of this world who, claiming that this is not so, in their assertions of moral superiority run the risk of being thought humbugs or worse. 'As for bodyline, as the Australians called it,' he wrote later, 'he [Jardine] thought this type of bowling was legitimate and within the rules.' But then Warner went on: 'My own view was that it was wrong, both ethically and also tactically, and that Larwood often "wasted his sweetness on the desert air" by sending down, for example, 39 out of 42 deliveries on the line of the batsman or just clear of him, as he did at Sydney in the first Test.'[10] For double – or triple – talk this takes some beating. It is, at one level, disloyal to Jardine and the team. (Having said that Jardine operated within the law he added: 'I think, however, he would agree it was stern action.') At another it equivocates between ethical values and pragmatism: would it have been all right for Larwood to do it if he had got a wicket every ball? And it raises the question of what Warner did about it when he was there on the spot.

Presumably Warner, like other MCC members, though they deplored Jardine's actions privately, felt that they must observe the code in public. Douglas was, after all, the sort of fellow one had been at school with. Even within the team there were notable dissidents. G. O. Allen, an amateur, declined to bowl to Jardine's packed leg-side fields. He did not decline to play, however, nor did Jardine force the issue. This was another example of the double-standards: gentlemen are allowed consciences. White gentlemen at least. The Nawab of Pataudi was less fortunate. 'I see His Highness is a conscientious objector,' Jardine remarked mockingly after the Nawab had refused to field in the leg-trap. Pataudi had also apparently announced publicly: 'Jardine is said to have many admirable qualities. However, I've been on tour with him for many months and I've not yet come across one.' The Nawab, who had made a century in the first Test, was dropped, after he failed in the second, for the rest of the series.[11]

So, triumphant if not entirely united behind their leader, the MCC tourists returned home. They found in the summer of 1933 that the idea of bodyline had spread. Warner later recorded how at Old Trafford Constantine and Martindale of West Indies gave the England batsmen a 'taste of their own medicine'. And as Bradman wrote, 'A humorous sidelight was the reversal of opinion by players when they themselves had to face it.' There was a notable exception. Jardine, the patrician, Warner tells us, 'played it magnificently – better probably than any other man in the world was capable of doing – but only by a hair's breadth did a very fast ball miss his chin.' Hammond was less fortunate: he had his chin cut and had to retire for a while. He announced plainly that if that was how Test cricket was to be played he wanted none of it.

Once he returned home Warner felt free to make his views known. In a letter to the *Daily Telegraph* he drew a distinction between bodyline and anything that had gone before. James Agate, the drama critic, had said he hoped 'the Australians are now raking the bush for some Hercules who can bowl faster than Kortright in order that, without regard to length and aiming solely at the batsman's head and heart, he shall, next season, try on the England goose the sauce that has been deemed proper for the Australian gander.' Warner deprecated this, not, of course, on any nationalistic grounds but because 'the courtesy of combat would go out of the game.' It wasn't cricket, and it wasn't good for the Empire. 'Admitting [bodyline] is within the law – there are many things in cricket which by the laws of the game are right but which are "not done" – is it worth while if as a result of bodyline, England and her greatest cricketing Dominion are to "fight each other"?'

The ludicrous thing was that those, like Warner, who controlled this noble game should shrink from legislation. In a letter to *The Times* Leonard Crawley, himself a fine batsman, at the height of the controversy expressed what seems the merest commonsense in response to the crude emotionalism of the virility cult which dominated thinking on the subject. 'Your correspondent,' Crawley wrote, 'urges the point that "Cricket is not played with a soft ball, and that a fast ball which hits a batsman on the body is bound to hurt." Rugby football is also considered by some a fair training ground for manly and courageous virtues. And yet in the event of a player wilfully hacking, tripping or striking another player, instead of going for the ball, the referee is required by the laws of Rugby football to order the offender off the field on the second offence.'

But this was not MCC's way of dealing with affairs. For one thing they weren't convinced that anything wrong had happened. E. W. Swanton published new evidence in his book *Follow On* (1977) of the frantic representations made behind the scenes, notably by the Governor of South Australia (Sir Alexander Hore-Ruthven, later Lord Gowrie). These in all probability led to critical comments about body-line being made by J. H. Thomas, then Secretary of State for the Dominions. But in the end the MCC were still in two minds whether it was better to continue to play cricket against Australia or to stand firm on the ludicrous assertion that bodyline was legitimate. They voted to invite Australia for the 1934 tour by only eight votes to five.

The Australians, not surprisingly, were divided about coming. In a significantly phrased letter Hore-Ruthven wrote to P. F. Warner asking him to 'Keep Jardine out of the picture on any plea you can find. I know the difficulties of not appearing to let him down, but the question is so vital that some excuse must be found for leaving him out.'

Not letting Jardine down (or 'not appearing to' as Hore-Ruthven put it) had extended to appointing him captain of the 1933–34 team to India. He had no Larwood with him but he did have E. W. Clark, a fast left-hander who had bowled bodyline in the summer. MCC were clearly not concerned about losing another part of the Empire. Perhaps they thought Jardine a man after the Indians' own hearts: after all, Lord Harris had been a profound influence on Indian cricket. And C. K. Nayudu, who was to captain India, was 'a man of exceptional character totally and ruthlessly dedicated to the game of cricket'.[12]

Nayudu held the belief that cricket was an ancient Aryan game. He could quote sacred texts to prove it, and he played cricket as though it were one of the battles described in ancient epics. He had the true

Harris-Jardine attitude to physical pain. Struck in the mouth by a ball which broke two front teeth, he refused medical assistance, brushing the broken bits of teeth off the pitch with his bat (presumably in case the ball might pitch on them and deviate awkwardly) and remonstrated with the distressed bowler for easing up with his next delivery. Not letting the bowler know you were hurt was important. When hit on the chest by a short ball from G. O. Allen Nayudu made no sign: it raised a bump but next time Allen pitched short he hooked him for four.

So Jardine would feel at home. (MCC hearts may have fluttered a little when they received a cablegram signed 'Indian Board of Control' which began 'Selection of such a team disgusting insult to India.' But it was a plea for more star players to be sent – and it was a hoax.) In fact, it may be that he fitted into the bizarre pattern of Anglo-Indian and internal relations admirably. Apart from the wicket-rolling incident referred to earlier, Jardine also overruled the Viceroy on another occasion. Relations between the Viceroy and the Maharaja of Patiala were extremely bad; at the height of the dispute Jardine insisted on picking Patiala, who was an MCC member, for the team against Delhi.

Jardine was as uncompromising on the field. When V. M. Merchant was hit on the chin he left the field for repairs and came back at the fall of the next wicket. Jardine by then had a slow bowler at one end, but when Merchant returned shakily to the crease Jardine brought back his two fastest bowlers. It was reminiscent of the low point in Australia when Woodfull, the Australian captain, was injured by Larwood bowling to an orthodox field and Jardine immediately switched to a ring of leg-side fielders. However, doubtless to the disappointment of some of his friends back home, Jardine was making quite a success of the Indian tour.

In England meanwhile it was being decided that bodyline was, one way and another, an embarrassment. In November 1933 a joint meeting of the Advisory County Committee and the Board of Control for home Test matches agreed with the county captains that though 'no alteration of the law was desirable' an obvious direct attack by a bowler on a batsman 'would be an offence against the spirit of the game'. The county captains agreed to eliminate it. The chief remaining problem, therefore, was the question of who would captain England against the reluctant 1934 Australians. In January 1934 Warner wrote to Sir Alexander Hore-Ruthven ('Dear Sandy') in characteristic style about the problem of Jardine. 'It is hoped he may retire at the end of the Indian tour, but in many quarters here – where they do not know the truth – he is a bit of a hero.' Perhaps Jardine's disinclination to stay in Warner's pocket was another factor. 'He rose to his position on my shoulders, and of his attitude to me I do not care to speak.'[13] As a backstairs plotter Jardine clearly had things to learn.

Warner need not have worried. Jardine was unrepentant and uncompromising. He cabled MCC from India that he had neither the desire nor the intention to play against Australia. Warner and Hore-Ruthven doubtless drank each other's health *in absentia*. The selectors were not yet out of the wood, but the rest was easy. They only had Larwood and Voce, the two professionals, to worry about. And Larwood, who must have been bemused by the machinations of his betters, obliged them by being unfit for the first Test of 1934 and then obliged them even further by lashing out in a newspaper article in which he said he wouldn't play against the Australians even if he were selected. (Warner, ever-assiduous in presenting judicious accounts of life at the top in cricket, recorded the view of *Wisden* that Larwood had 'put himself outside the pale of playing for England' and gave his own view 'that Larwood might well have said, "Save me from my friends" – and he had some bad ones.'[14])

One of the bad influences Warner had in mind was presumably A. W. Carr. Though discarded for England in 1926 Carr was still in 1934 captain of Nottinghamshire, for whom both Larwood and Voce played. He thought the MCC were shilly-shallying and should have stood by Jardine and Larwood. He sympathised with Larwood's frustration and anger and was sure the selectors were only seeking an excuse to solve their remaining problem, Voce. Carr was causing his own county committee as well as MCC some anxiety through his attitude to the decision of the previous November about bodyline. MCC had had 'complete confidence' that the captains 'would not permit or countenance bowling of such type'. It was not cricket and the gentlemen would make it a point of honour not to allow it.

Carr did not see it that way. Nottinghamshire shattered the code against Lancashire at Trent Bridge on 16–19 June (Larwood's article came out on the 17th and things seem to have been rather hectic). There was no love lost between the two clubs anyway. They had begun quarrelling with each other in 1883 and the tradition renewed itself periodically. Warner – inevitably – wrote an account of the game from which it is clear that he was not displeased at what happened. He was amused that retribution had struck.

> Presently I came across Duckworth. He was not on crutches but he was lame, one of his arms in a sling and he was bandaged in several places. 'Whatever have you been doing?' I asked, and he replied, 'Haven't you heard about that match with Notts at Trent Bridge?'
>
> *P. F. Warner* – 'I heard there was a bit of a fuss, tell me about it.'
>
> *G. Duckworth* – 'It was tough I can tell you. They bowled bodyline at us.'
>
> *P. F. Warner* – 'What, your old friends, Larwood and Voce?'
>
> *G. Duckworth* – 'Aye and they nearly knocked out Mr Lister and our skipper, and I got a few. The worst was here (pointing to his neck which was bandaged). If they had bowled properly they would have won, but Bill Voce bowled some bad 'uns amidst the bouncers, and when they went in to bat they were all so angry that they got out for 146.'
>
> *P. F. Warner* – 'But you used to lecture when you returned from Australia, defending bodyline bowling and saying it was all right.'
>
> *G. Duckworth* – 'Maybe. But it's tough – too tough – and makes trouble. I'm not for it now.'[15]

Warner adds: 'Duckworth was a bit of a character.' At this distance of time he seems to have been a more open character than Warner.

The Nottinghamshire committee wasted little sympathy on the Lancashire enemy and rejected their complaint. However, it was a different story when the Australians came to Trent Bridge in August to play the county. Carr and Larwood were not playing, ostensibly because they were not fit. Voce, who was still within the pale and therefore technically eligible to be chosen for the fifth and decisive Test, was. On the Saturday he staked a claim by taking 8 for 66, bowling to a leg-side field but not 'to a degree warranting any suggestion of intimidation,' according to the *Melbourne Star* or *The Times*. But in the Australian second innings Voce whirled a few around their ears in the two overs he bowled before bad light stopped play on Monday evening.

In retrospect it is hard to escape the conclusion that this gave the selectors and the peace-makers at MCC their excuse to pass over Voce for the Test. The Australian tour managers took full advantage. That night they complained to Nottinghamshire's honorary secretary, Dr Gould, a medical man. Quite independently of this (so the Notts committee claimed) the acting captain Lilley had reported that Voce had been suffering pain *on the Saturday*. So it was decided that Voce should be examined and Dr Gould declared him unfit to play. The Australians also complained to MCC and correspondence hurtled about between them and Nottinghamshire and the Australian Board of Control. Voce did not play in the final Test in which England put up a very poor performance and Australia regained the Ashes.[16]

The Trent Bridge episode led to great dissension in Nottinghamshire, with public meetings and votes of 'no confidence'. But it all blew over in time. A. W. Carr was sacked; the awkward fact that Voce had signed a statement saying he was fit to play was explained away, and eventually MCC did what they should have done in the first place – they declared bodyline illegal. The instructions they issued to umpires, though Warner thought them very clear, were anything but. They defined 'direct attack' as 'persistent and systematic bowling of fast short-pitched balls at the batsman standing clear of his wicket'. What batsman stands clear of his wicket, asked Bill Bowes?[17] And 'persistent' and 'systematic' were matters of opinion, not fact.

But at least it was better than relying on gentlemanly feelings. It was gentlemanly feelings that had, as much as anything, brought in bodyline in the first place. A. W. Carr quoted approvingly from two letters he had received at his time of trouble. One from a life member of MCC recalled how he had learned cricket at Eton from R. A. H. Mitchell, the greatest of the University batsmen in the first fifty years of the Oxford v. Cambridge match: 'What do you think he would have said to leg-side bowling? I think I know: "Hit it, boy".' The other was from a master at a 'well-known school': 'I was glad to see you had the guts to back up your pros, Larwood and Voce. An officer who lets down his men is beneath contempt.' Lord Harris had died in March 1932, aged 81, but his spirit was still abroad.

EIGHT

BORN LEADERS: LORD HARRIS AND LORD HAWKE

F BEAUCLERK WAS THE most disreputable of the leaders of MCC and Warner the most circuitous, Lord Harris was undoubtedly the most powerful and dictatorial. Amongst his many notable achievements in the pursuit of illiberal causes perhaps the most celebrated were hounding out of the game anyone with a suspect bowling action and relentlessly tracking down irregularities in the registration of county cricketers. As with his definition of amateurism, his opinions on these points, though very firmly held and expressed, were not entirely free of ambivalence. There were even muted suggestions that, on the qualifications issue, he was not above using his position at MCC to further the interests of his county, Kent.

These foul innuendoes were easily disposed of. That it was, on the contrary, logic, loyalty and opposition to Bolshevism that motivated him is clear from his 1922 pronouncement in *The Cricketer* referred to above in Chapter Five, on the subject of Jeacocke and Hammond. 'The Kent Committee does not conceive it to be its duty to hunt about the country for cases on suspicion,' he wrote, 'but where it knows its facts it does think itself bound, in loyalty to its comrades the first-class counties, to ask for an enquiry through the Committee of the MCC.' It was not true that Kent had invited Mr Jeacocke, illicitly playing for Surrey, to play for them instead. As for Hammond, 'We know that he was born in Kent, and that his bonafide residence was with his mother in Hampshire. His occasional residence at school in Gloucestershire was no qualification, for the counties had specifically barred such residence.'

'I am glad to say that my conscience does not prick me,' Harris concluded. Nevertheless there were those who thought it should have done. Because Hammond's soldier-father happened to be stationed in Kent when his son was born, an outstanding young cricketer was being kept out of the first-class game, they argued. And it was far from being the only instance. On one occasion Lord Deerhurst, President of Worcestershire, encountering Harris in the Long Room at Lord's is said to have observed icily: 'May I congratulate you, my Lord, on having b . . . . . . d the career of another young cricketer.'

Harris had a long career in highly influential positions in the world of cricket, but it is arguable that his finest hour was from 1890 to 1895 when he was Governor of the Presidency of Bombay. He quickly decided that the youth of India needed 'some healthy, active pastime as a counter-attraction to pice and politics'. Ignoring the abuse of the native press who accused him of leading youth astray and grossly neglecting his other duties, he set about building a structure for cricket. With characteristic modesty Harris tells us that 'it required some courage to push cricket into real popular prominence. It was popular enough amongst the masses, but it needed a lot of coaxing before the classes would admit that there were such moral lessons to be acquired by youth from playing it as to justify their giving their patronage.'[1]

The leaders of the various racial communities must have thought it was only a game. Lord Harris soon put them right. He sorted out as well their curious attitudes towards status and the observance of customs – such nonsense as a young Hindu bowler employed by the Bombay Gymkhana who insisted on leaving despite an offer of more pay because he had been warned that he would lose caste if he continued to play with beef-eating Englishmen. Such superstitious rubbish had to be swept aside. The Parsees and the Europeans took the lead but the Hindus and Muslims responded well to his urgings, and before he left he had acquired grounds for all the communities, and gradually they began to play against each other, first in Bombay and then in other cities.

Harris's influence on Indian cricket was considerable, and beneficial. In later years he was instrumental in persuading MCC to send out the first official tour. His impatience with local susceptibilities in India is in marked contrast with his belief in the importance of local customs and fine gradations of caste in the cricket clubs of England, but perhaps that was the only way for a colonial administrator to act. When the socially-conscious Calcutta Cricket Club tried to apply their own customs to MCC in 1926 Harris firmly intervened. This club, having been charged with the responsibility of choosing a representative team, picked seven Europeans and only four Indians. That was up to them, but when they went so far as to invite only the amateur members of the MCC team to a function the captain Arthur Gilligan told them that on the strict instructions of Lord Harris he could accept only those invitations which included the whole team.

It seems likely that Harris was motivated less by democratic feelings than by the desire to establish a proper sense of values, in which the British were clearly on top. Back in 1896 he had been fiercely opposed to Ranjitsinhji's selection for England despite his lineage, wealth and Cambridge education. Lord Harris was only thwarted in his opposition because the responsibility for selection for games away from Lord's fell to the local county committee; when Lancashire showed their customary independence by picking Ranji for the Old Trafford Test, Harris was furious. It may be that his opposition was simply part of his general zeal for strict attention to residential qualification, but an article in a recent *Wisden*[2] by a gentleman who remembered Lord Harris in those days suggests that the real objection was not that Ranji was not English but that he had a dark skin.

Ranji's dedication to the Empire and the English way of life was equally as fervent as that of Harris himself, so there were the makings of an ironic situation in 1929 when Ranji's nephew Duleepsinhji came into prominence. India was herself trying hard to get recognition as a Test-playing country, so there was an argument for discouraging Duleep from playing for England. Those who were of a mind to keep him out of the England side told him that if he played for England he would never be allowed to play for India. Others made excuses why it would not be desirable for him to play against South Africa: certain politicians objected, it was hinted. So the difficulties grew, and the pressures on the young man mounted to such an extent that he felt like leaving England altogether. However, his uncle insisted that he stay, and since Ranji controlled his future that was that.

Ranji wanted Duleep to play for England because that was where he had learned his cricket; in any case, he pointed out, there was no top-class cricket in India. Ranji thought young Indians had a duty to join English clubs if they were allowed to so as to try to break down prejudice. They should mingle with the English and hope that some of the English national characteristics would rub off on them. Lord Harris, on the other hand, does not seem to have been at all enthusiastic about this. Edward Docker in his absorbing *History of Indian Cricket* suggests that Harris, 'while sternly believing that an Englishman had a duty and an obligation in India, didn't wish the association to be too close lest it contaminate.'

This arms-length attitude explains why, though Harris's influence on Indian cricket was strong, it tended to work against European domination, which, given a more liberal attitude to race, would perhaps have been the natural tendency. The Indians had only started playing cricket because the British did, and people like Lord Harris had thrust it upon Indian youth to do them good and to consolidate the Empire and make the Indians more like the British. However, discreetly but firmly government influences (as distinct from those of other European residents) were exercised in favour of 'nationalist' policies in keeping with the underlying belief in the white man's burden.

Consequently Indian cricket blossomed into an exotic version of eighteenth-century English patronage (or twentieth-century Packerism). It began with rich Indian citizens emulating the Europeans, who had their exclusive clubs, by starting private clubs of their own. Then the native princes took it up for themselves or their sons. They imported professionals from England, built private cricket grounds, and in due time hired their own teams. They became intensely jealous of each other, quarrelled, stole each other's players, and, of course, bought their way into and around selection procedures for any prestigious activity there was.

The most famous patrons were the Maharajas of Patiala. When the 1926–27 MCC side played at Baradari Palace they were, says Edward Docker, 'fortified by the knowledge . . . that the Maharaja's 300-odd wives and concubines were likely to be attentively watching.' MCC did not try too hard to get their host out. In an earlier game Patiala had seemed to be caught in the slips off Maurice Tate. He stayed put and Tate said nothing. Afterwards somebody asked him why he hadn't appealed. 'Don't be a fool,' said Maurice. 'We shall be staying at this chap's palace later on. I don't want to be poisoned.' Even if he had appealed it would have been unlikely to make much difference. As Edward Docker put it: 'The Maharaja was the cynosure of all eyes as he strode to the crease, jewels flashing in the sun. The people adored him and if, plumb in front of the first ball he received, he was given not out by the umpires, who cared?'

When it came to competition for the captaincy of touring sides to England no expense was spared. Patiala's chief rival was the Maharaja Kumar of Vizianagram. 'Vizzy', as he came to be called, had begun in his early twenties building up and buying contacts and founding powerful teams to win the various competitions. But in 1931, despite an offer of 50,000 rupees towards the cost of the trip to England, he was outbid by Patiala who brought in 50 players from all over India, staged his own trials, and virtually took over the selection boards. The touring side announced the following February was headed by the Maharaja of Patiala (captain), Prince Gyanashyam of Limbdi (deputy captain), and, in the ignominious and unusual position of deputy vice-captain, the Maharaja Kumar of Vizianagram. Vizzy withdrew 'for the sake of the future of Indian cricket', expressing regret that his recent loss of form should have deprived him of the honour which must otherwise have been a certainty for him but assuring the selectors that since, as luck would have it, he would be in Europe in the summer for reasons of health he would be available to advise the team 'if called upon'.

In March Patiala himself withdrew – it had never seemed likely that his political activities would allow him to go – and the selectors, with Vizzy out of the way, chose in his place a person of suitable rank, the Maharaja of Porbandar. Porbandar was, by all accounts, a charming young man, and if he had any disqualification at all as captain of an international touring side it was that he could not play cricket very well. This proved a more serious handicap than the selectors had supposed. Mounting criticism in the British press of his performances led Porbandar to withdraw from the playing arena.

By the time of the Test the deputy captain Limbdi was injured, so the leadership devolved on the less aristocratic but more capable C. K.

Nayudu. The Indians gave a good account of themselves. Without the princes, though, the team broke up in disorder, fighting, drinking and exchanging insults: the chief trouble seemed to be that a commoner had been elevated above the others and they resented it. Consequently, though they earned a reputation for dashing cricket, the 1932 tourists failed to realise their full potential.

As soon as that tour was over Vizzy began his preparations for the next one in 1936. When MCC visited India in 1933–34 he hired a team that beat them; he brought Constantine to India in 1934; he tried to sabotage Patiala's idea for a trophy named after Ranji by devising another one to be called after the Viceroy, Lord Willingdon; he bought up all the best players for a tournament; he installed himself on the selection board for the 1936 tour and eventually, through all kinds of machinations including buttering up the Viceroy, he got himself made captain. The team reflected the promises he had made to influential people; and his tour manager was the Viceroy's ADC, who was seeking a period of leave at home.

There was no vice-captain and no touring team selection committee. Vizzy picked the teams. Altogether he had 21 players which meant that some of them hardly got a game. (Meherhomji rarely played because there were two other wicket-keepers.) By contrast Vizzy played in the first 17 games himself: he dare not allow any potential rival to lead the side.

The team lost five of the first eight matches and drew the other three. The Indian press began to call for Vizzy to step down. Then came the culmination of a series of incidents involving Amarnath, one of the greatest of cricketers. Amarnath spoke harsh words about his leader in Punjabi, which, on translation, Vizzy decided were such a serious affront that Amarnath should be sent back to India. As a captain Vizzy was a disaster. As a player he managed an average of 16.21 for the tour, with the help, it seems, of a good deal of friendly bowling. One county captain found it very embarrassing. Vizzy had given him a gold watch before the match, but after bowling a full toss and a couple of long hops the embarrassed opponent decided he must bowl properly before it became too obvious, and out Vizzy went.

He was more successful off the field. Vizzy was knighted during the summer in return for the services he had rendered, and was obliged perforce to leave his team for at least one match. It was against Lancashire and under the captaincy of C. K. Nayudu that the tourists got themselves in a position to win their first county match. Then the star fast bowler, Nissar, began to bowl very badly. The rumour in the Indian dressing-room was that Vizzy had called him from London instructing him to bowl nothing but full tosses. Nayudu took Nissar off after two overs deciding he'd better bowl himself and the tourists emerged triumphant.

After the team returned home having won only one other match – by two runs – Vizzy had to face a judicial enquiry into the tour. The conclusion, that the miserable performance of the team was largely the result of the unsuitable choice of captain, seemed fair enough, if belated.

It would be interesting to know what Lord Harris, looking down from the Elysian cricket fields, thought of Vizzy's performance, for it was one of the less desirable results of Harris's own policies. No doubt he would have claimed that if only Ranji had known his place and Duleep had known his duty, Vizzy need never have happened. Still less need the ultimate horror have occurred, forty years later, when the Pakistani professional, Asif Iqbal, became captain of Harris's own county, the once-fastidious Kent.

Skin colour, as the West Indies and South Africa were also to demonstrate, was but another complication in the gentlemen and players pattern. From the mid-nineteenth century the English cricket establishment lived in a dream-world seeking to shut out the horrors of the industrial revolution and its aftermath. The Empire was an extension of the stage on which fantasies could be enacted. And, given the crumbling social fabric at home, even in the dream-world, it was a necessary extension.

Harris's dire warnings of Bolshevism were issued at a time when the captaincy of England was itself in danger of falling into the hands of the socially unqualified. By 1921 there was such a dearth of experienced amateur talent that the 49-year-old C. B. Fry was being canvassed for the post, and it needed the six-months-older Archie MacLaren to beat the Australians. Fortunately, the staunch P. F. Warner, though no longer available to play, was able to dedicate himself in retirement to the preservation of true values, first as Editor of the new and strongly un-Bolshevik magazine *The Cricketer* and later as chairman of selectors.

There was also the formidable northern eminence, Lord Hawke. Lord Harris, the old joke ran, was Archbishop of Canterbury, and

Lord Hawke was Archbishop of York. Unfortunately as an ally he was something of a liability. When he eventually died in 1938 his passing was like that of the last dinosaur. Even Warner, in an otherwise fulsome tribute, had to admit that the departed Hawke 'sometimes dwelt too much in the past', adding in a masterpiece of understatement that 'on occasions he made speeches which were carelessly phrased and which did not convey his exact meaning.'[3]

This had been a particular problem to Warner in his efforts for the cause at *The Cricketer*. Lord Hawke's annual utterances at the Yorkshire county dinner were not always helpful. In 1924, for instance, his favourable reference to the contribution of professionals to the game had shocked a regular contributor who regarded this as 'a slightly veiled sneer at the amateur cricketer'.

What Hawke intended was doubtless no more than to blow his own amateur trumpet, for he prided himself inordinately on his sponsorship of the professional, like a selfconscious later version of the early patrons employing their own gardeners and coachmen. And this was the basis of Warner's defence. In the March 1924 issue he wrote: 'No man has done more to raise the status of the professionals. It is almost entirely due to him that the professional cricketer of today is the smart, civil, excellent fellow we know him to be.' He paid tribute to the results of the 'tradition of sobriety, discipline and good fellowship which Lord Hawke was the first to inculcate'. The great, but unspoken, advantage was that these excellent and useful fellows knew their place.

Unfortunately at the following year's dinner Lord Hawke spoke of this advantage out loud. 'Pray Heaven no professional may ever captain England!' he cried for all the world to hear. 'What no doubt Lord Hawke meant,' wrote Warner in the February 1925 issue, 'was that it will be a bad day for England when no amateur is fit to play for England.' This version would certainly have sounded less reactionary but in the context it would have meant precisely the same thing: the assumption was that if an amateur was fit to play he should be captain. Warner's main concern, however, was the support such controversy might offer to the efforts of 'some people' who were intent on stirring up class warfare. Lord Hawke was not to blame: 'people with balanced minds do not attach the same importance to remarks dropped in a speech as they do to what is written.' The real villain was Cecil Parkin, the Lancashire professional, who had taken to journalism and suggested that Jack Hobbs should captain England. Parkin had no business 'pirouetting into the limelight' in this way, provoking the wrath of all right-thinking people.

Warner assured his readers that he regarded Parkin's remarks as offensive not because he was a professional but because they were 'entirely contrary to the spirit of the best of games'. Fortunately the *Weekly Dispatch* had felt unable to publish a further article by Parkin as at the last moment he had been advised not to publish; and, as the *Dispatch* put it, 'as the advice came from that excellent sportsman, Sir Edwin Stockton, the President of the Lancashire CCC it naturally prevailed.' Despite this Warner felt so strongly that, in addition to his editorial comments, he also wrote a signed piece saying more or less the same thing over again, supplemented by a repetition of his praise for Hawke's championing of the professional. As to the captaincy, he reminded readers that there were duties off the field as well as on, and the responsibility was 'better shouldered by an amateur than a professional'.

1924 had been a troubled year. Parkin's first offence, fully described in *The Cricketer*, was to complain of humiliation in the first Test match against South Africa, when the new inspirational captain A. E. R. Gilligan put everyone on to bowl except Parkin. 'I feel I should not be fair to myself if I accepted an invitation to play in any future Test match,' wrote Parkin, adding perceptively: 'Not that I expect to receive one.' Calling for unreserved apologies from Parkin and unspecified action from Lancashire, Warner returned to the subject a few weeks later pointing out to Parkin that if he did not make amends 'the cricket world will regard him as the first cricketing Bolshevist and will have none of him.' It is not recorded whether Trotsky or Zinoviev, following Lenin's death in January 1924, thought of making Cecil Parkin an offer to join them in their efforts to combat the ever-growing power of Stalin.

The extent to which the citadel was vulnerable to seditious ideas was, however, illustrated by a particularly painful occurrence. For the most part *The Cricketer*'s correspondence columns had given evidence of firm support for Warner's defence of civilised standards. But there were exceptions. A 'Lancastrian Sextette', whom a southern correspondent suggested were really one person claiming to represent a number, chose this moment to complain about southern bias in the selection of teams. And even more seriously a Balliol man not only suggested that Parkin's complaints were justified but saw him as a victim of mistaken policies which had preferred A. E. R. Gilligan as captain of England over P. G. H. Fender, which he ascribed to 'the petty jealousy entertained by the authorities at Lord's towards the Oval, and the snobbishness current at the self-constituted headquarters of cricket which make the appointment of a captain who has not been at a public school or a University undesirable in their eyes.' Warner, though publishing the letter to demonstrate his sense of fair play, commented: 'We are pained and grieved that an Oxonian should be responsible for such biased ignorance and such wrong-headed and fantastic ideas.' To no one's surprise the Oxonian turned out to be a northerner.

But Parkin passed beyond the pale. 'Loyalty to one's captain and one's comrades is the beginning and end of a cricketer's creed,' Warner pronounced. These are words with which it is not always easy to reconcile his subsequent actions. Having demonstrated the incompatibility of journalism with active participation in the game, he went on to combine his own journalistic career with an ever-more prominent role at MCC. In 1926, as Chairman of the selectors, he had the opportunity to demonstrate loyalty to his captain, and also to put into practice the ideas Lord Hawke would have expressed if he had had Warner's diplomatic abilities.

The choice of A. W. Carr as captain and Warner's enthusiastic messages of support – when things were going well – were based on the mystical belief that captaincy was an in-born quality, and consequently an amateur preserve. It was a belief increasingly difficult to sustain. The innovation of co-opting two professionals, Jack Hobbs and Wilfred Rhodes, on to the selection committee shows how the world had changed since before the war. Hobbs was 44 and Rhodes was 49 but they were still dominant figures in county cricket which was now, for the successful, an organised affair played rationally and shrewdly by experts. Yorkshire had won the championship four years running since 1922, usually playing ten professionals, under an undistinguished amateur captain. The economic climate was making it a professional game, but there was no tradition of professional leadership. The gifted amateur who could afford to play regularly was in short supply.

Thus any amateur who had a good season in county cricket could expect to be sought after. A county captain who made runs was well-placed for the England job. Carr, recording that in 1925, by far his best year in county cricket, he had hit fifty-two sixes, was aware that he was 'pretty well set for the captaincy of England in 1926, and it would be an affectation to pretend that I was surprised when it came my way.'[4] Nor was it likely that the two great pre-war figures from the professional world, Hobbs and Rhodes, would be eager to seek office for themselves or their fellow-professionals. (Rhodes, indeed, had retired from Test cricket, and only came in for the last Test when there was nothing else for it.)

Ironically enough, Hawke's assertion of feudal principle seemed to have been overthrown shortly after he had made it. Carr fell ill just before the Manchester Test, and with the only other amateur at hand the inexperienced G. T. S. Stevens, the accolade fell on Hobbs. It is hard to imagine that in Australia, in similar circumstances, if a legendary cricketer like Hobbs, with vast experience and acumen and great personal popularity, had acquired the captaincy in this way he would have been lightly set aside. If the original captain had returned, then perhaps it might have been justified. But this was not the case. As Warner, with bland disregard for the true circumstances, wrote: 'Carr . . . had been suffering from a severe attack of tonsilitis, and with the greatest regret we came to the conclusion that he should stand down.'[5] Instead the selectors gave the captaincy for this match, on which, as Warner said, 'the prestige of English cricket seemed to depend', to A. P. F. Chapman, who had been on the fringe of the team hitherto.

It is interesting that Carr, who was naturally hopping mad about being passed over for the laughing cavalier Chapman, certainly did not favour the appointment of Hobbs, who was, he says, 'a rotten captain'. How did he know? He claimed to have 'seen him in charge of a side several times'. Whatever Hobbs's performance as a captain this proves little. Occasional captaincy is not the same as regular tenure and to be a professional captain in an amateur world must have been extraordinarily difficult. Carr goes on to reveal the true reason for his belief: 'But then, I am afraid, most pros are not much good at the job.' They lacked, evidently, those officer-like qualities that G. D. Martineau's military model of cricket attributes only to amateurs.

It was the merest rationalisation. As the professionals were debarred from leadership – except in unfavourable circumstances – there was no way of telling whether they would be any good or not. Australian, and subsequent English, experience has shown that there can be good leadership amongst the humbly born. But even before Carr and Martineau there had been good English professional leaders. As we have seen, in the days when amateurs tended not to want to commit themselves to long spells away from home or business, the early touring teams were led by professionals. First William Clarke and later George Parr seem to have managed the All-England touring side very well. Indeed Richard Daft and Alfred Shaw, two of the greatest cricketers of their day, regarded Parr as the best captain they had played for.[6] Bernard Darwin offers an explanation that typifies the orthodox attitude: 'For one professional to manage an eleven of professionals has never been an easy task and this cannot have been an easy team for George Parr to drive. Fortunately, he was something above most of them in social position.'[7]

'A Country Vicar', contributing his delightful antediluvian memoirs to the periodical stream of dream-world literature in *The Cricketer*, wrote most movingly in 1924 about the Yorkshire of his youth. From 1873 to 1892 though brilliant individually they never took first place. The cause of their failure, he felt, was 'in a word – drink!' And the remedy was equally simple: 'What the Yorkshiremen really needed was strong leadership . . . they were always led by a professional; and it is strange but true that men in the lower walks of life will never obey, readily and implicitly, one of their fellows. They require someone to whom they can look up.' They found what they needed in 1883 in the Hon. M. B. Hawke who, succeeding his father to the peerage in 1887, eventually established sufficient regard for the position that the team won the championship at last in 1893, after which his 'firm fearless leadership' received its just reward eight times before he finally stepped down in 1909.

Hawke himself made occasional contributions to the dream-world. In the 1924–25 *Cricketer Annual*, for instance, he cleared up the whole debate on North v. South in a few paragraphs by his personal assurance, backed up by a quotation from Lord Harris, that there was no question of prejudice. The trouble was the shortage of amateurs in the north, leading to a less enterprising spirit. Also the climate made the wickets slower, and there was 'a notable variation in the temperament'. It was not conspicuously logical, but it was a sharp warning to the Bolshevists, north or south.

The article reveals no signs of excessive modesty or lack of self-appreciation. If Hawke had had any tendencies in that direction they would scarcely have been encouraged by the review, on the opposite page, of his recently published reminiscences, 'Lord Hawke's name is a household word wherever cricket is played,' it began, 'and he has done more for the game than anyone that ever lived.' Such was the way the mutual admiration society operated. Several paragraphs are devoted to reproducing quotations of a highly flattering kind about P. F. Warner, a life-long friend, including 'a deserved tribute to the loyal and impartial way he is rendering great service to the game by his excellent journal *The Cricketer*'. (The frequent references to the sterling qualities of the editor which characterise the early issues of this periodical are sometimes made to seem even more oleaginous by disclaimers from Warner and denials of any departure from strict objectivity by the contributors. An example of this objectivity occurred in 1924 when Neville Cardus made his first appearance. His article about Lancashire's Diamond Jubilee coyly insinuated: '. . . with the Editor's permission I should like to say that Lord's never loved him and his dear old Harlequins cap more than Old Trafford.' The syntax may have been shaky but the heart was evidently in the right place, and three weeks later Cardus's own *Days In The Sun* was assured of a warm welcome as 'altogether a charming book' by a 'gifted author'.)

The gifted author of *Reminiscences and Recollections* was doubly fortunate. It was appropriate, the review suggested, that the book should be published by Williams and Norgate, for 'the head of this famous firm is Sir Home Gordon, who needs no introduction to *The Cricketer* and who, for five and twenty years, has been one of Lord Hawke's most intimate friends.' However, making due allowance for all these environmental factors that must have tended towards self-indulgence on the part of any author, the suspicion lingers that Lord Hawke contributed a good deal of it himself.

Hawke's autobiography must rank amongst the least modest books ever put together. It is full of tributes to himself, which he drags in under any pretext: flattering newspaper articles, after-dinner eulogies from sycophantic commoners, and even 'quotations' from anonymous and for all anybody knows non-existent admirers. Many are tributes to his dashing leadership and manly bearing, but there are also incredible references to his compassionate and fervent support of the less fortunate – voices he claims have been heard in the crowd (by whom is not revealed) saying things like 'Is that the great Lord Hawke then, him that's a friend to rich and poor alike but more of a friend to the poor?'

One of the best sentences is about the great Wilfred Rhodes: 'The presentation of his portrait to me was the crowning tribute to his wonderful career.' But there are many other delights such as 'I believe I have done more than anyone else to raise the standard and self-respect of the splendid paid section of first-class cricketers'. Advising ladies on how to comport themselves, or paying his wife a most generous compliment – 'I think I can safely say I have drawn a prize in the matrimonial lottery. Even in golf my wife and I are well-matched' – Hawke is superb.

His memoirs are worth reading, not for any literary merit, nor even for their frequent flashes of unconscious humour, but chiefly as an antidote to romantic illusions about the past. Whether Hawke is decrying the deplorable habits of the young women of the 1920s, performing what he calls American 'nigger-dances' or being patronising about great players, he dispels all nostalgia. The overriding impression is that this mediocre cricketer believed he had outstanding natural gifts as a leader and that Yorkshire and the world were extremely fortunate to have him. Whether he had such gifts and whether they were more valuable than cricket ability must remain a matter of conjecture. What is certain is that he had two great advantages over his professionals – money and power. That he used them to the full is clear from Hawke's own account.

He was proud of originating his own incentive bonus scheme. Talent money was by no means new. In 1778 the *Morning Post* had recorded: 'We hear the noblemen and gentlemen of the Grand Cricket Club have established a fund for the purpose of rewarding such players as particularly distinguish themselves.' Hawke's 'invention' was, however, a characteristically egocentric up-to-date version, and one that added to the already considerable personal power of the amateur captain over the players. His contribution was 'the mark system, which was entirely my own idea . . . I gave marks according to my view of the importance to the side of what was done. Not only did I reward good batting and really excellent bowling . . . but I also allocated marks for fine wicket-keeping and smart fielding.' His usual award was 2s. 6d. and five shillings the limit.

The system was admired and copied by many in later years. In his autobiography, *Long Innings*, P. F. Warner tells of a match against Yorkshire in which he was caught at slip by 'Long John' Tunnicliffe. It was so splendid a catch, he says, 'that as I walked away I heard Lord

Hawke say "Ten shillings for that one, John".' Either Warner's hearing or his memory must have been at fault or else Hawke was feeling particularly generous. However on the 1932–33 tour Warner seems to have been inspired to see if the method could be adapted to his own purpose. Jack Fingleton was a journalist and Warner, who wrongly suspected him of leaking a story to the press, enlisted Harold Larwood's aid. 'As we were going out on to the field in your second innings,' Larwood told Fingleton, 'Sir Pelham said to me, "Larwood, I will give you a pound if you bowl Fingleton out quickly."'[8]

The talent money system, personally administered, was still being spoken of approvingly in 1935 by A. W. Carr. He tells us the most anyone got out of him was 'Dodge' Whysall, who notched up £40 in 1929, Nottinghamshire's championship year. The amateur captains were judge, jury and treasurer combined. It was a characteristic embellishment of a system in which the players had to take whatever wages their counties thought fit, without appeal, and the amateurs treated them with the unheeding condescension they gave to their domestic servants or local greengrocer.

Yet it has to be said that Lord Hawke's methods, in their time and place, worked. Perhaps it is recognition of such realities that explains why Yorkshire, of all counties, persisted with the notion of amateur leadership for so long. No doubt Lord Hawke's long reign is partly responsible. His own dominance of the committee and the team's remarkable record of success made it unlikely that his approach would be lightly set aside. The result was for many years a triumph of pragmatism which survived even the emergence of the new-style professionals replacing the old.

Rhodes, arguably the greatest all-round cricketer of his day and certainly one of the smartest cricketing brains, was confined to the role of 'senior pro', the RSM of the cricket field, the successor to Old Nyren. Would he not have done better on his own? The question has more point when applied not to Hawke himself but to his successors. There is a legend that one of the many nondescript amateurs who followed Lord Hawke as Yorkshire captain was found hanging about a corner of the field at a loose end until rounded up by a friendly 'pro', who told him: 'Come in, sir, Wilfred's declared.'

The social conventions were perhaps not ripe for Rhodes to come from behind the throne. But what of the vastly different, polished and sophisticated Herbert Sutcliffe? Even he never became captain. It is true that when a successor had to be found for Major Lupton in 1928 Sutcliffe, to the alarm of the traditionalists, was offered the post. The terms in which the offer was made are interesting. The Secretary F. C. Toone wrote:

> Dear Herbert,
>
> At the Committee meeting yesterday you were appointed Captain for 1928 without your status being altered.
>
> It is hoped that this will be agreeable to you and that you will accept the same and be happy and successful in your new and honoured position.[9]

History does not record why he declined, but the presumption must be that he did not relish the prospect of the controversy it would cause. It was certainly not that Sutcliffe believed that professionals were incapable or unworthy of the distinction. Bill Bowes, who was a young MCC groundstaff player getting an occasional game for Yorkshire at the time, recalled that Sutcliffe had been deeply disappointed when Jack Hobbs had not asserted his logical right to the England captaincy (to the extent, in effect, of refusing the honour). Perhaps the way he expressed his disappointment may explain Sutcliffe's own refusal: 'Lord Hawke lifted professional cricket from there to there,' said Herbert, raising his hand from knee to shoulder level. 'Professional cricketers lifted it to there,' he continued, raising his hand above his head, 'and even Lord Hawke always wanted it back again.'[10]

Sutcliffe felt that for the sake of the professionals Hobbs should have accepted, notwithstanding the personal embarrassments and worse this would have caused. Yet he was not, when it came to the point, prepared to go to the stake himself. Who can blame him? It is significant, perhaps, that his reply to Yorkshire was sent not to the secretary but to Lord Hawke himself. His cable from South Africa read: 'Official invitation received yesterday. Many thanks you and your committee. Great honour. Regret to decline. Willing to play under any captain elected.'[11] And so the choice fell upon W. A. Worsley, later Sir William, about whose cricket little has been permanently engraved on the tablets.

Bowes in his book *Express Deliveries* describes Sutcliffe as something special off the field as well as on. 'There was something in his walk, his carriage that compelled attention. Here was no ordinary man . . . Eyes turned to him automatically. One could hear the hurried whispers – yes, whispers – "It's Herbert Sutcliffe!" And professionalism was important to him: Herbert was a great player, but beyond even his great performances on the field I respect and admire his belief in the honour of professional cricket.' There is of course one big difference between captaining England and captaining a county: the county job is a matter of week-in-week-out relationships with one's employers. It seems likely that Sutcliffe felt the honour of his profession would be better served by not subjecting it to the day-to-day scrutiny of Lord Hawke, whose presence brooded over Yorkshire.

The presence continued to brood until long after the Second World War, and Yorkshire kept up the tradition of amateur captaincy when many more obviously gentlemanly counties had abandoned it. It would need a digression of unjustified length to attempt an explanation of this. Is there something in the Yorkshireman's heredity or environment that encourages conservatism? Did the very substantial membership of the club, producing a guaranteed income that must have been the envy of other counties, give a security to successive committees that sustained them in reactionary attitudes? Were memories of the 'nine drunks and a chapel parson' still so fresh in the 1920s that even the suave and dignified Sutcliffe could seem a threat? Was it Yorkshire's historic destiny as custodians of cricket's Holy Grail to preserve all its ancient customs?

Such questions are scarcely capable of rational solution, and devotees will prefer their own explanation of the paradox that this most professional of counties clung so firmly and so long to amateur leadership. However, two points seem worth considering. Like the Indian tourists of 1932 the Yorkshire professionals seemed to need an authoritarian figure from outside their own ranks to subdue their fratricidal tendencies. And, as a corollary, the syndicalist spirit amongst the hard core who in effect ran the side for decades made the quality of the leadership, in cricketing terms, supremely unimportant.

As long as they were winning matches, they were entitled to ask each other, what did it matter who was captain? Indeed there were real advantages in amateur leadership, though of a different kind from those proclaimed by the idealists. Bill Bowes described how in 1929 when he was a raw recruit the seasoned professionals George Macaulay and Emmott Robinson bamboozled the skipper, W. A. Worsley, by congratulating Bowes effusively at the end of every over during a long spell in which the batsmen were hitting his best balls to every corner of the field. They were not anxious to be put on to bowl themselves on an unrewarding pitch. It was a bonus for such professionals when in the 1930s they acquired in A. B. Sellers an amateur captain who could exemplify the general will and the general ethos.

Be that as it may, for many years the last thing that seemed to concern either committee or players was the captain's contribution as a player. Until the Second World War the county was so strong that it hardly mattered. For fifteen years after, the skipper's contribution in runs and wickets was the least of their worries. In N. W. D. Yardley, Yorkshire had the best amateur performer since F. S. Jackson as their captain, but the team achieved dismal results under him. W. H. H. Sutcliffe, amateur son of Herbert, was by no means a bad player, but he held the reins too lightly. Yet when in 1958 with the senior professionals getting out of hand the committee brought in J. R. Burnet, the second-team captain and a distinctly second-rate player, he quickly put things right, and the following year Yorkshire won the championship outright for the first time in thirteen years.

Burnet's success was founded on Hawke-like standards of discipline. Recalcitrant professionals had to come to heel or leave. The Committee enthusiastically supported the return to normality. The club had turned the corner at last, it appeared, and seven championships in ten years satisfied all but the insatiable. In the process, also, the momentous change to professional captaincy took place at last, with inches to spare before the distinction between gentlemen and players was finally abolished. It was dictated, in the end, by sheer necessity. However great the need for an amateur disciplinarian at the helm, by 1960 it proved impossible to find one. For one thing amateurs of any kind had virtually disappeared; but for Yorkshire there was a painful new factor. Committed as they were to the staunchly patriotic policy of picking only men born in the county, they could no longer afford the luxury of carrying a passenger against less scrupulous opponents who employed not only Yorkshire exiles but, increasingly, foreign super-stars.

In retrospect, this grudging acceptance of the realities looks to have been too little and too late. When it did come, the change to professional leadership involved no concessions to contemporary notions of good industrial relations, and the number of Yorkshire exiles increased and improved in quality. By 1971 when D. B. Close, the captain, himself joined this category, it became evident that the chickens were coming home to roost; and when his successor, Boycott, was dismissed in 1978 there had been ten years without a championship win and nine without success in any competition.

One of the remarkable achievements of the Yorkshire cricket establishment over the years has been to make their counterparts at national level seem enlightened and progressive by comparison. Amongst the candidates available to Yorkshire for the leadership in the 1950s before the rot set in was Leonard Hutton, an even greater batsman and possibly an even shrewder professional than Sutcliffe. Perhaps he might not have made a good county captain. Perhaps he would still have retired, prematurely as many thought, in the face of injury and ill-health. Perhaps not even a distinguished and vastly experienced professional, loaded with international honours, could have exercised sufficient moral authority over the truculent descendants of Peate, Peel, Macaulay and Robinson. It was never put to the test, and the abortive search for a true successor to Brian Sellers continued, a task commanding the whole-hearted personal attention of Sellers himself, inspired no doubt by the keen-eyed gaze of the committee-room portrait of Lord Hawke.

Yorkshire's attitude makes the action of the national selectors in 1952 in appointing Hutton captain of England seem even more of a daring and radical experiment than it was. The social implications of a professional appointment were nothing like so great for the intermittent phenomenon of a home Test match as they were for county cricket (a tour abroad was another matter). Nevertheless it was regarded by many as a further step down the slippery slope to Bolshevism. By 1951 the England captaincy had fallen into the enthusiastic hands of F. R. Brown. One of nature's gallant losers – a stereotype dear to British hearts – he had gone beyond reasonable expectation in Australia the previous winter by actually winning the final Test once the series had been comprehensively lost. This pleased everyone greatly, especially the Australians, who made much of Brown's achievement, doubtless in the hope of many more such results in the future. The death in June of the Rt. Hon. Lionel Tennyson, who had exemplified the same courage in adversity against Warwick Armstrong's 1921 Australians, evoked powerful emotions amongst loyalists.

The selectors were more realistic. Victory over the unexciting South African tourists of 1951 could not conceal the sad fact that

Brown's days as a Test cricketer were numbered. There was no amateur successor available who would not have been an embarrassment to
a side full of illustrious professionals. So, on 26 May 1952 the Board of
Control announced that Hutton would lead England in the first Test
against India. Perhaps Lord Harris might have been reconciled to this
on the grounds that English professionals outranked even aristocrats
of darker skin, but Lord Hawke would have found little consolation
even in the elevation of a Yorkshireman. Their followers took it badly.

Hutton may not have been the most Galahad-like of cricketers, but
he deserved better support than he got in and around MCC. In fact
the belief in the mystical qualities of amateur leadership was set aside
with such bad grace as virtually to ensure that the experiment would
fail. 'Much unofficial – and some quasi-official – opposition to the
appointment was surprising and all but shocking,' John Arlott, not
given to intemperate outbursts against authority, was later to record.
'In some quarters,' he went on, 'reaction towered far above that form
of team-support which is sometimes called patriotism. Len Hutton
never did anything braver, sounder or more balanced than keeping his
eye firmly on his objective and ignoring this malevolent snobbery.'[12]

That the root-and-branch of it all was snobbery is confirmed by the
testimony of Walter Hammond, professional turned amateur, who
had laid down the burden of captaincy only five years before. In the
year of Hutton's accession he wrote: 'Apparently it is only the nominal
status, not the man or his characteristics, to which objection is taken.
I can say this because I captained England, after most of a cricket life-
time as a professional. I was the same man as before, or perhaps I
even had a slightly declining skill by that time. But because I changed
my label all was well.'[13]

NINE

THE MAGIC CIRCLE

BY THE TIME THE mantle of England leadership had fallen on Hutton the days of the formal division between amateur and professional were numbered. It was, of course, no great upsurge of democratic fervour that prompted the decision to abandon this great principle in 1963 but simply the harsh realities. The privilege of having one's initials before one's name no longer compensated for the obvious disadvantage. Colin Cowdrey, as a young amateur, was aware that the joke, if there was one, about Yorkshiremen not playing cricket for fun was on him. In his autobiography he describes how he spent a long and difficult morning in an Australian Test watching a masterly and astute display by the great man batting at the other end: 'As we walked off he said, "How are you, then?" I said, "It's hard work." His reply was a classic Huttonism. "Aye, and what's more you're not getting paid are you?"'[1]

Yet for all but the most exceptional, and fortunate, players the professional's lot was never anything but hazardous, insecure and poorly paid. Before the war the county scene, with unemployment rife in the world outside cricket, was a miserable affair for many. Bruce Hamilton's novel *Pro* is blood-curdling in its melodrama, but it communicates well the essentially precarious nature of the pre-war professional's life, dependent on amateur whims, modified by box-office requirements and journalistic 'angles'.[2] Still there were advantages, even for the run-of-the-mill professionals. It was a healthy existence.

When Derbyshire in the 1930s were said to be able to whistle down the nearest pit-shaft and bring up a fast bowler they were not just strengthening their team but performing a social service. In earlier days the rewards of playing for a good county were infinitely better than the alternatives of the coal-face or the textile mill. But, obsolete class distinctions apart, there were unnecessary and unsatisfactory features of the system that bore no relation to events in the world outside cricket.

In 1952 Walter Hammond described a scene that contrasts starkly with the modern image of sporting figures as celebrities, well-heeled modern folk-heroes, owning a chain of boutiques before they are thirty: 'Any English professional today, if you can get him to say what he really feels, will admit at once that the present professional system here is unsatisfactory and not in the best interests of the game. A large part of the career of a "pro" these days is beset with anxiety, and at forty or before he is thrown into an unreceptive world. If he is one of the lucky few who have enjoyed a Benefit, then he may be financially secure . . . It is the others I am thinking about. Some take public houses. Some try to get employment in sports shops, or as commercial travellers. Some are lucky enough to be appointed to the umpires lists. Some get jobs connected with their old club – Strudwick, for example, became scorer to Surrey. Some get jobs as cricket coaches. But there are a good many more who cannot put their cricket past to any use at all. Do you know the kind of jobs offered to such people? Nightwatchman; caretaker; window-cleaner. And so on.'[3]

But it was the decline of amateurism and the end of the feudal dream rather than the economic needs and social aspirations of the professionals that commanded attention. The authentic voice is that of Neville Cardus. 'It is not known,' he wrote in *Second Innings* in 1950, 'and will now never be known, what Rhodes and Robinson in their hearts thought of Sutcliffe, who made his hair resplendent with brilliantine and wore immaculate flannels and on the whole comported himself with an elegance which in the Yorkshire XI was unique and apocryphal . . . Our Sutcliffes and Hammonds, with their tailors obviously in Savile Row, have taken us far far beyond the echo of Billy Barnes and his rough heavy-handed company of paid cricketers of the eighties and nineties.'

Cardus's writings are highly important in the mythology of cricket. For one thing it was he as much as anyone who created the intelligentsia of the game, giving respectability to attitudes that would otherwise have remained inarticulate or seemed merely snobbish special pleading. And he wrote with all the conviction of a convert to an old-established religion. Not being of the purple himself, either as a cricketer or socially, his reverence for those who were was all the more heartfelt.

It had to be the genuine purple, though. Cardus was not himself a member of the magic circle and he took his revenge on those on its fringes whenever he could. He enjoyed Lord's enormously but was acutely aware of the extent to which he was accepted there: 'But at last I made Lord's my headquarters, though never a member of the MCC and never free to go into the pavilion during a Test match except by special dispensation.'[4] He tells of MacLaren, the former Test player, brushing aside his exclusion from the best circles because of his press commitments and making courtly gestures to the tea-ladies. He makes it clear that his own cultural standards set him above cricket, that it is, with him, though a thing about which he knows a great deal, in the end an affectation, a world about which he has chosen to write with amused tolerance, a facet of human life that happens to afford subject-matter for his art.

Above all Cardus resented deeply the *nouveaux riches*, the not-quite gentlemen. This characteristic vein in his writing no doubt relates to his own early experiences. At any rate he recalled in his autobiography how as a poor boy in Manchester he used to field out for the local 'gentry' at the nets: 'I hated them very much; and years afterwards I bowled them out with a relish that counts amongst my most satisfying memories.' He had an even greater source of vengeful joy: 'And not every player in those days used a "box". I am not ashamed to confess that I seldom hesitated, as soon as a batsman came to the crease to let him have a quick one bang in the penis.' It is an unusual, and in cricket literature an unusually frank, expression of the virility cult.

In this, however, Cardus is reflecting the true morality of cricket;

and he is also reflecting the origins of the modern first-class game. In the feudal concept there is a rapport between the lord and his serfs, and it is the bourgeoisie who are the intruders. The stories Cardus wove around cricket used a literary convention older than Shakespeare in which the rustics are clowns, pointing up the true nobility of the serious characters by making shrewd homespun comments, and occasionally, without forgetting their place in life, discomfiting their betters.

His description, in *Second Innings*, of Harry Dean of Lancashire is comic and affectionate: 'He wore blue serge and a watch chain across his waistcoat and strong boots; with a strong Lancashire accent but with speech formed in Sunday School, capital letters and all. "The reason why we young 'uns learned t'Principles was that we played with wise Men. It were an Education to bat wi' Maister Spooner."' It is also patronising. In his fictional world of cricket the true gentry are benevolently autocratic and dashing, the old-style pros know their place, and it is the suede-shoed modern suave interloper trying to blur the distinction who is the threat. 'The advent into cricket, and into the Yorkshire XI of all places, of a Herbert Sutcliffe was a sign of the times; the old order was not changing, it was going.'

Cardus's aversion from the pretensions of the brilliantined, Savile-Row-suited new model professional seems quite irrational. It is somehow even more objectionable than the conventional yearning for the golden age – as if he took exception not to 'the spread of professionalism' as such but rather to the professionals making a decent living or speaking good English. He is intending to be severely critical when he writes: 'The county cricketer has become in certain instances a man of bourgeois profession.'

Even Lord Harris in his 1909 exposition of the distinction between amateur and professional did not see it as part of his business to require professionals to be working-class clowns. They might not be gentlemen but they were entitled to their livelihood: 'In the republic of cricket the prizes go to the best and the best can demand – perhaps successfully – the best terms. Well, that is the reward of efficiency, and "ca' canny" is not likely to upset the natural rule at cricket.' But then Harris was, of course, born to the purple.

These prejudices of Cardus provide a sharp edge to otherwise fatuous generalisations like: 'An innings by Lord Aberdare comes straight out of Debrett's. And an innings by Richard Tyldesley comes straight out of

West Houghton.' (What about an innings by Hammond or Woolley?) And they help to explain why he was so taken with MacLaren: 'The royal arrogance of him could brook no compromise; never did his proud temper suffer him to wait for an easy ball.'[5]

A story that otherwise seems merely silly turns out to be significant as a lament for feudalism: when a Yorkshire professional offers the Lancashire amateur a long-hop to reach his hundred MacLaren cries, 'Long hops be . . . Look, here, Ted my lad, I'll hit your best balls anywhere you like.' (We have to assume that MacLaren was good enough to tell a deliberate long hop from an accident, quixotic enough to decline the offer, and ungracious enough to spurn it publicly. We have to assume also that a Yorkshire professional would do such a thing in a Roses match.) It is as if the young master is dazzling the servants.

Feudalism does not of course require totally uncritical admiration: indeed there is a sense in which it is important for the feudal lord to have human failings to demonstrate his humanity. Thus in a very funny passage Cardus tells how MacLaren came a cropper. The great aristocrat is elaborately taking guard in a match against Warwickshire and surveying the scene like the lord of the manor. The bowler is a plebeian. 'The rude inglorious Hargreave chewed a blade of grass while MacLaren attended to these ceremonies. He then slouched to his bowling place, ran a few steps and wheeled over his left arm casually, as though in the nets . . . When MacLaren returned to the pavilion not a soul made a sound by word of mouth; but one or two members stood up as a sign of respect.'[6] But the essence of the joke is MacLaren's greatness. It is a feudal joke, like little Lamborn crying out 'It was tedious near you, Sir,' to the mighty Duke of Dorset.

Cardus may have underestimated the sophistication of the early players. Perhaps it is unfair to refer to Albert Knight, the Leicestershire professional, but in 1906, in an altogether splendid book, he produced a piece of rhetoric on the subject of amateurism that even Cardus could scarcely match. 'Matthew Arnold,' he wrote, 'musing over the beautiful city which did not appreciate his interpretation of the Faith of the Centuries, wrote of Oxford as "The home of lost causes and forsaken beliefs, of unpopular names and impossible loyalties". If this were true of theologies, that Oxford bent not her knee to the passing Zeitgeist, but set aloft her lonely light amid the mists of Tubingen criticism, she may do the same for sport.' In other words Knight thought the true amateur was all but extinct! He saw many virtues in amateurism but politely deplored the influence of the MCC in giving the weight of its authority to 'the maintenance of distinctions which in county cricket have little or no true validity'.[7]

Polite and discreet dissent was as far as the professionals were prepared to go for many years after Knight's time. One of the most significant ways in which the cricket establishment was able to make its dream-world a reality and ignore the industrial revolution was in avoiding the unpleasantness of trades unionism. The Trades Union Congress met for the first time in 1868 but the activities of this body had as little impact on cricket as did those of Karl Marx, who in 1861 had organised his subversive conspiracy 'The International', or of his protégé Henry Myers Hyndman whose Democratic Federation wanted to enlist the aid of the proletariat in overturning society. ('I could not carry on unless I expected the revolution at ten o'clock next Monday morning,' said Hyndman, who some believed had only turned socialist out of pique at being left out of the Cambridge University cricket team.)[8]

There was one trades unionist amongst the cricket professionals, but unfortunately he had to fight the battle all on his own. This was S. F. Barnes, arguably the greatest bowler there has ever been and certainly one of the most contentious. Born in 1873, Barnes was a man ahead of his time in seeking that his talents be recognised and rewarded fairly and in resenting class distinctions to the point of mutiny. In cricket he was a solitary, and for the authorities an embarrassing rebel. Barnes first played for Staffordshire in 1894. He was asked to join the groundstaff but thought the terms they offered were inadequate, so in 1895 he went to Rishton in the Lancashire League playing on Saturday afternoons only. He was asked to play for Warwickshire, but when he went into the dressing-room for his first match the other players ignored him, through jealousy of the money he was getting at Rishton. The next time he was invited to play for Warwickshire was by a telegram which arrived just before Barnes was setting off for his club match: by the time he got home that night there was another message. 'Do not come. An amateur is playing.'

He did not emerge again from league cricket, with Rishton and Burnley, until 1901. By then he had been spotted by Lancashire, whose captain, the belligerent MacLaren, must have admired Barnes's aggressive approach to cricket. He played several times in the 1901 season and in the final match took six wickets for 70. This was the year in which MacLaren, having difficulty in getting together a team to tour Australia that winter, had fallen foul of Lord Hawke and the Yorkshire committee. He still had one place to fill and the season was over. He tried once more to recruit another bowler, but without success. In desperation he turned to Barnes who had gone off to finish his contract in the league. The telegram taken out to him on the field at Burnley caused a sensation.

So it came about that Barnes's ninth first-class game was a Test match. After a moderate initial performance he did well in the second Test with 5 for 65, but the 64 overs he had to bowl were more than he was used to. His knee trouble when he broke down in the third Test was thought by some to indicate a lack of enthusiasm. Back home again in 1902 and playing for Lancashire his recurrent knee trouble and mixed performances led *Wisden* to suggest that he gave up too easily. He played in the third Test of 1902 and took 6 for 49, but was then dropped and was not picked again for five years.

Thereafter Barnes was in and out of Test cricket and in and out of the leagues. The usual trouble was money. Despite his 131 wickets for an average of 16.85 for Lancashire he was not picked for the tour of 1903–4. His variable form, induced by heaven knows what real or imagined grievances or by physical injuries, earned him the reputation of being unreliable. He bowled one over only when picked for the Players in the prestigious match against the Gentlemen and then retired. *The Times* thought it unfair that he should claim a fee and then not pull his weight.

He quarrelled with Lancashire because he wanted more money than other players who did less work. Since Lancashire terms were £3 a week in summer and £1 in winter, he worked out that £8 a week in the summer for Church in the Lancashire League, working only on Saturdays, was a better proposition. So he pressed his case and delayed signing for the following year despite strong pressure from the county, until the very end of the season. Lancashire said he would not be picked and therefore would not be paid for the last match unless he signed. Barnes still didn't sign but he turned up for the match, changed and made to go out on the field. In the end MacLaren had to order him back to the dressing-room.

This episode tells us something about Barnes and the kind of man he was, but it also tells us a lot about the system. It was a throwback to the days of hiring fairs when farmers looked for bargains amongst the labourers, who put themselves up for hire. It was the last straw for MacLaren, who must many times have rued the day he came upon Barnes. The combativeness that MacLaren admired was not reserved for opponents on the cricket field. It is easy to understand why the selectors were not enthusiastic about choosing Barnes for tours: sulking and, if necessary, downing tools or going sick are even harder to deal with when playing resources are limited. MacLaren, though doubtless anxious to have his gamble justified in picking Barnes for the 1901–2 tour, soon realised his error. As Bernard Hollowood wrote in *Cricket on the Brain*: 'Even MacLaren was upset by Barnes's surly intractableness. When warned that the ship carrying the English team was in danger, the captain reacted philosophically: "There's one comfort," he said. "If we go down that bugger Barnes will go down with us."'

After the contretemps on the Old Trafford balcony, Barnes, amid universal criticism, went back to the League and Staffordshire. His performance was so outstanding that, again as a last-minute choice, he got on the 1907–8 Australian tour. He bowled more overs than anyone on either side and the great M. A. Noble declared: 'Barnes is the best bowler in the world at the present day.' Back in England in 1909, though playing only three Tests, he still bowled more than anyone else. If he could have been paid according to how much work he had to put in, much of Barnes's resentment would have disappeared. As it was he had frittered away his best years in disputation. At the age of 38 his selection for the 1911–12 trip was the first time he was chosen to tour other than as a replacement. His performance in the first Test, when he had to follow the captain, J. W. H. T. Douglas, who had pre-ferred to open the bowling himself, was not very good, but when restored to what he felt was his rightful position he had five wickets for six in the second Test. Thereafter he was, when fit, an automatic choice for England until the war.

Barnes appears to have thrived on dissension. He continued play-ing, in the leagues and for Staffordshire, for another fifteen years after the war. He played in no more Test matches but at the age of 51 he took 8 for 41 for Minor Counties against the South African tourists and he went on playing for Staffordshire, a legend in his own lifetime, until he was over 60. He was combative to the last.

But Barnes was exceptional, not only in his talent but in his attempts to fight the system. Most professionals lived with it as best they could. And it was a good best for some. George Hirst and Wilfred

Rhodes had been content, when they retired, to become coaches at public schools. Their successors, the new-style professionals, Sutcliffe and Hutton, did not seek to burn down these establishments: they sent their children to them. In due course Sutcliffe, H. and Hutton, L. begat W. H. H. Sutcliffe and R. A. Hutton, which no doubt gave their parents almost as much pleasure as the money they had made out of the game. So for the successful there was the prospect of steady progress. The unsuccessful, *ipso facto*, had to keep their mouths shut. No one cared much about the in-betweens. There are more rebels these days. John Snow is perhaps the nearest modern equivalent to Barnes: not quite so ready to down tools perhaps (nor treated in quite such a niggardly fashion either) but able to switch off according to his own sense of priorities. 'Snow . . . seems too often for comfort to agree to bowl grudgingly, as if some liberty were being taken with his contract,' as Alan Ross put it.[9] Significantly Snow was one of the first to sign up with the Kerry Packer circus as surely Barnes would have been if he had had the chance.

The cricket authorities have seemed to see no connection between preserving the lofty values they have claimed for cricket and removing social and economic injustices. It would be wrong, however, to suggest some dastardly, cunning conspiracy to oppress the masses. For the most part it was amateur muddle added to certain assumptions about the superiority of amateurs. C. B. Fry has given in his autobiography an amusing account of the bizarre and haphazard way in which England teams were selected at the turn of the century. The exercise was conducted largely on an 'old boy' basis. Fry himself had been doing well in the late 1890s without attracting the attention of the right people. 'The upper reaches of cricket,' he writes, 'and especially the well-fenced area known as Test Match cricket, are inhabited by familiar names that appear to be its natural denizens.' The 'old boy' basis was tempered, however, by idiosyncrasy. In 1899, unknown to 'the big boys', Fry made 80 for W. G. Grace's London County team against the Australians and 'the same W.G. being at the age of 49 [he was actually 51] still captain of England, plumped for me as his first choice as a batsman.' Not content with that, W.G. took it upon himself to co-opt Fry on to the selection committee. Lord Hawke, the chairman of the committee, was not best pleased, but reluctantly he eventually admitted Fry on a trial basis.

Now even this bizarre manner of proceeding appears to have been an improvement on the past when there was no national selection committee at all. The method whereby the Test teams except for the Lord's Test were chosen by the county committees on whose grounds the games were being played seems to have been useful only because it allowed the independent-minded Lancashire committee to choose Ranjitsinhji. That decision of 1896 may have hastened the end of the old system but it had also by then become obvious, even to the counties, that it was not a good way of building up team spirit to have four different selection committees. The new national selectors, however, were scarcely models of efficiency and thoroughness.

One important issue, whether W.G. should stand down as captain, was decided in an extraordinary fashion. Fry, the co-opted member, arrived late to be confronted with the question of who should open the innings. Fry, having suggested MacLaren, found that he had been giving a view about the captaincy, and W.G. dropped out. Even more extraordinary, the decision to bring in MacLaren as a batsman also meant that he came to succeed W.G. as captain. Whether he was the right man or not is impossible to say but Fry honestly admits that one factor never entered their minds: 'It was quite forgotten that by order of seniority and on the score of at least equal merit, F. S. Jackson ought to have had the reversion of the captaincy, even if Archie MacLaren was brought in to raise the batting strength.' This monumental lapse was not calculated to improve the team's morale or relationships between Jackson and MacLaren, and to the outside world it must have looked like a vote of 'no confidence' in the heir-apparent.

The amateur tradition in cricket had the same defects off the field as on. Even loyal supporters had to draw heavily on their reserves of complacency and goodwill to excuse the state of affairs that had been reached in the 1960s. Indeed, E. W. Swanton, doyen of cricket writers, whose tolerance of the established order and reverence for the nobility were such that he believed the MCC Australian tour of 1962–63 was 'admirably managed by the Duke of Norfolk' – a view not universally held – had his patience strained by the goings-on at headquarters in the 1960s. In a considered judgement on the period he felt obliged to refer to 'the malaise that was at this time affecting the top echelons of cricket'.[10] Swanton was not complaining about amateurism. On the contrary. Yet what he was complaining about was the result of long years of amateur domination.

Walter Hammond in his book *Cricket's Secret History* gives a good example: 'The need for at least one professional among the selectors was demonstrated in 1948. In the second Test that season against the Australians, selectors watching the game at Lord's noticed that Len Hutton seemed to be drawing away from some fast balls on the leg side, particularly from Lindwall. Hutton was dropped from the next Test not so much because of any failure in his own batting as because it was felt by one of the selectors that younger batsmen might be infected by this idea of getting away from fast bowling. What the selectors did not know, but every professional cricketer (and a good many other people) in the country knew quite well, was that Hutton had received a sharp knock on the hip-bone from Johnston, which slowed his footwork and also make him loath to risk a second blow in the same place. Many batsmen would have retired after getting that injury. Len knew the side needed runs, so he carried on, and his courage cost him his place in the next Test.' Whoever the influential selector was, the result of his advice was disastrous. Hutton's replacement, a very ordinary county cricketer called George Emmett, brought in for his first and only Test, made 0 and 10. It was lunacy to have left out Hutton in the first place. He came back and did well and in the final Test held the side together. Then and afterwards, until his retirement, he was by far England's most consistent batsman.

The villains of the piece in Swanton's account are mostly professionals. In 1969 in circumstances reminiscent of the MacLaren-Jackson episode, the heir presumptive, Tom Graveney, was passed over in favour of Illingworth, and the first Graveney knew of it was when he read it in the papers. The chairman of selectors was Alec Bedser, who after a long and distinguished career as a professional, in times when the distinction between gentlemen and players was still preserved, had embarked on a further period of service to the game on retiring to become a successful businessman. Swanton gives Bedser most of the blame for publicly embarrassing Graveney which, he thinks, provoked Graveney's subsequent act of defiance – playing in a match on the Sunday of a Test match – and his dismissal from international cricket like a small boy sent out of the room for putting his tongue out at the teacher. Bedser should have known better, it is suggested, particularly as he himself was left out of the Test side in Australia by Hutton on the 1954–55 tour and had been considerably hurt to learn about it from the cold print of the team sheet for the second Test.

Swanton in criticising the top echelons of cricket did so in terms that echo Martineau's concept of first-class cricketers as a military organisation. 'There used to be a terrible Army phrase,' writes Swanton, 'called "man management" under which heading were set down certain elementary guidelines for handling people.' He nowhere gives even so much as a hint of any thought that amateurs would have handled these things better than professionals. Yet the after-image persists of nostalgia for days of yore when good officers and gentlemen looked after their troops.

The reality is that former professionals have scarcely been allowed further into the magic circle than Old Nyren was at Hambledon. E. W. Swanton in his second volume of autobiography was at pains to suggest that the MCC had changed with the times. Its ten sub-committees, he suggested, 'form a democratic cross-section which would pass the scrutiny of most fair-minded men.' More than fifty years before, Lord Harris had made the same claim. 'To some it might appear,' he wrote, 'that MCC is a highly aristocratic and autocratic body. I venture to assert that it is thoroughly democratic.' Harris's justification for this is significant: he refers to the trouble MCC took to consult local councils before issuing any edicts. This, of course, reflects the power of the counties, which historically has been such a strong influence on cricket, and the balance of interests continuing from the eighteenth century and the days of the country party. 'Democracy' used in this special sense has nothing to do with the involvement of the lower orders.

Any concession to the second of the two nations has come tardily and as a result of financial pressures. Gate money has been gratefully received and, in recent years, so long as the basic three-day county game remained inviolate, has given rise to variants which, though doubtless entertaining, have seemed something less than cricket. Sponsorship, another influence in this, has seemed no shame. The last bastion is the committee room, and this has been skilfully defended. Professionals, even though they no longer exist, still know their place in the corridors of power. They pick the teams nowadays, and some of them are honorary members of MCC, an innovation attributable to G. O. Allen during his twelve years as Treasurer; but they held no important committee chairmanships even after MCC had adjusted to the Welfare State.

It was the 1964 Labour Government and its creation the Sports Council that brought limited change about. In June 1967, 'in order that the Minister of Sport could establish relations with cricket', as *Wisden* characteristically put it, MCC agreed to modify its structure. In fact the Sports Council introduced the possibility of grants to cricket. By a coincidence S. C. Griffith, the Secretary of MCC, had announced in a speech that winter: 'We have for some time been considering an organisation which will ensure that every cricketer and administrator – Test, county, service, university, club and school – and umpires – at whatever level will feel eventually that their voice can be heard by the Governing Body.'

Already MCC had brought into being a National Cricket Association, a loose grouping of the various interests listed by Griffith (the schools had the Headmasters' Conference as well as the English Schools' Cricket Association, the gentlemen as well as the players). From early in the century there had been an Advisory County Cricket Committee and a Board of Control for Tests, serviced by MCC administrators. Under the new arrangements these bodies came together as the Test and County Cricket Board, and this and the National Cricket Association became the two wings of the new MCC Cricket Council, the Governing Body.

For some years the difference was not sufficient for *Wisden* to separate the Cricket Council from MCC except in a sub-paragraph. The lay-out reflected the realities. The MCC committee men were joined by simulacra from the NCA but the differences were scarcely perceptible to the naked eye of outside observers. The President, Treasurer and Secretary of MCC took over the comparable, highly influential, offices on the Cricket Council.

By 1974, though the structure became formalised enough for a separate page in *Wisden* (five members of MCC, five from the TCCB and five from the NCA, plus a minor counties representative), the transubstantiation of the MCC hierarchy remained. The same names seem to crop up in one guise or other. The democratisation of cricket, if it has happened at all, has taken a different form from that of the outside world. The addition in 1977 of a representative of the Irish Cricket Association, though it would have surprised the Rev. Mr Pycroft, involved no risk of opening the gates to the rag-tag and bob-tail. The dominant category, apart from a sprinkling of gentry and some committee men from the counties, appears to be ex-amateur cricketers, and notably Old Blues.

One of the features of early cricket, it will be recalled, is that the camaraderie of the playing field, the decorous coming-together of the classes so lauded by the early writers, did not extend to the committee room. In principle, even now, after all the inroads of the vulgar modern world and the abolition of the hallowed distinction between gentlemen and players, this still seems to be the position.

As far as selection of Test teams is concerned, shrewd appreciation of commercial realities has ensured that ex-professionals play a prominent part. (Since they tend, like Alec Bedser, to be ultra-traditional in their outlook there is little danger of mob-rule asserting itself.) But, as to policy, which quintessentially means the preservation of the old social values in the structure of the English game, there is no hint of class mobility.

The excitement at Lord's must have been intense in 1978 over the election of a successor as chairman of the TCCB to D. J. Insole of Cambridge and England. The choice lay between three other Cambridge Blues – George Mann, Raman Subba Row and O. G. Wheatley. Mann prevailed, and the other two will doubtless have their hour.

Insole, on laying down the burden of office, had been awarded the prize of managing the 1978–79 tour of Australia. The advent of Kerry Packer meant that the post could not be left to the former professional, Barrington, but needed full ambassadorial status. That the captain, Brearley, though also a Cambridge man, was suspected of a tolerant attitude towards the circus was an unfortunate complication, but as the next chapter will suggest, a cross that had to be borne. The grip of amateurism persisted.

There were murmurings from malcontents. An article by Albert Hunt in *New Society* pointed out in November 1978 that 'ironically, although the amateur traditions still seem to dominate in questions of selection and management, they don't extend on to the field of play.' The last remark is a reference to the attempts of 'the England captain, Brearley, in his head-protector, facing bowling well short of fast on an easy-paced wicket, and doggedly trying to play himself into some kind of form' before the forthcoming Test matches. Hunt regarded this as an unchivalrous denial of the crease to a member of Brearley's team who also needed practice, the unfortunate Geoffrey Boycott.

This dyed-in-the-wool professional had never understood (perhaps never considered) the word 'compromise'. The pursuit of perfection, to which he was wholly dedicated, would perhaps have been an alien concept to the establishment, even if Boycott had been inclined, or equipped, to present it to them in an agreeable package. A saint would have had some difficulty in gaining acceptance on these terms. As it was, this manifestly frail human being found himself not only passed over as captain for Australia but even as vice-captain, an affront that provoked the *Guardian* to editorial thunder.

Boycott swallowed his pride and went to Australia. All that was left to him was to make runs. As Hunt reported, he fended off the probings of the media with dignity and tried to concentrate on his task, clearly aware that if he did not make more runs than everyone else he would be regarded as a failure. But he was also aware 'that runs don't come by magic' and indeed had always – in spite of frequent derision – sought to practise and prepare himself for the big occasion. Hunt's article claimed that the 'amateurs' Insole and Brearley unreasonably denied Boycott the opportunity: 'The amateur traditions expressed them-selves at Melbourne in what seems to have been an almost frivolous regard of the professional needs of England's leading professional bats-man.' It was a warped view perhaps; but Barnes, S. F., would have believed it.

TEN

LOYALTIES AND MODERN VALUES

THE EVENTUAL ACKNOWLEDGEMENT IN 1963 that it was no longer possible to sustain the formal distinction between amateur and professional in first-class cricket, however painful it may have been to diehards, seems in retrospect to have made little difference to the way the game has been conducted. At the time the outside world, on the brink of the Beatles era, no doubt regarded it as an outward and visible sign that even MCC saw the need for change. In fact their pre-occupation, then as afterwards, was with the preservation of the obsolete pattern of county cricket.

To everyone else it was clear that the county game was in a bad way. The central issue was not whether the county basis still had any mean-ing for the public, but whether the three-day game meant anything. The average man – highly important at the turnstiles – could not hope to see a game the whole way through even if he himself was prepared to stick it out for three days. Perhaps he could get away on Saturday. He might have been glad to do so on Sunday if there had been any games. But in mid-week he had little or no chance.

After the war there had been a brief flurry when the public, starved of sport for six years, welcomed back cricket as a sign of return to normality, but then the game sank to a poor state in the 1950s and 60s. What seemed to many the obvious remedy – to reduce the programme drastically and concentrate on week-ends – was, though frequently discussed, never seriously considered by the cricket authorities. Instead there was a frantic quest for popularising devices and constant tinkering with the regulations. Smaller boundaries, bonus points, fines for slow play – all kinds of things were tried in an attempt to revive interest in the county championship. Alas, though closely followed in the newspapers, it was rarely watched. The regular clientele was chiefly composed of retired persons, clergymen and actors.

The pressure for change did not come from novelty-seekers, radicals or hard-nosed modern men with no respect for tradition. It came from people who loved the game but despaired of what was happening to it, people who, though as nostalgically inclined as the next man, were prepared to face reality for the sake of the game. A good example was Major Rowland Bowen, whose dedication to cricket was unquestionable, who had a healthy respect for tradition – as distinct from ancestor-worship – and who campaigned long and hard for moderate reforms that would enable county cricket to contend with the modern world.

Writing in 1970 he had to record complete failure: 'Twenty years ago I wrote a detailed memorandum which pointed out, with the knowledge of those days, but without the hindsight of these, that factors such as full employment and the taxation of the well-to-do would make the continuation of the first-class game impossible along the then lines: the lines it still follows. I suggested a two-divisional county championship . . . with promotion and relegation. I suggested two-day cricket of long hours at weekends, on public holidays, and in mid-week in August: I pointed out that the number of days needed for a county to complete a programme was well within the weekends, public holidays and during the individual's own annual holiday. I showed that the true amateur, who has hardly ever played in England (though he has overwhelmingly done so overseas), would be able now to play: that the waste of money on ill-paid mediocre professionals could be concentrated in retaining two or three outstanding players per county . . . There were a few murmurings about this scheme, nothing was ever done, and when I elaborated some parts of it in 1963 . . . I knew already that it was too late; for in the meantime there had been vast social changes in England.'[1]

The 'solution' the authorities preferred – emphasising where their interest really lay – was to leave the county matches untouched but intersperse them with a variety of one-day over-limit competitions. In the process they sold their souls and became a part of show-business.

One of the first innovations, designed to improve the fading image of county cricket, was the importation on a big scale of star players from overseas. Another was that the new competitions were sponsored by tobacco and drinks firms, razor-blade manufacturers and so forth as an aid to selling their products. One-day games, in themselves, were a splendid idea, but they took a form (whether at the behest of the sponsors or not is not clear) that narrowed the range of skills that cricket had developed over the years and also, together with the overseas stars, inhibited the development of young English cricketers as potential Test-match players.

The wholesale importation of overseas cricketers, while it raised the standard of play, reduced the opportunities for local youngsters. The one-day games, though they improved fielding standards beyond recognition, encouraged tactics and styles of batting and bowling that were of little use for winning Test matches. One of the arguments for keeping county cricket has always been that it is a nursery for Test players. (Test cricket is important to the authorities not only for its own sake but because it makes a profit which is used to subsidise the county game.) Whether the county system is really helpful is doubtful. There are disadvantages in playing cricket six days a week season after season. The experience it gives is invaluable but it can lead to staleness, fatigue, injuries and sometimes a kind of world-weariness. The new one-day games mixed in with the county programme added another burden to the work-horses.

Only the most doctrinaire would argue against the one-day game, as such, though very short games do not give batsmen a chance to build an innings. Nor is it quintessential to cricket that there should be two innings a side: the two-innings game is subtler and fuller but a single-innings game has all the main ingredients. The real objection is to the artificial rules based on over-limits. 'Many are more anxious to have maiden overs credited to them than to win a match,' complained Frederick Gale in 1871. The over-limit game actually encourages this approach by making it possible to win without taking a wicket.

Over-limit cricket puts a premium on negative bowling and on frantic and idiosyncratic batting (such as edging the ball through where the slip fielder would be in a normal game). It reduces the range of possibilities of the game. True, it has improved the art of fielding. It may also be more exciting, at times, than other types of cricket, but it is less sophisticated and often more stereotyped and limited than the full version.

It would be wrong to put all the blame for the recent decline in cricket crowd behaviour in England on this type of cricket. Nevertheless spectators at over-limit games increasingly tend to behave like Association football crowds, chanting and running on to the pitch, waving banners and so forth. Cricket, despite its ancient claims to superiority, appears to be coming to terms with the plebeian taste for tribal war-chants and with the vulgar apparatus of show-business – stars, agents, publicity, ballyhoo, mass media, adulation and hysteria.

The indications are that so long as the county structure remains intact the cricket establishment is ready to make the adjustment. There was a straw in the wind in 1972. The events of the 1970–71 and 1972 England–Australia series had included such things as systematic swearing at each other by the two teams, the England captain wagging his finger at an umpire, a beer-can deluge, a flouncing off the field, extreme ill-feelings because of peculiar umpiring and at Headingley in 1972 a very, very peculiar wicket. Yet they were sanctified by the inclusion of a laudatory article by a former Australian captain in the biblical pages of *Wisden*. 'Everyone will have their own ideas on this question of whether or not controversy harms cricket, but over the last two series between England and Australia I think the game has come out of it very well . . . I doubt if cricket has ever had such beneficial publicity through all avenues of the media and rarely has the financial return been better for the game's administrators,' he wrote.[2] This is a philosophy capable of sustaining the growing sensationalism of the later Roman Empire's circus ring.

The needs of cricket as a contest have always been to some extent at odds with the notion of providing entertainment. Most perceptive advocates of the first-class game have accepted the responsibilities implicit in this tension. Roy Kilner, the maverick Yorkshire professional of the 1920s, was quite clear about this: 'People have to be educated up to it,' he said. He likened it to understanding Shakespeare or appreciating other things of value. Children may not find them immediately appealing or understand them in all their subtlety but wise parents and teachers persist all the same. As E. V. Lucas put it, 'Cricket is not big hitting or consistently bright batting, although big hitting and bright batting are a part of cricket. Cricket is big hitting and bright batting, plus no hitting and anxious batting, plus even dull batting, plus bowling, plus fielding, plus strategy, plus chance. That is the game: all these ingredients are essential.'[3]

But Lucas also points out another fundamental – 'the very important one of untiring, unrelenting rivalry'. Festival cricket has never been more than an end-of-season diversion, attractive only because of the contrast with the seriousness of what has gone before.

Fervent partisanship can subdue a crowd's yearning for brighter cricket because it injects an excitement of a different and more powerful kind. In the 1977 Test series between England and Australia it was the slow-scoring Boycott who held the stage. Indeed, once at the crease he scarcely left it and the English crowds loved every moment. There were two sides to it: his own painful struggle for rehabilitation, which sustained many of his personal admirers, but also and above all his gradually growing dominance over the opposition. In contrast the Australian Greg Chappell, the most attractive batsman on either side, made very few runs, and there were no complaints about that from the spectators.

For the true devotee this partisanship can produce unbearable tension and can diminish his enjoyment of his own team's performance or even his appreciation of his own personal hero's style. Neville Cardus suffered acutely in this way: 'I loved Spooner so much that I dare not watch him make a stroke. It is a curious thought – I probably *never* saw him at the moment which he actually played a ball.' When Lancashire were playing Yorkshire his agony sometimes led him to distinctly unchristian hopes which he nevertheless expected the Lord to sustain: 'I closed my eyes and prayed that God would make George Hirst drop down dead before bowling the next ball.' Indeed he called upon the Almighty not only for the immoral but also for the impossible. 'Sometimes I got myself into difficult positions with God. There was Victor Trumper, for example, next to MacLaren and Spooner my most adored. He was an Australian and I was a patriotic English lad. I wanted him always to score a century, but I also wanted England to get him out first ball and win the match.'[4]

These ethically disreputable goings-on occurred at the turn of the century, but the dilemma will be recognised by many a contemporary addict. The discomfort it causes may well be of social origin. Apart from the young it may occur in its acutest form in the less elevated social groups. Consider, for example, this account of a 1939 Test match by a superior spectator irritated by a vulgarian: 'In spite of West Indian wickets which fell like ninepins the woman was ill-satisfied. She groaned loudly when a ball from Robins shaved the stumps without displacing the bail; she screamed with delight when another luckless batsman returned *quam celerrime* to the pavilion. It was victory she wanted, and to her husband who protested mildly at infrequent intervals, she said, "I can't help it. I want England to win." And yet there was something noble in her character. There must surely be some stuff in a woman, who, having paid two shillings at the turnstile only a short while ago, is willing, nay anxious, for the match to end at half-past three, in order that her team might win.'[5]

The lady may have been exceptional (and male chauvinists will have their own view of the situation) but the tensions of partisanship tend to be more acute for the working classes in general. This is hardly surprising. The bourgeoisie have always been able to hedge their bets – whether in wars, or civil strife, or in sporting mock-battles – for they have class loyalties and values (and the security to sustain them) that are denied the lower orders. For plebeians, allegiance to a team or a pop-star may be their only contact with any values outside the narrow concerns of the shop-floor or the street corner; and they are unlikely to have either the sophistication or the tradition of security to allow themselves the luxury of appreciating unproductive frills even in games. They are likely to have a limited appetite for good things produced by opposing teams.

Games have always been a serious business for the human species, though their true significance has not always been recognised. In contemporary Western society, shaped by the industrial revolution, they are the vehicle for millions of inarticulate and possibly unattainable dreams. Cricket, like any other sport seeking to survive in a specialised world, has to take into account the different and possibly conflicting loyalties of administrators, participants and spectators.

Viewed in the light of the orthodox mythology of the game, the masses needed to keep the turnstiles clicking are likely to seem fickle and potentially anarchical. The loyalty of the non-participant contemporary supporter is not easy to satisfy because it is apparently irrational. It craves short-term results but it is capable of withstanding setbacks provided the object of loyalty offers some prospect of escape from the ultimate horror of boredom (especially if this holds out the promise of vicarious mastery). These factors often seem nowadays to be more important in establishing allegiances than, say, the sense of identity with a place which could once be taken for granted.

It may still be easier for little Yorkshire boys to identify with their heroes than for youngsters in counties that have filled their ranks with all nationalities. Certainly this was the case in 1938 when the Rev. Hugh Hunter of Keighley wrote to *The Times* describing how he had called out to a small boy slogging a ball in a village street, 'Hullo, Bradman.' The boy soon put him right: 'I'm not Bradman, I'm 'utton.' Mr Hunter apologised instantly. Even today many people in Yorkshire cling on to the tradition. This has persisted despite the not very successful efforts of the county's players in recent years, so there may still be a residual intrinsic belief in Yorkshireness.

Throughout England the strong county loyalties which helped to shape cricket have been seriously eroded by urban growth. Towns have their own loyalties. These are associated more with soccer, which, not surprisingly, is much the more popular game in the twentieth century. Yet it is doubtful if even urban loyalties have any real meaning by now. Soccer teams, though called Manchester or Newcastle, have long since ceased to have any local significance in terms of the origin of players. The partisanship survives of course and local pride is apparently bolstered by the achievements of imported gladiators. But how local the pride actually is, is problematical. It would be just as easy to explain in terms of working-class group solidarity against an unknown and therefore hostile world outside the group. Certainly easier communication and transport means that support for teams comes from far and wide. Manchester United, as any police force will confirm, have rabid fans throughout Britain, and even further afield – industrial workers cocking a snook at the malign forces that oppose them.

So it should surprise no one that in cricket the introduction of West Indians, Pakistanis and South Africans to county sides has in no way lessened the banner-waving enthusiasm of supporters of Leicestershire or Kent. When cricket crowds intone tribal chants and swarm on the field in soccer-style their springs of action seem to relate not so much to pride in their birthplace as to less tangible but equally powerful modern equivalents – hero-worship, the desire for vicarious achievement, the search for identity and for excitement in soul-destroying, and utterly boring, industrial society.

Show-business has an ambivalent role in this. Clearly it can, and does, recognise these human longings and use them for commercial purposes. It remains to be seen whether, confronted with a true loyalty to a significant social or political grouping, the show-business ethos can survive. Currently the dominant partisan loyalty is the national one, still strong everywhere and fervent in emergent nations. This could be the biggest obstacle to the success of the Packer-style super-games intended to overshadow the Test matches, especially as there is a post-colonial edge to encounters with England in the other cricket-playing nations.

Another question, though, is whether sponsored games of this kind can be genuine. The logic of show-business is that in a five-match series the teams should always stand level by the time the fifth game starts. Modern entrepreneurship can subdue apparently natural laws, but if the illusion, at least, of genuine contest cannot be sustained there could be a bigger-scale repetition of the story of William Clarke's All-England XI. Gradually as the novelty wore off the venture became less profitable, and long before then it had become necessary to stage-manage some of the games.

On the other hand entrepreneurs have things going for them, too. The large sums of money available to the commercial sponsor are likely to attract, at least temporarily and perhaps always, the best players. This will not solve the problem of team loyalty, but it may help. The Packer approach seems well suited to a return to the old single-wicket competition. Hero-worship is a powerful force, and the problem of allegiance is less complicated in an individual contest than in a team. Representative teams, which evoke group loyalties, are under greater obligation to be truly representative of something other than an arbitrary, commercially-determined grouping.

One of the features of cricket, of course, is that though it is very much a team game, and one in which notions of team spirit are strong, it is also a series of individual man-to-man encounters. So there is some friendly territory for the Packer circus to occupy. There may well have been recognition of this in the reaction of the cricket establishment to the Packer threat. Once the court case had been lost the Cornhill Insurance Company came forward with a plan to invest a million pounds in the Test matches (henceforth to be known by their founder's name), so that English players chosen to play would have their income multiplied by five.

These events are a reminder that when games become industries, as they have done in the present century, then the loyalty of the player as well as that of the spectator has to be seriously considered. Ranjitsinhji, near the turn of the century, could write in his Jubilee Book: 'The true artist regards his art, not as a means to an end, but as an end in itself. For him the art is not only his work but his pleasure.' This was the situation of those who 'would rather play cricket than do anything else, even though it is the means whereby they live'. Ranji acknowledged certain moral considerations: 'Men ought not to get income out of games. They ought to be so employed that their means of livelihood is also a benefit to their fellow-men and society. They ought to be helping to supply some of the world's requirements.' (He quoted a headmaster rebuking a faulty Latin scholar: 'You may some day make a good professional cricketer. You probably will. But you will never make a useful citizen or a Christian English gentleman.') Ranji nevertheless did not believe that 'the life of one who devotes himself to cricket is altogether wasted or quite useless to his fellow-men.' He suggested that the 'innocent and healthy amusement' in such games as cricket and football could not be offered to the masses unless there was 'a class who devote themselves entirely to the games'.

The argument scarcely arises today. In a world of specialisation it is taken for granted that the leisure industry, of which cricket is a part, should offer expert practitioners an opportunity to make a lot of money. The poorly-paid masses who sustain the leisure industry, so far from resenting or deploring the money earned by performers, look to it with admiration and approval. It is an outlet for the unfulfilled aspirations of the young and an agreeable reminder of what might have been to the old. Few see anything wrong in sportsmen seeking rich rewards: it is an inversion of 'There but for the grace of God.' Even sceptics subdue their reservations on the grounds that the productive life of professional sportsmen is very short, so that they have to cash in while they can.

But bought loyalty can be re-sold. Much of the public debate in 1977 when Packer launched his circus plan was, understandably, about whether the cricket authorities were right in seeking to ban those who contracted out to Packer from playing in the official competitions. However, this drew attention away from an issue of loyalty: the conduct of England's captain, Tony Greig, who not only signed up for the circus himself but encouraged others of the team to do so. (His explanation that these activities began only when the current Test series had ended, so that he was technically no longer the captain, lacked conviction.) Greig, a South African, had seemed an amazing choice to many even before this. Some thought the choice was confirmation of MCC's sympathy with apartheid. Some contrasted the authorities' attitude to Greig with their treatment of D'Oliveira, a different sort of South African. Others, neutral politically, pointed out that Greig was not a normal resident of England before or during his appointment as captain but a carpet-bagger playing cricket all the year round in some country or other. This practice in itself was no longer remarkable but it seemed strange to find the England selectors, so scrupulous in their observance of the high moral code, happily swallowing this camel when they had strained at so many gnats. One way and another Greig's defection seemed loaded with significance.

Could greater loyalty have been expected from a native Britisher, as John Woodcock suggested in *The Times*, or was Greig merely a representative contemporary trend-setting hero? Does everything depend on money nowadays? It may not be a law of nature that money should be put above other considerations but our materialist society and its inequalities make it seem so. During the summer of 1977 the first two England cricketers known to have been made an offer by Packer and refused it were Geoff Boycott and Chris Old, both of Yorkshire – the only county still insisting on a birth qualification.[6] The romantically-inclined may take comfort from the thought that the Puritan ideal of the Yorkshire club even today encourages and sustains values above the sordidly material.

Their satisfaction may be diminished somewhat, however, by the irony that Boycott, putting his county before Packer's gold, found that it bought him nothing when a year later the county dismissed him as captain. The inescapable conclusion is that even the fierce Yorkshire loyalties have been strained in recent years.

An important factor in these events, in other counties as well as Yorkshire, is the extent to which county committees have tended to assume the mantle of the early patrons – without their personal financial obligations – and to have as simple a view of industrial relations as Sir Horace Mann once did. Yorkshire is merely a spectacular example that happens to have come to public notice. There the committee, apparently operating according to Lord Hawke's blithe assumption of God-given right, have involved themselves in recent decades in a series of episodes in which, however worthy their motives, their concern for the human dignity of their employees has seemed gravely deficient. When Illingworth asked for a contract – scarcely in 1968 a revolutionary concept – he was told, it seems, to bugger off; and two years later, Close, the club captain, was given ten minutes to resign if he wanted to avoid the sack. The senior players leaving or being sacked in the 1950s and 60s would have made a championship-winning side in themselves. The rights and wrongs of individual cases may be arguable, but they amount to an unimpressive record of industrial relations by any standards. The moral seems to be that waving the flag is not enough, even if it has a White Rose on it.

At national level, also, the legacy of back-door work of the Warner kind has created an atmosphere in which loyalty must find it hard to flourish. With Greig it clearly did not flourish at all and perhaps it would not have done in any case. Without seeking to excuse Greig's behaviour, however, there is a sense in which he and the cricket establishment deserved each other. Furthermore, he turned out to be on the side of the angels, legally at least, because of the authorities' Stone Age philosophy of industrial relations.

Kerry Packer's super-star commercialism appears likely, if it succeeds, to change the game beyond all recognition. This the MCC seem to have been ready to countenance long before Kerry Packer came along. In their anxiety to protect the underlying social values of 'more than a game' and 'it's not cricket' they have spared too little thought for the game itself. Insofar as Packer's venture has exposed the irony there may be that much to be said for it. But whether the price to be paid will be worth it is another matter. It is hard to believe that Greig's approach to life is good for cricket.

The irony itself should surprise no one. Students of history will recall that before, and even during, the Second World War there were in Britain those amongst the privileged who were in grave doubt about whether country or class should come first. Communism seemed a bigger threat to what they held dear than Adolf Hitler. The Nazi leader was indeed admired in certain circles. Rudolf Hess believed sufficiently strongly that the upper classes would negotiate a peace with Germany that he flew to Scotland in 1941, with the war at its height, to make the offer.

It seems likely that a similar phenomenon was at work, giving rise to the lack of patriotism to which John Arlott referred, at the time of Hutton's accession to the England captaincy. Any old amateur, though preferably one from the south, was to be preferred to this north-country realist. And even when the convention of gentlemen and players was finally abolished the preference of the selectors and their overlords continued to be for ex-amateurs, university men and other 'natural' leaders.

That the actual selection committee included more and more ex-professionals affected this little if at all. The selectors were not selected for their radical outlooks, and the membership and leadership of the Cricket Council and the TCCB themselves showed no sign of veering to the left. In fact the chief modifying influence on the traditions of Lord Hawke and Lord Harris has been commercialism, reflecting the growing dependence of the establishment on clicking turnstiles and sponsorship in order to sustain the old pattern of six-day-a-week county cricket. Paradoxically this pursuit of the old feudal dream has made them more dependent on professional expertise, and more vulnerable to the alien philosophy of Packer and Greig.

The objections to Hutton because of his Yorkshire origin remind us that the two nations concept has always had a geographical as well as a directly social aspect. Northern resentments – righteous indignation or paranoia according to taste – surface periodically in many aspects of life. In cricket Yorkshire feels them more strongly than any, and the fact that at least some of their wounds are self-inflicted helps the situation not at all. By 1978 a decade in the wilderness had eaten into the Yorkshire soul. Failure to come to terms with the over-limit game, leadership crises, bloody-minded management attitudes, persistence with the Yorkshire-born when every other county was thronged with foreign stars – all these led to pent-up frustrations which gave added force to Yorkshire chagrin at the national selectors for their stubborn failure to recognise the supremacy of Geoffrey Boycott. A *Guardian* editorial on 4 August 1978 was both skittish and superficial: 'Yorkshire is afflicted from time to time with feelings of persecution by effete southerners. Test selectors are traditionally seen as archetypal southerners, if not by their counties of origin, then certainly by contamination from southerners.' Professor Robin Pedley of Southampton University, who had the previous day written a letter admonishing the selectors, was unmasked by the *Guardian* as, despite his address, 'as Yorkshire as Ilkley Moor'.

Yet, at the risk of being tarred with the same brush, it seems pertinent to suggest that accusations of simple chauvinism miss an important point. Yorkshiremen feel not only that their cricketers, if God were in his Heaven and all were right with the world, would win all the time, but that they are the custodians of the true faith. This means, amongst other things, that Yorkshire people are suspicious of outsiders who claim cricket is more than a game, yet then betray it. The more socially conscious may be inclined to suspect that the effete southerner has perpetuated the myth of more than a game for his own malign purposes. As Professor Pedley's letter, in support of Geoffrey Boycott, and Boycott's own behaviour, show, many Yorkshiremen have a different idea of loyalty from that of the cricket establishment.

The Pedley letter is worth quoting in full, together with a reply from an address in Surrey (presumably inhabited by a genuine southerner).

Sir, – The man John Arlott praises so fulsomely as England's captain is one who, on his own admission, refused to undertake not to sign for Packer while he was captain of England, who persists in his admiration for the dismissed Greig, and who still wants 'compromise' with Packer.

Most reprehensible of all, however, is the attitude of both Brearley and Arlott towards Geoffrey Boycott. Boycott is by far the best batsman in England, and the only batsman in the world who has scored his hundredth 100 in the cauldron of a Test match (against Australia, too).

He has a higher career average than any other batsman with a hundred 100s except Bradman, and a higher percentage of hundreds per completed innings than Hutton, Sobers, or Compton. Can anyone doubt that if Brearley wanted Boycott in the England side he would be included?

Does anyone doubt, either, that it was the absence of Brearley and the presence of Boycott which put the steel in the England team's resolution in Pakistan which prevented Packer's men from playing? Boycott's loyalty and ability are being scurvily rewarded, and the shameful behaviour of the England selectors calls for the courage of a Marlar, not the apologetic whitewash of an increasingly reactionary *Guardian*.

(Prof.) Robin Pedley.

The reply:

> Sir, – Professor Pedley lauds Geoffrey Boycott's supposed loyalty to England. Has he really so short a memory?
>
> It was Boycott's own decision to make himself unavailable for England when the pressure was really on and his undoubted talent was really needed. Messrs Lilley [sic] and Thomson were clearly too much for his loyalty at that stage.
>
> Moreover during last winter's tour, which the professor admires so much, he proved himself to be tactically naive both as a batsman and more important as a captain. Far from putting steel into the England side, he has inflicted it with dourness and even worse, selfishness.
>
> Brearley's poor run of scores is unfortunate, but look at his record as captain of England. Most of all, it is the England players both past and present who have had to suffer the vagaries of Boycott's temperament. I am confident that there are many who like me would prefer to do without his brand of cricket in the future. – Yours faithfully,
>
> David Helsen.

Between them these letters include references to most of the current controversies in cricket and hark back to themes discussed in earlier chapters. The topical issue, whether Boycott or Brearley should captain England, was not as straightforward as those seeking to prove a simple thesis might wish. For Boycott, though a remorselessly good and utterly professional batsman, had become over the years a captain and a player about whom there were two opinions even in Yorkshire, and only one in most other places – that he was more than a little self-centred. Nevertheless his experiences in Test cricket (in which by the early 1970s he was the sheet-anchor of poor batting sides and in the opinion of many the rightful heir to the captaincy once Illingworth's Indian summer came to an end, but was passed over in favour of lesser men) must have played their part in adding a few more layers of protective covering to the central enigma of Boycott's character. Though the reasons for his withdrawal from the international scene were shrouded in mystery the general assumption was that it was at least in part a protest at the elevation of M. J. Denness of Kent.

This appointment, one of the selectors' less successful efforts as it turned out, did seem to fit the simple thesis – that despite the abolition of amateur status the preference was still for gentlemen leaders, preferably Old Blues, and failing that public-school men, even minor public-school men, and, of course, southerners. (Anglicised Scotsmen, in certain circumstances, also qualify.) After Hutton's retirement in 1955 until the start of Illingworth's four-year reign in 1969 there was only the brief and abruptly terminated hour of Close to break the monopoly of May, Denness, Cowdrey and M. J. K. Smith. Once Illingworth was gone the forces of reaction took over again. Or so it must have seemed to the wearers of White-Rose-coloured spectacles.

Others saw it differently. The Editor of *Wisden*, Norman Preston, took a particularly poor view of Boycott. In the 1975 edition, after commiserating with Denness whose limitations the previous winter's Australian tour had exposed, he declared roundly that Boycott's presence had not been missed. 'After being chosen amongst the sixteen for the tour he withdrew some weeks later, explaining that he had still not got over the pressures and tensions of international cricket and that he was not confident of being able to stand up to the rigours of a long Australian tour.' Casting doubt on Boycott's ability to face bouncers, Preston went on to say: 'Indeed Boycott by his deeds and words has all England wondering whether he will ever be a force again in Test cricket.'

Denness, still in office at the start of the 1975 season, had such a poor game one way and another in the first Test that he had to repeat his gesture of the previous winter in offering to stand down. So the selectors turned, Mr Preston informs us in the 1976 *Wisden*, 'to Greig, the tall, volatile captain of Sussex, born in South Africa of a Scottish father'. Though unproven tactically Greig had, according to Mr Preston, 'many splendid qualities'. These splendid qualities, as we have seen, were to include recruiting the best players from the team to play for Kerry Packer.

And so to Brearley, who on his first exposure to Test cricket, the 1976–77 tour of India, after a long and moderately successful career in Cambridge University and Middlesex cricket, had been made vice-captain and achieved, thanks to one innings of 91, an average of 26.87. As captain against Australia he did better (27.44) but perhaps not quite so well as the returning prodigal Boycott with 147.33. But England won the Ashes and it was Brearley who led the tour to Pakistan and New Zealand that winter. He unfortunately broke his arm before making any big scores or winning any Test matches and had to hand over the captaincy to Boycott. And Boycott, proving that real life is not like fiction, had only limited success when his big chance came.

But Professor Pedley's strictures during the 1978 season cannot entirely be written off as the outcrop of deep-seated Yorkshire persecution mania. After the fourth Test of the summer even John Woodcock in *The Times* seemed somewhat apologetic about Brearley's average – less than 20 for his last 12 Test innings – though his preference, to enable Boycott to return after injury, was to drop Roope who had an average of nearly 45. Until then, even though Boycott was fit again, the excuse had been made of 'not altering a winning team', though this meant retaining a batting line-up in which only one of the first six had scored a Test century.

But cricket ability was not the only consideration. Throughout his travails as a batsman Brearley's supporters had made much of his social and tactical excellence as a captain. 'Because England are at ease under Brearley and play the better for being so, it is much to be hoped that he will, as it were, pull through,' wrote Woodcock.[7] The gratuitous 'as it were' seemed indicative of the despair the situation was clearly beginning to induce. On the BBC, the air was heavy with cultivated southern accents invoking the mystique of captaincy and playing up and playing the game regardless of bumping pitches, blinding light or jammed Gatlings and dead colonels.

Ironically, whilst the erstwhile liberal John Arlott was being panned by Professor Pedley and defended in the *Guardian*'s editorial columns, elsewhere in the paper the utterly conventional Henry Blofeld was stating the truth of it: 'It is always an embarrassment when the captain is not really worth his place, but particularly so when it means that it prevents the selectors from giving a young player . . . the chance of Test experience with a tour of Australia ahead.' John Arlott himself, once the team was announced, became judicial: 'the selectors would scarcely have retained credibility if they had left out Boycott this time. He is so clearly the outstanding England batsman of the day that it is not possible to pick a true England team without him. If Brearley does not recover his form – indeed, even if he does – a considerable weight of northern opinion will expect Boycott to captain the team to Australia this winter.'[8]

That Boycott, recalled, duly made his 108th century and England, having previously achieved no more than 38, had an opening stand of 111, is of only incidental interest, for the issue clearly concerned other things than Brearley's form.[9] The selectors' loyalty to him was remarkable, especially since, as the Pedley letter suggests, Brearley's own loyalty was of a kind that some thought capable of embracing Packer as well as the TCCB. The advent of his benefit year, some believed, helped prevent his joining Packer, though the more cynical suggested that since he could scarcely have been required as a player in super-cricket, but rather in some advisory or administrative role, there was no particular hurry anyway. Mr Helsen in his reply invokes the other kind of loyalty – the stiff upper-lip variety – and neatly illustrates how, despite the superficial irony of the situation, it is in the end unsurprising that the cricket establishment should be so complaisant about their captain's attitude to Kerry Packer and his World Series Cricket.

Financial morality had never been a noticeable feature of first-class cricket. In the long history of under-cover payments, deals with Packer were merely a modern variant. Nor with regard to their own response to super-cricket were the authorities in any position to preach morality to others. In the ancient alliance between MCC and the counties there had always been tension, and so it proved on this occasion. The reaction of Sussex to the initial shock of Greig's defection was to re-appoint him their captain for 1978. Kent, though they deposed the Pakistani Packer player Asif Iqbal as captain, kept him on as a player. Indeed, having won the championship in 1978 aided by the English Packer players Woolmer and Underwood, freed from Test match calls, Kent decided to retain them for 1979. Their argument, that if they didn't other counties would sign them, said little for the Kent Committee's ethical standards or their assessment of those of their rivals. It was no surprise when later it was announced that Alan Knott, the former England wicket-keeper, temporarily unseated by a new discovery, Downton, would be returning to Kent despite his signing for Packer. Some counties at least placed other values higher than loyalty to England, it appeared.

Internationally the story was similar. The original united front soon seemed more like a façade. In a long article on the same day as his assessment of the Boycott-Brearley question, John Arlott summarised the latest state of affairs with regard to World Series Cricket. Compromise was now the order of the day. Arlott's explanation – 'the strong stand of England and Australia has been markedly weakened by the fact that, since Pakistan and West Indies clearly want coexistence, the ICC can no longer present a united hostile front' – was undoubtedly correct as far as it went. Pakistan, for instance, with virtually all their top players in the Packer net, could scarcely allow themselves to take the field against India, unscathed, without them. But it underplayed the division within the English ranks.

In England neither patriotism nor the true game (as proclaimed in Yorkshire) appeared to weigh as heavily as self-interest and the click of turnstiles. Furthermore, as the Pedley-Helsen correspondence reveals, the self-interest is overlaid with values and loyalties that go back to the feudal origins of cricket. Gentlemen and players, the mystique of captaincy, dashing amateur batsmanship, the two nations, North and South – all are there. And so too is the virility cult. Not the least significant feature of Mr Helsen's criticism of Boycott is his suggestion that Lillee and Thomson 'were too much for his loyalty at that stage'. This indeed was the allegation of Greig, an insinuation that earned him suspension for a while. That the evidence does not support Greig is not the point. It is manliness, and C. B. Fry on William Gunn, and Bradman and Australian squealers over bodyline, all over again.

John Arlott's thoughtful article advocating coexistence insufficiently touches on another aspect of the advent of World Series Cricket. Acceptance of Packer is acceptance of show-business loyalties. The cricket establishment had travelled far along that road before Packer's name was even mentioned in connection with the game. The counties need not be surprised if, in adjusting to the ethics of World Series Cricket, the loyalty they receive is of the kind they give. Hampshire soon tasted this medicine when first their South African batsman, Barry Richards, and then their West Indian bowler, Andy Roberts, withdrew. Arlott described this as a domestic matter, but John Woodcock in *The Times* thought it rather more significant. 'At the way Roberts and Richards, two players who owe so much to English cricket, have walked out on them, Hampshire members and players are equally indignant,' he wrote,[10] urging the county to resist re-entering the overseas market and to encourage young English players instead.

The different approach may partly be due to John Arlott's position as President of the Players' Association. Always the cricket writer and broadcaster whom the county players respected most, Arlott managed to reconcile his journalistic and official positions in a dignified and honourable way (and with less recourse to legerdemain than P. F. Warner in earlier days). Naturally, however, the Players' Association's angle was that of securing maximum financial benefit for their members, who included Greig as well as Boycott. Compromise with Packer would certainly mean more money for some, particularly as the official game seemed likely to attract more sponsorship. Greig, indeed, had claimed that his defection was in the best financial interests of all; and he received support from some unlikely quarters. In August 1977, under the inelegant heading 'Er, that dragon is St Kerry', *The Economist* reminded its readers that Greig, having said that all cricketers would gain once commercial interests were competing with the existing cricket establishment, had been 'vituperatively attacked by that establishment and its captive newspaper correspondents' but had subsequently been proved right. 'The Cornhill Insurance Company (whose bid has been too quickly accepted) last week offered English cricket more money than it has ever had before.'

The weakness in the argument is that it was likely to be the stars, such as Greig, who chiefly benefited from this competition rather than the still downtrodden run-of-the-mill county players, even if the conventional game survived the Packer take-over bid. The aim of the Players' Association in 1978 was to use the situation to secure a minimum wage for county players, a proposition that could be conceded only in principle with no guarantee that there would be money to pay it. Smaller playing staffs were seen as one possible outcome. And it was not only captive newspaper correspondents who found the idea of Packer and Greig having the best interests of the game at heart somewhat improbable. The Warwickshire staff wrote to the Chairman of the committee urging the county not to re-engage Dennis Amiss, an English World Series Cricket man, for 1979: 'We do appreciate the very difficult situation in which the committee finds itself owing to the incredible action of many other counties. We would, however, hope that the club committee will not similarly bow to parochial pressures,' they wrote.[11]

Interestingly *The Economist* found John Woodcock's chauvinism unacceptable: '"Greig was reared in South Africa," blandly explained one international cricket writer, which "is not the same as being English through and through".' Clearly Woodcock had failed to perceive the universality of commercialism.

The complex nature of loyalty in the 1970s could scarcely be better revealed. It was an odd situation in which the 'captive newspaper correspondent' of the establishment, John Woodcock, could propound – on Packerism, on what the counties' attitude to star overseas players should be, and on Greig – views that would be shared by Boycott, whilst fervently supporting the claims to the captaincy of Brearley, whose values were of an entirely different kind. Modern cricket prefers those of *The Economist* and of commercialism, as distinct from the professionalism by which Boycott clearly set great store. And, as Herbert Sutcliffe had suggested to Bill Bowes forty years before, the establishment was never prepared to allow the professional his full due.

Faced with the prospect of an alliance between the establishment and show-business, the ideals of C. L. R. James, quoted in the first chapter, in which cricketers would return to the community and do a job of work along with their fellows, take on a new appeal. But they are correspondingly less likely to be realised. Those who held so dear the myth of gentlemen and players and cherished the legend of the golden age of the amateur, appear, by their chosen approach to defending the citadel, to have banished the amateur from the first-class game for ever.

During the second New Zealand Test match at Trent Bridge in 1978 a working party of the TCCB produced proposals for reform of the structure of the English game. (Though actual reforms are virtually unknown, working party proposals are plentiful.) One of these called for the formation of a natural partnership between the professional and amateur games. This, when read out during an interval in the play to the BBC radio commentary team, was greeted with snorts of derision by T. E. Bailey, the former amateur, always noted for his honesty. How could there be a natural partnership, he asked, when the first-class game was solely concerned with money?

ELEVEN

BEYOND THE BOUNDARY IN THE WEST INDIES

SHOW-BUSINESS, WHETHER SPONSORED by Kerry Packer or anyone else, will have to contend with the phenomenon of partisanship and its impact on players and crowds. Traditionally the British are supposed to be moderate in their enthusiasms, priding themselves on their balanced outlook. They tend to blame 'the newspapers' or 'the media' for any departures from accepted norms. 'It should be admitted at once,' wrote John Arlott in 1953, 'that under the influence of topical sensationalism the defeats of Test teams have been regarded as national disasters, to the annoyance of those disinterested observers who, reasonably, doubt the sense of values of those who think the result of a cricket match means anything at all outside its immediate circle.'[1]

Now this is a valuable comment in a number of ways. It reminds us that nations do not actually collapse if their sports' teams lose to other nations. And it reminds us that games should be looked at within their own frame of reference and not as indicators of social or political attitudes. But it is unmistakably the statement of a secure West-European.

Liberal, well-intentioned, and concerned that all others are not the same, Arlott's statement leaves out of account the limited outlets there are for the insecure to express themselves. Judged by contemporary standards he also seriously underestimates the force of nationalism and the importance more demonstrative patriots attach to symbols of their cause. To many millions of people today cricket and football matches are not about whether eleven players overcome eleven others. Like it or not, national honour is on the line.

The games people play have always tended to be invested with national characteristics. Before there was international competition and winning became the first indicator of a nation's prowess, it was possible to take national pride from the very nature of the games. Cricket, as we have seen, was presented as a reflection of national virtues before there were any Test matches. Its failure in Ireland was thought significant. Pycroft regarded as indicative of cricket's essentially Anglo-Saxon superiority that it could 'hardly be said to be naturalised in Ireland'.

The feeling was mutual. In the 1880s Dr Croke, Archbishop of Cashel, wrote a letter of support to one of the founders of the Gaelic Athletic Association, Michael Cusack, in this fashion: 'One of the most painful, and at the same time one of the most frequently recurring reflections that, as an Irishman, I am compelled to make in connection with the present aspect of things in this country, is derived from the ugly and irritating fact that we are daily importing from England not only her manufactured goods but, together with her fashions, her accents, her vicious literature, her music, her dances, her manifold mannerisms, her games also and pastimes, to the utter discredit of our own grand national sports and to the sore humiliation of every genuine son and daughter of the old land. Ball-playing, hurling, football-kicking according to Irish rules, "casting", leaping, wrestling in various ways and all such favourite amusements may now be said to be not only dead and buried but, in several localities, to be entirely forgotten and unknown. And what have we got in their stead? We have got such foreign and fantastical sports as lawn tennis, polo, croquet, cricket and the like, very excellent, I believe, and health-giving exercises in their way, still, not racy of the soil but rather alien on the contrary to it as are indeed, for the most part, the men and women who first imported and still continue to patronise them.'[2]

The winning, not the game, is now of first importance in most countries. New nations, or old ones emerging from foreign domination, have displayed a fervour requiring no stimulation from 'topical sensationalism'. The 1972 *Wisden*, for example, described the aftermath of the first victory of the Indians in England: 'The flight plans of Ajit Wadekar and his men for the return journey to India were altered at the last minute to take them first to New Delhi, for the Prime Minister expressed the wish to meet the players and congratulate them personally. When they arrived in Bombay they were taken from the airport to the city in a motorcade with thousands lining the seventeen-mile route to cheer the heroes. A leading newspaper raised a fund for the captain and his team. Handsome gifts in cash and kind reached them from people known and unknown.'

As international competition has spread and the post-colonial needle has grown sharper, reactions of this kind, amongst people and politicians, have become more common. On the field also the tension has grown, being reflected just as much in the behaviour of English teams as in their opponents'. In the first Test of 1971, for instance, the England fast bowler John Snow, much-publicised as a sensitive poet, deliberately barged into the Indian batsman Gavaskar as he, half Snow's size and as far as is known unpoetical, was trying to make his ground for a quick single.

English crowds are also much more demonstrative than in the past.[3] Their attitudes and behaviour have been affected to some extent by the number of immigrants from the former colonies who identify strongly with overseas teams. Test matches in England against West Indies have recently produced more vocal support for the visitors than the home team. Overseas the passions aroused can be frightening. In India, for example, partisanship has been a vital factor in upsetting the equilibrium of more than one MCC side. 'The strain of trying to find their way in a crucial Test match in Calcutta while 70,000 bayed at each ball created a memory that will stay with all of them', said *Wisden* of the 1972–73 English tourists.[4] In 1977–78 there were riots on successive days at Lahore in the game between Pakistan and England.

All emergent nations regard success in international encounters as important status symbols. Former colonies may be expected to play that little bit harder against their former overlords. Non-white former colonists may have added reasons, racial and social. So, one way and another, of all the places where cricket has been played it has probably meant most to the people of the West Indies.

There were cricket clubs in the West Indies at least as early as 1806. These were presumably solely for the white colonists. Slavery was not made illegal until 1833 and it was some years afterwards before it died out. Such a social division would not quickly lead to racially-mixed cricket clubs. The islands, too, were separated from each other. However, Barbados played British Guiana in 1865, Trinidad began to compete in 1869, and a West Indies team toured Canada in 1886. It was not until 1895 that an English team – all amateur – ventured into the Caribbean. In 1897 two teams deciding to make the trip got in each other's way. (According to Rowland Bowen, this arose 'through the stubborn and ill-mannered mulishness amounting almost to insufferable arrogance on the part of Lord Hawke.'[5]) In 1904–5 professionals were taken out for the first time, under Lord Brackley, and the amateurs in the party misbehaved themselves – the first of many unhappy incidents associated with the visits of English teams.

The colour bars, which operated until the First World War, were reinforced by economic factors. Inter-island cricket and competitive club cricket were strictly amateur, which had the effect of keeping out black cricketers. In 1900 P. F. Warner, born in the West Indies, accompanied his elder brother to England as part of a touring team that included L. S. Constantine, father of the great Learie and the descendant of slaves. But as the formal barriers began to go they were replaced by the less tangible restrictions of an elaborate class structure in which shades of colour and money had their place.

C. L. R. James's book *Beyond a Boundary* gives a fascinating account of the complexities of it all. James tells how in his own island of Trinidad there was great disappointment amongst the black people when Piggott was left out of the 1923 touring side. Piggott was a wicket-keeper and a natural genius, but he seems to have been socially unacceptable. 'The only excuse current at the time,' writes James, 'was the following: "You can't depend on a man like that; who knows when you are looking for him for some important match you will find him somewhere boozing." It was untrue. It was also stupid.'

The real trouble, apparently, was that Trinidad could only expect a certain number of places in the team and Piggott would have upset the balance of the island's contribution and offended the white folks. There was a hierarchy of cricket clubs in Trinidad: first came Queen's Park, mostly white, often wealthy, with a few coloured people mostly from old mulatto families (and a rare anonymous black, who had acquired money and status, usually when too old to play). Shamrock was almost all white, usually from old Catholic families. Maple was for the brown-skinned; it was middle-class but more interested in colour. Shannon was for the black lower-middle-class. Constabulary always had a white inspector as captain leading a team of black other ranks. Stingo was all-black and had no social status at all.

Piggott was, of course, a member of Stingo. Two other selections, John and Small, were also Stingo players, and Constantine and Pascall were from Shannon, slightly up the social scale, but black. And this was the difficulty: 'Piggott would have meant three Stingo and two Shannon. All would have been absolutely black. Not only whites but the Queen's Park Club would have been left out altogether.'

James writes compellingly about Piggott and about Telemaque, another neglected social inferior, and the great fast bowler from the Stingo Club, George John, who career straddled the First World War and who 'incarnated the plebs of his time, their complete independence from the values and aspirations that competed in the spheres above.' One of the most revealing passages describes Wilton St Hill, a light-brown man of the lower-middle class but a member of the Shannon Club for blacks. Someone once said to him: 'Maple would be glad to have a man like you.' He replied: 'Yes, but they wouldn't want my brothers.' They were darker than he was.

St Hill was born in 1893 and by 1922 was 'a great batsman and universal favourite.' He worked in a department store, which was not very rewarding, and he conceived the ambition of going to England. He seemed certain to be picked on the next tour. James was once stopped in the street by a shoemaker and his mates. They talked of St Hill. 'One said weightily: "You know what I waitin' for? When he go to Lord's and the Oval and make his century there! That's what I want to see." It was,' wrote James, 'the instinct of an oppressed man that spoke.' But St Hill was left out of the 1923 team and 'it was as if a destined Prime Minister had lost his seat in the elections.'

The situation was complex. St Hill had not done well in the trials: his supporters would have been hard pressed to say who should have been left out for him, since it was recognised that the other islands had to have their share. But despite their doubts their deep suspicion of prejudice rankled. 'We became convinced in our own minds that St Hill was the greatest of all West Indian batsmen and on English wickets this coloured man would infallibly put all white rivals in the shade. And they too (West Indian whites, that is) were afraid of precisely the same thing, and therefore were glad to keep him out.' H. G. B. Austin, the white captain, was chiefly held responsible, and in a curious way the excellent choices he made, such as Francis, a fast bowler, and the young Constantine, did him no good. St Hill supporters almost wanted his selections to fail: 'We were sensitised, on the alert for prejudice.'

Ironically, after a good season in 1926 against the English tourists and successful trials, St Hill was chosen for the 1928 tour – and he failed. It was left to Learie Constantine to fulfil the people's hopes and St Hill's frustrated ambition of staying in England and playing in the leagues. Even success had its bitterness. James, who knew Constantine well, tells us: 'I believe that if Constantine had had not only honour but a little profit in his own country he never would have settled abroad . . . Had his skin been white like George Challenor's, or even light, he would have been able to choose a life at home.'

Constantine had the usual difficulties of a black cricketer in the West Indies. He was not rich and so couldn't afford to play in the inter-colonial tournament, and if he wanted to be selected for an overseas tour he had very little chance to show his paces. There were also other obstacles. In 1925 Constantine had quarrelled with the Queen's Park Club of Trinidad, so when Barbados invited him to play in a Test the Club found an excuse not to forward the invitation to him. Again in 1934–35 when he was away in Nelson he never received his invitation to play against England: it was left to MCC to force the issue by threatening to withhold a subsidy.

Constantine had to endure the poor standard of captaincy that went with the assumptions of racialism, including the young Grant who came straight from Cambridge to captain West Indies on the 1930–31 tour of Australia not knowing anything about West Indian cricket and not having seen many of the side before. 'The question of appointing a captain was a major engagement for the Board of Control,' Constantine wrote. 'The coloured man was not good enough and in fact no coloured player would play happily under him, it was said.'[6] This echo of the classical English view of gentlemen and players was a proposition that, since it was never put to the test, began to lead to more and more discontent.

According to James this growing dissatisfaction was the underlying cause of the crowd disturbances that took place on the 1953–54 and 1959–60 MCC tours. Though he perhaps overstates the case his account is a useful corrective to the slightly baffled air of most English versions. Compare for instance James's comments on the 1953–54 series with those of Roy Webber.[7]

Webber: 'A strong MCC team under the captaincy of L. Hutton left for the West Indies in an attempt to gain some prestige in the Caribbean . . . It was in many ways an unhappy tour and the players of both sides were concerned in incidents which did not assist in good relations.'

James: 'The 1953–54 MCC team was actively disliked. This was not due merely to unsportsmanlike behaviour by individuals. There is evidence to show that the team had given the impression that it was not merely playing cricket but was out to establish the prestige of Britain, and, by that, of the local whites.'

Webber: 'In the first Test at Kingston physical attacks, luckily not too serious, were made upon the wife and son of one of the umpires in the match, and the only reason put forward was the fact that the official had given J. K. Holt out l.b.w. when only six runs short of his maiden Test century.'

James: 'In Jamaica in 1953 the umpire was threatened when Holt was given l.b.w. at 94. Holt . . . is a black man, his father was the W.G. of Jamaica. Stollmeyer was threatened when he refused to ask the England team to follow on.'

Webber: 'This [the intimidation] did not give the umpires much joy in their duties, and several decisions were given against England in the Tests which the touring players felt were incorrect . . . in the third Test at Georgetown C. A. McWatt was given run out on the fourth day when the West Indies were trying hard to save the follow-on, and the crowd were so displeased with the umpire's decision that they hurled bottles and packing cases on the playing area.'

James: 'The fate of the match was not at stake . . . England had made 435. From seven for 139 the score had been taken to 238 when a run-out precipitated the disturbance. Ram and Val were the remaining batsmen [i.e. bowlers who could not get many runs]. All witnesses agree that the decision had been given, the batsman given out had reached the pavilion, the incoming batsman took guard. It was only then that the bottle-throwing began.'

Webber: 'Under these circumstances it is little wonder that the England players were inclined to be a bit edgy in temperament, and things that should not have been said were allowed to happen.'

There appears to have been no one particular cause of the episode, but rather an accumulation. First, following unsatisfactory umpiring in the colony match against British Guiana (as Guyana was then called), the England captain, Hutton, had asked that the local man be replaced for the Test. This was understandable, but it presumably did little for the England team's popularity: the English complaints about the umpires had already become the subject of a calypso. Second, England had scored 435 having taken two days over it. Third, they used delaying tactics to keep the number of overs down when West Indies batted. Fourth, Everton Weekes, a West Indian hero, bowled at 94, waited whilst the umpire, unsighted, checked with his colleague what had happened. Weekes later apologised and was exonerated, but as the Australian Ray Robinson afterwards wrote: 'Who can tell what thoughts were set up in the crowd at the unusual sight of an appeal for bowled being necessary to dismiss a star batsman six runs short of 100?'[8] Fifth, as Robinson adds, 'more than likely, betting added to the confused din.' Finally he quotes Senior Superintendent A. H. Jenkins, the Welsh officer in charge: 'We think it was an instance of mob psychology. One stupid man, probably drunk, threw the first bottle, followed by a lot of other stupid people.'

James is at pains to point out that none of the incidents had anything to do with lack of etiquette by West Indian players or with the crowd being angry because their team was losing. He insists that there was no comparison with the situation in Australia in 1903, when in the first Test Clem Hill's dismay at being given out just when his side looked like staging a recovery sparked off uproar in the crowd: nothing of the kind had ever taken place in the West Indies, he tells us.

Nor, he assures us, were any of the incidents 'a political demonstration against an imperialist Britain. It was more complicated than that: the cause was the conviction that here, as usual, local anti-nationalist people were doing their best to help the Englishmen defeat and disgrace the local players. That is the temper which caused these explosions and as long as that temper remains it will find a way to express itself . . . Those suspected of anti-nationalism are usually rich whites and their retainers. Local politicians, editors, officials, police-men, selectors, umpires are under scrutiny.'

That was also the trouble, says James, on the 1959–60 tour. On 30 January 'there crowded into the Queen's Park Oval over 30,000 people . . . [who] had come to sun themselves in West Indies batting, 22 for none the previous evening. Alas, the West Indies batsmen col-lapsed and were 98 for eight. At that stage Singh was given run out. The crowd exploded in anger, bottles began to fly: soon they flew so thickly that the game could not be continued.' The West Indies were 300 behind. 'Not a soul on the ground believed that Ramadhin could make twenty. They would have cheered Singh as a hero if he had made ten.'

Again the causes were complex, with frustration, local pride, rum and betting playing their part. The first wicket to fall was that of Hunte, a renowned moral rearmament man, caught off his boot by Trueman, whose outspoken comments to and about umpires and opponents had been widely publicised; Hunte had stayed at the wicket until given out by Umpire Lloyd, a Yorkshire-born instrument engi-neer – a decision roundly booed by the crowd. Kanhai was l.b.w., then the great Sobers was caught at slip for 0. Solomon was run out, and his partner, Worrell, the black man's choice for captain, upset by this, was caught behind the wicket. Both Butcher and Alexander were l.b.w. At 98 for eight the crowd were betting on whether Ramadhin or Singh would put up the 100. Singh was run out by a yard and he simply kept on running to the pavilion.

But the dismissal of a local hero was the last straw. The first bottle flew over, then the beer cans, soft fruit and whatever else came to hand. The uproar was very much worse than in Georgetown six years before. 'Go on, Wes, you're in,' said Alexander to Hall, but Hall took another look at the flying bottles and said: 'I'm not going out there for anybody's money, man!' The England players and the umpires were marooned in a sea of spectators until they were escorted off by police. Then came the riot squads and mounted police: there were 30 hospi-tal casualties and 60 other people needed treatment, until things quietened down after 45 minutes.

C. L. R. James assures us again that this was nothing like the first Test in Australia in 1903: the West Indian players had observed the code. His contention that the demonstration was not against the England team is borne out by Ray Robinson, who points out that no attempt was made to harm them. Indeed, James suggests, the atmosphere in that respect was different from 1953–54 when MCC were unpopular. Some had feared that this unpopularity would rub off on May's team; but 'Such fears proved needless. Before long the 1959 team was so popular that when May in Jamaica committed the blunder of refusing Kanhai a runner, although the match was at stake, nobody bothered very much. There were a few boos and that was all. It must be quite clear that such politics as there were in the [Port of Spain] outburst, and it was drenched in politics, did not in any way involve either Britain or the MCC. My belief is that consideration for the MCC moderated it both at the time and afterwards.'

If it was drenched in politics, no one knew better than C. L. R. James. There were those who thought he had done a good deal of the drenching. As editor of *The Nation* he was waging a fierce campaign for a black captain of West Indies. As before in Australia, the captaincy of the cricket team had a special importance in helping to shape the West Indian national identity. Inter-island rivalry, subsequently reflected in separatism, was intense. James, though conscious of this, was more concerned with the interrelated social and racial question.

The argument about the colour of the captain's skin, muted before the Second World War, began in earnest as soon as Test cricket resumed afterwards. 'It is still confidently affirmed,' wrote James, 'that in 1947–48 Jamaica refused to play against England at all if George Headley, a black man, was not made the captain as he had every right to be.' The black men themselves, professionals and with a living to make, usually in England, may not have been so sure. In 1950 another row over Headley was complicated by his financial needs. Black frustration mounted when 'there were public subscriptions to bring Headley home from England to get him to play in the trials and to try to have him picked for the 1953–54 series and get him elected captain. Hopes were high and the disappointment was all the greater. That is why Holt's run-out decision near his maiden century mattered so much. It was another sell-out for the black man.'

Then it was the turn of the great black trio – Clyde Walcott, Everton Weekes and Frank Worrell – to be passed over for men like Jeffrey Stollmeyer, Dennis Atkinson and Bruce Pairaudeau, light-skinned colleagues who had much less talent. In 1958 Walcott wrote: 'The public feeling seemed to be that the West Indies Board did not relish the prospect of having a coloured captain but I do not think this was in fact the case. Much more likely, it seemed to me, was that West Indies were following the old-fashioned precedent of standing out against the professional captain: a precedent which, despite Len Hutton's reign as captain, still has its roots deeply laid in England.'[9]

In the West Indies it was a distinction without a difference: the whites were the amateurs. Walcott, fully aware of this, was perhaps still hoping to be the first to break the barrier. Tact, with further disappointment, gave way to candour. James quotes a private conversation some time later. 'Suddenly Clyde, who is always circumspect in his speech, blurted out: "You know who will be captain in England in 1963. You see that Barbados boy, Bynoe, who went to India? He has only to make fifty in one innings and he will be captain."' James adds, in case one had not suspected it, 'Bynoe is white.'

In 1959–60 it was F. C. M. Alexander, a light-skinned Cambridge graduate, who was the enemy. James's explanation of events has to contend with one very awkward point – that Frank Worrell had in fact been offered the captaincy in 1957 but had declined it because of his studies at Manchester University. That did not prevent James writing in a piece that appeared in *The Nation* the day before the Port of Spain riot: 'I want to say clearly beforehand that the idea of Alexander captaining a side on which Frank Worrell is playing is to me quite revolting,' and adding: 'That Worrell was not captain in 1957 in England was a scandal known to everybody.'

Those on the establishment side who did not avert their eyes took him severely to task. Alan Ross, the poet and critic, was particularly harsh. 'Who but a malicious xenophobe' could write such things in the middle of a Test match, he asked, adding: '*Revolting* is the parlance of the irresponsible agitator.'[10] Now whatever else he might have been C. L. R. James was no xenophobe, still less a malicious one. Nor was he irresponsible: on the contrary he was deeply concerned, and, it would seem, genuinely revolted. The reforms he was seeking reflected deep feelings going back half a century.

Beyond a Boundary offers a much less sinister, indeed some would think sentimental, view of things. 'West Indians crowding to Tests bring with them the whole history and future hopes of the islands. English people have a conception of themselves breathed from birth. Drake and mighty Nelson, Shakespeare, Waterloo, the few who did so much for so many, the success of parliamentary democracy, those and such as those constitute a national tradition.' James is fully aware at how little these traditions may be valued, but, he says: 'We of the West Indies have none at all, none that we know of. To such people the three W's, Ram and Val wrecking English batting, help to fill a huge gap in their consciousness and their needs.' Perhaps it is not the whole story. Few stories ever are. And there is no doubt that deeply-held convictions can sometimes lead to distorted perspectives. To the nationalists even the somewhat unsavoury character Roy Gilchrist was a cause to be taken up when he was sent home from India for trying to flatten batsmen rather than wickets. James and his supporters thought the Board were picking on a plebeian hero, a rough diamond perhaps but one who, in a side led by Worrell (whom he was said to worship), would have been a reformed character and was therefore entitled to be allowed back into the fold.

Yet it would be hard to argue that James was not on the side of the angels. He had set himself a difficult task in taking on the white establishment without resorting to the cruder standards and methods of racial politics as such. For one thing his view of cricket was deeply traditional. His consequent fervent advocacy of the higher ethics of cricket, as promulgated by MCC and exemplified by W.G. and his Edwardian successors, modulated by his view that the world had taken a turn for the worse in 1929, needed to be reconciled with his deep emotional longings for justice and an overt end to prejudice, in cricket as in politics. The conflict caused him personal anguish. In 1960 the scent of success was in his nostrils but he was nervous nevertheless. 'I didn't like the look of things after the bottle throwing, I didn't like it at all.' So in a long open letter to the cricket authorities he used the riot to ask for a public enquiry to look into eight matters ranging from overcrowding, through the Gilchrist affair, to 'the conviction now deep-seated that the Queen's Park Club represents the old régime in Trinidad'. Sincerely, but not entirely convincingly, he added: 'In the campaign I am carrying on against Alexander instead of Worrell as captain I shall exhaust every argument before I touch the racial aspect of it.'

When the battle for the captaincy was won the West Indies found, as everyone else does, that a new régime merely creates the opportunity for reform and advance but does not guarantee it. It was Worrell, not Alexander, who led the touring side to Australia in the winter of 1960 and Worrell not Bynoe who was captain in England in 1963. It did not stop the riots for long. Nor did it stop MCC touring parties, with problems of their own, ill-informed and ill-equipped to deal with crises, rushing in where angels might well have feared to tread. No doubt Hutton, the captain of England, and Trueman, his fast bowler and a great nuisance on the 1953–54 team, believed in the Yorkshire tradition that cricket was not played for fun, but it is doubtful if either of them realised how seriously it was played in the West Indies.

It is crystal-clear that Colin Cowdrey, who led the 1967–68 team to the Caribbean, long after the colour of the West Indies captain's skin had ceased to be an issue, had little concept of what was involved. Very few Englishmen would have done. Poor Cowdrey had had a difficult enough time before he got to the Caribbean. But for Close's misbehaviour he would not have been captain, and the chairman of the selectors had said so publicly. Yorkshire lips curled in scorn. Cowdrey's own must have tightened when M. J. K. Smith was offered the honour before him. So Cowdrey, always the bridesmaid, had been thrust into the bride's veil at the last minute and was aware above all else that he had to show people back home that by results on the field he deserved the accolade. In a detailed account of the preamble to the tour Cowdrey does not once mention West Indian politics as a factor in his thinking. He was chiefly concerned with a Five-Tour plan, with himself as captain, to put England back on top of the cricket world.

Unfortunately for him (and for James's purist views about the cause of trouble in earlier tours) the second Test at Kingston, Jamaica, produced a worse riot than anything previously experienced. Even the gentlemanly Cowdrey makes plain what he thinks about it. 'I have heard a number of attempted explanations for the crowd's violent mood that day. One was that it was a local political demonstration, entirely unconnected with cricket; and another that it was a Communist-inspired plot. I cannot deny either. All I do know is that coincidentally the West Indies cricket team was falling apart at the seams when it happened.' West Indies had made 143 in reply to England's first-innings total of 376 and were following-on: 'they had lost half their side for 204 in the second innings when Basil Butcher touched a leg-side catch to Jim Parks behind the stumps. As so often happens in these circumstances Butcher did not actually see the catch completed and, quite justifiably, paused to check whether he was out or not. His hesitation proved fatal. The crowd completely misinterpreted his action and exploded.'[11] The next minute there were bottles raining on to the field and when the commotion showed no sign of abating the police used tear-gas. It was far worse than Sydney in 1903 or anything previously seen on a cricket ground.

We can scarcely avoid the conclusion that partisanship, stark and unmitigated, prevailed, both in the riot itself and in the aftermath. By the time the game started again, an hour and a quarter later, the England team were badly shaken; Garfield Sobers played a great innings and West Indies saved the game. Indeed, with Sobers on form with the ball, too, England were 30 for 4 at the end of the scheduled time to end the match. It had been agreed to extend the match if necessary when it looked as though England were going to be deprived of a victory. Sobers, within his legal rights but perhaps not quite in the spirit of the Badminton book, now decided to claim this time. England, with 68 for 8, just survived.

Even more blatant was the episode in May 1978 at Kingston, Jamaica. It was the final day of the final Test and the West Indies, who had their Packer men in the side for the first two matches, had already won the series against a gallant but weakened Australia. But in the fifth Test they were 258 for 9, needing 111 to win, when the crowd stopped the game by rioting. It was sparked off by Vanburn Holder who, after being given out, remained at the wicket for a while before reluctantly walking away. Hundreds of bottles were thrown on the pitch, and some stones. Chairs and a garbage can followed. Finally some 2,000 spectators stormed the pitch, amid a hail of rocks, bottles, chairs and even a 40-gallon oil drum. Police had to fire blank rounds over the heads of the crowd, and it took over a hundred of them 40 minutes to restore order. Play was abandoned for the day, and it seems clear that this was the crowd's intention.

Worse still, although the Jamaican authorities tried to finish the match the following day one of the umpires arrived late and then declined to stand, as did the reserve. The other umpire, Wesley Malcolm, who had given Holder out the previous day, was given a police guard. (Malcolm had only been chosen for this Test because the Australians objected to the original choice, and he was clearly no favourite with the crowd.) So the Australians had to forfeit the match, and, it would appear, mob law prevailed.

In the end, then, it is hard to accept unreservedly James's starry-eyed version of the lofty standards of West Indian behaviour.[12] More important, though, his description of the social background of cricket in the West Indies explains how important to black people winning a cricket match against white people can be for reasons only incidentally connected with cricket. The story of West Indian cricket, in the post-war period in particular, provides one of the most vivid examples of the contrast between myth and reality. It is James's intense desire to relate the behaviour of his team and his people to the exalted philosophy he associates with the public-school tradition of cricket that leads him to make such elevated claims in the first place.

The various tensions inherent in West Indian society have shown themselves in cricket. In the past the myth of 'it's not cricket', 'sportsmanship' and the like has been important enough, as part of the inheritance of colonialism, to constitute one extreme. Partisanship has in large measure replaced this lofty concept – in so far as it ever existed – and the ethics of national honour contend with the ethics of show-business.

This tension is the greater because of the strong tradition, from Constantine and Headley onwards, of star West Indian cricketers seeking their fortune overseas. The resignation of a group of senior players – Packer men – from the official West Indies team in the middle of the 1978 series against Australia shows how acute it is. And it must surely have been a factor in 1979 when 'Riot halts Supertest' became a commonplace headline during the Packer series. What seems certain is that the influence of the mythology of 'it's not cricket' and the golden age is on the wane.

TWELVE

THE SOUTH AFRICAN CONNECTION

THE YEAR AFTER HIS experience of West Indian politics Colin Cowdrey was again the central figure in events concerning a country where cricket and the colour of cricketers' skins were thought highly important. There were no riots this time, but that was because the tour never took place. Cowdrey's Five-Tour plan for the rehabilitation of English cricket suffered a setback in 1968 when MCC, after prolonged debate, reluctantly struck South Africa (in pencil only) off their visiting list.

It was a year when upholders of the tradition that cricket is 'more than a game' seemed to argue that it was only a game after all and that the politicians ought to let them alone to play it. South Africa had always occupied a special place in the affections of the cricket establishment. Although A. W. Carr didn't think much of the country when he went there in 1922–23 (he thought it a poor imitation of London), he liked the people – 'the South Africans are fine sportsmen, as we understand the word.' This understanding of the word has to make allowance for a certain idiosyncrasy in the sportsmanlike behaviour of the South Africans: their treatment of people with dark skins.

In 1956 one of the most prolific of cricket writers, A. A. Thomson, wrote: 'It is always delightful to meet South Africans.' He recalled his pleasure, forty years earlier, at riding in a rickshaw 'drawn by a Zulu chieftain in gleaming war paint and horned headdress', described the South Africans as 'lively and warm-hearted hosts', and added with unconscious irony that 'as cricketers, they are colourful and good-natured guests'.[1] South African teams have been notable for their lack of colour ever since their first tour to England in 1894 when an outstanding cricketer, T. Hendricks, was excluded on racial grounds.

It is arguable that the South African Government's policy of apartheid could have been averted if Britain had been firmer in the past. The British Government sanctioned a colour bar in Natal before the Boer War and shirked using dark-skinned troops from other parts of the Empire against the Boers. They allowed the Boers only one concession in their eventual 'unconditional' surrender – no coloured voters.

South Africa had one very great asset – gold. This seems to have come to the notice of the cricket establishment in England and may explain why the Springboks were admitted to the magic circle of Test cricket in England as early as 1907. The disastrous Triangular Tournament with England and Australia in 1912 was staged on the initiative of the South African millionaire Sir Abe Bailey.

To prepare for the Triangular series a South African team visited Australia in 1910–11 and tried a mild experiment in racial integration. They included a coloured man, C. B. Llewellyn, who, though born in Natal, had played as a professional for Hampshire. According to Rowland Bowen, Llewellyn 'was tormented by his white fellow-tourists to such an extent that for peace and quiet in the hotels where the teams stayed, he had to take refuge in the WC's and lock himself in.'[2] 'This kind of thing should never be forgotten,' says the forthright Major Bowen, 'when South African cricket is referred to.'

As Bowen knew, however, it *has* usually been forgotten. The 1920 edition of the Badminton book, notable for its exposition of the game's high moral code, included a new chapter on the South Africans by the Editor, P. F. Warner himself. It made no mention of race relations but it did make a fulsome reference to the 1910–11 visit to Australia which it hoped would be the first of many (because such exchanges help 'maintain the camaraderie and solidarity of Empire which carried us through the fiery furnace of Armageddon'). Warner spoke favourably of Llewellyn. But he also spoke in glowing terms of J. H. Sinclair: 'No wonder he was a popular favourite . . . In any history of South African cricket James Sinclair takes a very prominent place.' Poor Llewellyn's chief tormentor on the Australian tour was this same James Sinclair.

Subsequent events give a nice twist to the motto Warner chose to head his chapter – *Ex Africa semper aliquid novi*. At the time Warner lauded Sinclair, South African cricket was not only segregated: it was stratified. It was not until after the Second World War, when the Empire had come through its second Armageddon (with slightly diminished solidarity), that the various strata – African, Cape Coloured, Indian, Malay – came together as 'non-whites'. They had much inferior facilities, no say in how the highest class of cricket was run and no chance of selection for the national team.

But this perhaps was the least of their worries. After the 1948 electoral victory of the Afrikaner National Party the doctrine of apartheid was applied with increasing force. By 1960, when a narrow majority of the white electorate voted in a referendum to become a republic, these whites, one-fifth of the population, enjoyed one of the highest standards of living in the world. This they had achieved largely by the extension of the Pass Laws and the colour bar denying Africans trade union recognition and comparable standards of life in general.

With the advent of 42 new African states to the United Nations in 1961 world opinion became more and more hostile. South Africa left the Commonwealth but was still encouraged to play cricket with England and the other white countries. That was to be expected. Insofar as cricketers cared about politics at all they inclined to the right.

One of the few cricketers to criticise the South African set-up, openly at least, was Jim Laker. His book *Over to Me* was thought scandalous in 1960, but it is characterised by an unsentimental, unhypocritical belief in fair treatment on and off the field: he wants it for himself but, unlike many more theoretically charitable folk, he concedes the rights of others to it.

In South Africa he was clearly disgusted by an episode in which, when he was travelling in a car driven by his team-mate, Alan Oakman, a black man on a bicycle rushed out of a side-street and got himself run over. Crowds gathered, but they were more interested in getting the cricketers' autographs than in the black man on the ground. When a policeman arrived and sized up the situation the first thing he said was: 'He was drunk, wasn't he?' Spotting a neighbour of the victim he said: 'You live near this nigger – he's always drunk, isn't he?' Then, Laker tells us, 'Slowly, fearfully, the black head nodded.'

MCC's official attitude was that of 'building bridges'. If they hoped thereby to exercise a liberal influence they were mistaken. The Prime Minister, Dr Vorster, declared in 1967 that there would be no mixed sport in South Africa, no matter how good the players were. Nor was he prepared to allow mixed Springbok teams to travel abroad. (Cricket teams visiting South Africa could be mixed provided there were no political implications that might harm internal relations.) Meanwhile in England Basil D'Oliveira, a coloured South African immigrant, had been picked to play in the 1966 Test against the West Indies at Old Trafford. He went on tour in 1967–68 but performed only moderately. Then in 1968 he played in the first Test against Australia at Old Trafford and scored a very good 87 not out in the second innings in a heavy defeat for England. The question looming ever larger was – should D'Oliveira be picked for the forthcoming South African tour, and would the South African government admit him?

During the match Colin Cowdrey, the England captain, had a talk with Sir Alec Douglas-Home, former President of MCC, who was newly returned from a meeting with Dr Vorster. His advice was, apparently, to pick the strongest team, regardless of any other consideration: Cowdrey 'should not be swayed by the press or public opinion.' MCC had written to Vorster in January asking whether D'Oliveira would be admitted if selected. There had been no reply but Sir Alec was opposed to forcing the issue by insisting on an answer. According to Cowdrey, Home 'added that he believed the moral issue was not Britain's to enter into. He was certain that to break off cricket relations with South Africa would have no effect on her attitude to apartheid, however long we refused to play against them.'[3]

This, if true – and Cowdrey says he recalls the sense of his remarks with complete clarity – explains much that followed that might otherwise seem baffling. Sir Alec was saying (a) that apartheid was no concern of Britain's, (b) that because, in his view, not playing South Africa would not stop apartheid, England should go on playing them and (c) that the South African government should not be embarrassed by being asked plainly whether D'Oliveira could go or not, presumably so that neither they nor the England selectors need face a situation which might never arise. Instead Cowdrey and the others were to choose their team without fear or favour.

It was exactly what Sir Pelham Warner would have advised, no doubt; and no doubt Sir Alec and Cowdrey and the rest all believed themselves to be facing issues squarely and being fair to everyone including D'Oliveira. But how they must have wished he did not exist or would break a leg or something! Cowdrey found Sir Alec's 'decisions', as he rather curiously calls them, 'very reassuring'. He 'respected his wisdom and integrity'. All Cowdrey had to do was be entirely uninfluenced by the outside world in choosing the team for the tour. 'Sir Alec's words sustained me greatly, when after choosing D'Oliveira in the twelve for the second Test at Lord's we left him out of the team on the morning of the match,' writes Cowdrey, adding wistfully: 'It was inevitable, I suppose, that a number of people leaped to the wrong conclusion.' Cowdrey explains that this, like all the other decisions about D'Oliveira, 'was purely a *cricket* decision. He was dropped from the side at Lord's, despite his excellent second innings at Manchester, because of his *bowling*.' It was a harsh doctrine to apply to an all-rounder.

D'Oliveira, though outwardly phlegmatic, can hardly fail to have been discouraged and perplexed. Not surprisingly he lost form and was out of the reckoning for the third and fourth Tests. It was a break for Cowdrey and the selectors, but their anguish began again when D'Oliveira ran into form with the ball. He took 5 for 39 and 6 for 29 against Hampshire. Alas, it seemed that for the final Test it was no longer bowlers England were looking for. Five other bowlers were selected, three fast men and two spinners (D'Oliveira was a medium-pacer.) Unfortunately for him the South African tour party was to be picked immediately after the Test.

'Those who suspected collusion,' wrote Cowdrey afterwards, 'were now convinced that the politicians had won . . . They were wrong.' The principle of selection by pure cricketing merit still had some surprises in store for those who thought this implied a rational and consistent policy. Cowdrey noticed that the Oval pitch suited medium-pace bowlers and sought the permission of his fellow-selectors to add another player to the possibles for the team. He approached Tom Cartwright, then Barry Knight of Essex. Neither was fit, so D'Oliveira was brought in as a last resort.

At that stage D'Oliveira's status was stand-by bowler in case the conditions seemed likely to favour his type of bowling. The chances were that he would still not play. Then Roger Prideaux, a batsman, fell ill at the last moment – and D'Oliveira took his place. He had followed a tortuous route through the minds of the selectors, with first one route blocked and then another. But he was there. With the eyes of the world on him D'Oliveira had his chance.

Amongst all the uncertainties and obscurities of this protracted saga one thing is certain. 'Dolly', as he was affectionately known, seized his chance. And it is from this point on that, however sound or credible their policy until then may have been, the selectors', and Cowdrey's, treatment of D'Oliveira began to seem to many fair-minded people not just insensitive or mistaken or self-deluding, but despicable. It was a vital match against England's oldest cricketing opponents. England had to win to save the rubber. When D'Oliveira came in with an hour to play at the end of the first day things could have gone either way. According to E. W. Swanton, 'He batted confidently and briskly that evening,' though Cowdrey suggests that 'He began slowly and rather tentatively.'[4] Both agree that having been dropped at 31 he went on next day to make a splendid hundred and eventually, after chancing his arm and giving three more chances, was ninth out for 158. There have been few more emotional scenes at cricket matches in England than that at the end of Dolly's innings. Later, on the final day, when it was touch and go whether Australia could hold on, he broke a vital partnership. Insofar as any man could win a Test match, D'Oliveira had won that one.

He was a national hero. But not to the selectors, meeting after the game to choose the party to tour South Africa. E. W. Swanton (who, it should be said notwithstanding his own political convictions, spoke out courageously against what was happening) expressed the views of millions. When a cricketer, amongst a group of twenty or so eligible for selection for a touring party of sixteen, gets a last-minute chance to prove himself and with all the pressure on him shows that he has the temperament as well as the skill, then he 'pretty well picks himself'.

Cowdrey did not see it that way. 'D'Oliveira himself, I feel sure, believed he had done enough to justify his selection for the tour,' he wrote. 'On purely cricketing grounds I was not so sure.' Of all the extraordinary cricketing grounds for doubt, Cowdrey's worry was that D'Oliveira's bowling might not be suited to South African conditions.

Poor Dolly. E. W. Swanton records a conversation with another selector during the Oval Test who had also referred to how different the conditions would be in South Africa (in a purely cricketing sense, of course). Swanton was astonished; as well he might be. If a South African is not likely to know about bowling conditions in South Africa, then who is?

Nevertheless as the world knows and to the shame of the selectors (D. J. Insole, A. V. Bedser, D. Kenyon, P. B. H. May, with M. C. Cowdrey and L. E. G. Ames, and A. E. R. Gilligan, President of MCC, and G. O. Allen, Treasurer) D'Oliveira was not picked. The full MCC Committee approved the team, without demur. Doubtless they all thought that was the end of the matter. They had followed Sir Alec's advice to the letter and what could be wrong with that? The doctrine of pure cricket ability had triumphed. It was strange to find that after all those years of contending that cricket was more than a game MCC should now be saying the opposite, and strange, too, to find apartheid as the beneficiary whilst a coloured South African with a reverence for the English way of life was the loser.

Cowdrey, before the selection, had talked privately to D'Oliveira 'to discover how he felt about the inevitable pressures to which he would be subjected if he were picked'. Apparently he 'was under no illusions at all about how the microscope would be on him every day, every hour, every moment' and he knew he had put everyone 'on the spot', but he was in the hands of people he trusted and he would accept their judgement. Cowdrey adds, hilariously: 'If this implies that, in the end, anything beyond cricket was involved in our debate over D'Oliveira, then I must firmly refute it.'

Most people felt, in fact, that if MCC were not prepared to offend Vorster by choosing D'Oliveira they should have said so at the outset and not engage in charades. And as E. W. Swanton makes clear, it was a charade. Lord Cobham (formerly Charles Lyttelton of Worcestershire, and afterwards Governor-General of New Zealand) had met Vorster in the spring and had passed on to the President, Treasurer and Secretary of MCC Vorster's assertion that it was highly unlikely D'Oliveira would be allowed in as a member of the team. So at least two of the selectors had known this all summer. No wonder the public, as Cowdrey plaintively records, reacted badly to D'Oliveira's omission and that some even sent abusive letters to the captain. His wife sent flowers to Mrs D'Oliveira and 'even this gesture made the front pages'. Cowdrey goes on: 'There was nothing to do but wait for the furore to die down and then go to South Africa and win.'

But the furore did not die down. The public and the media were outraged, the politicians were vocal, some members resigned from the MCC, and under the leadership of the Rev. David Sheppard, later Bishop of Liverpool, a group called for a special meeting of the Premier Club, expressing their lack of confidence in it and calling for no further cricket contact with South Africa until there was some evidence of progress on racial matters in sport there. (When the meeting took place Sheppard and his people took most of the honours in a low-level debate – as Swanton says, it suffered from the absence of both Sir Alec Douglas-Home and Lord Cobham – but the MCC's stand was vindicated by a big majority of support through a postal vote of its members.)

Meanwhile the final ludicrous turn of events was that Cartwright, a bowler, having dropped out, D'Oliveira, the batting hero of The Oval, was brought in. According to Cowdrey: 'Now, on cricketing grounds, pure and simple, from which we never deviated from first till last, he automatically came in to the party.' Dr Vorster, who at least did not go in for double-talk, said the MCC had bowed to pressure, declined to have a team thrust upon him and cancelled the tour. He clearly thought MCC had ratted on him and was furious that his allies had been got at by 'trendy lefties'. Cowdrey, though 'very sad', still hadn't had enough. He wanted to fly to South Africa to seek an audience.

Later, reflecting on the South African situation, Cowdrey posed the question: 'How long will it take to break down Afrikaner attitudes? I believe it will come in my life-time.' Short of some Methuselah-like performance by Cowdrey this seems unlikely. He went on: 'As Sir Alec said, "Things are moving faster than any of us fully realise".' Unfortunately they appear to be moving in the wrong direction. When Cowdrey wrote, 'The situation will respond more to warmth than to threats or demands from pulpit or cricket pavilion,' he spoke for many, including all those who mattered in cricket administration. The evidence is all to the contrary; but many in the cricket establishment seemed determined to offer the warmth anyway. For these people the D'Oliveira episode was a regrettable affair, introducing politics (i.e. 'radical' politics) into cricket. They saw no reason, however, why it should affect the long and happy association with South

African sportsmen for long. Indeed, they took it for granted that the suspension of cricket relations was temporary and looked forward to the South African tour scheduled for 1970.

The bridge-builders welcomed the fact that the South Africans were coming on a rugby tour in the autumn of 1969 and deplored the attempts of protesters to stop it. The name of Peter Hain, a 19-year-old white South African student, was particularly reviled. (One of the features of the South African approach had been a constant succession of schoolboy and youth teams, all white, touring England making friends and influencing people. Wilfred Isaacs was a prominent organiser of these ventures. In 1969 Hain had had the bad taste to lead demonstrations against one of Isaacs' teams. Few questioned Isaacs' taste. Though E. W. Swanton had suggested that it would at least be a gesture if Isaacs were to include a few non-whites, Isaacs explained that the arrangements had to be made long in advance and his team had already been chosen.) The rugby tour took place but at enormous cost, both in injuries to police and spectators and in the provision of police protection. One game in Manchester cost nearly £9,000.

The country divided on the question of the 1970 cricket tour. Important principles were at stake. The Minister of Sport had declared that the South African cricketers should stay away, but the South African Cricket Association had said they were coming anyway. Should the Government interfere? S. C. Griffith, Secretary of the Cricket Council, newly formed from MCC, reiterated the conviction 'that more good is achieved by maintaining sporting links with South Africa than by cutting them off altogether.'[5] The anti-apartheid supporters thought this was mistaken and morally wrong. There was trade-union agitation and over 100 Labour and Liberal MPs wrote to MCC saying they intended to join in protests if the tour went ahead. The tendency towards violence by some of the opponents of apartheid and the tours also caused heart-searching and anxiety amongst non-violent spokesmen such as Hain and Sheppard (then Bishop of Woolwich).

The Test and County Cricket Board met at Lord's in December 1969 and affirmed their intention to go ahead with the tour, expressing 'their aversion to racial discrimination of any kind' but also 'their intention to uphold the rights of individuals to take part in lawful pursuits'. In December also Jack Cheetham of the SACA announced that their tour party would be chosen 'on merit alone', which brought horse-laughs from the non-white South African Cricket Board of Control. (The team when eventually announced was all-white.)

A referendum of the Cricketers' Association in January 1970 revealed that 81% of English first-class cricketers supported the tour. In the same month a dozen county cricket grounds were damaged in a single night, and the MCC bought 300 reels of barbed wire. Estimates of the cost of protection ranged from £7,000 to £18,000 for a three-day match, which would have made a nonsense of the profit of £7,000 each county expected from the tour. The Cricket Council, financially if not morally concerned, announced a shortened tour of twelve matches. In April 'The 1970 Cricket Fund' was launched to try to get at least £200,000 to save the tour. Its committee included the Duke of Norfolk and Brian Close, the bad boy of 1967.

Meanwhile the Prime Minister, Harold Wilson, called the Cricket Council's intention to proceed 'a big mistake' and 'a very ill-judged decision'. He was against violence but hoped that everyone would feel free to demonstrate against apartheid. The Supreme Council for Sport in Africa threatened the withdrawal of thirteen African teams from the Commonwealth Games due to be held at Edinburgh in July if the South African tour went ahead. The Fair Cricket Campaign also came into being in April, under David Sheppard, to try to stop it. The TCCB informed all players chosen to play in the games that their lives would be insured for £15,000.

After a debate in the House of Commons on 14 May, the Home Secretary, James Callaghan, questioned the judgement of the Cricket Council and said he was having to weigh carefully whether, in view of the likely damage and violence, he ought to ban the tour. He had not so far decided that this would be justification for interfering with people's rights, but he asked the Council without loss of honour, having invited the South Africans, to uninvite them. Meanwhile there was only limited response to the 1970 Tour Fund and plenty of approaches from several sides urging the Council to consider their responsibilities as citizens.

South Africa earned the distinction of being the first nation ever to be expelled from the Olympic movement. The West Indies Board of Control deplored the tour. The Chairman of the Race Relations Board spoke against it. The Archbishop of Canterbury declared his opposition, and an announcement from Buckingham Palace said there would be no invitation there for the cricketers and no Royal Visit to the Lord's Test.

On 18 May with the tour due to start in a fortnight the Cricket Council decided that it should go ahead, but that after that there should be no further Test tours either way until South African teams were selected on an inter-racial basis. This did nothing to appease the opposition. In the end the Government had to 'request the Cricket Council to withdraw their invitation on grounds of broad public policy'. Only then and 'with deep regret' did they do so. They felt that they had been forced into submission.

Is it a coincidence that this, the most serious and sustained argument there has ever been about sport, certainly in Britain and probably in the world, concerned cricket? What was at stake, as it so often has been in arguments about cricket, was what cricket symbolised to those involved – more than a game, more a way of life. And is it a coincidence that the school of thought that exalts cricket as a symbol of true and lasting values has so often aligned itself with things that are manifestly 'not cricket'? Apartheid is one. It seems a feeble defence, when opponents of this savage and selfish injustice point it out, for supporters or 'neutrals' to argue that cricket is, after all, only a game and that politics has no place in sport.

Cricket-lovers from *Tom Brown's Schooldays* on have invested the game with profound political and social significance. It has been an emblem of the British way of life. Consider this passage from Colin Cowdrey's autobiography: 'The cover drive is the most beautiful stroke in batsmanship. Does that throw any light on why I am a self-admitted lover of all things British and traditional?' The thought process is obscure but the message is clear.

However, perhaps Cowdrey's cover drive – a handsome shot indeed – is the signal to leave political affairs and consider how the myth and the reality compare when it comes to the aesthetic aspects of cricket on which writers have dwelt so lovingly over the years.

THIRTEEN

CARDUS AND THE AESTHETIC FALLACY

THE ASSOCIATION OF AESTHETIC pleasure in cricket with romantic images and English traditions was, of course, the trade-mark of Neville Cardus, widely regarded as the greatest modern writer on the game. His Edwardian version of the Victorian apotheosis of cricket had fewer moral overtones – and indeed some irony and a deal of comic skill. It is thus a more insidious form of the 'more-than-a-game' argument and, despite its underlying social attitudes, a much more attractive one. Cardus was scarcely a man of the people, and as he grew older even his staunchest admirers began to think that, as Warner said of Lord Hawke, he was sometimes inclined to dwell too much in the past.

Nevertheless, because of his rejection – often quite explicitly – of conventional moral postures he presents a more credible picture of cricket as a game. He is conscious on the one hand of the elements of display and ritual and style; yet on the other he is aware of the fierce demands of the contest. He looks on them amorally. In this he resembles Ernest Hemingway on the subject of bull-fighting and at his best he can be almost as compelling. There are no stylistic similarities, of course. Cardus is too fond of what Hemingway called 'ten-dollar words' and has intellectual pretensions to match.

These pretensions seem sometimes to get him into a muddle. Though Cardus talks much of 'philosophy' it is doubtful if he had one himself – or, if he had, he could produce a new one every day. In 1920 in a piece grandly entitled 'The Cricketer as Artist' we find him claiming that 'love of technique for technique's sake is a characteristic in English cricket today,' and contrasting this with the Hambledon days when folk were simply, and without sophistication, concerned about winning. (That this was not true is not the immediate point.) The attitude in 1920, he suggests, was: 'Who cares about the tussle for championship points if a Ranji be glancing to leg?' As never before cricket was full of artists, forever trying to do things the hard way – 'the divine discontent of the artist'. The danger was that specialism would lead cricketers to become so obsessed with artistic technique that they would forget about the basic principles on which winning matches depend. 1920 was, he felt, the heyday of the 'cricketer-artist'. Yet in 1923 he was rebuking the counties, suggesting that cricket was in danger of becoming cannily utilitarian with too much of an eye to the main chance.[1]

Nor, for all his pretensions, does he make any serious effort to consider the nature of art or to spell out what he means by it. Instead he describes some of the characteristics of certain aspects of art and uses this as the basis for comment on one or other of his favourite characters or themes. What he is usually describing is style, which, though it is a thing all artists have, is not itself art. Thus, on his favourite lay-figure, Frank Woolley: 'Art, when all is said and done, is simply the expression of personality, through a stylish technique, making for our pleasure. Is not then Woolley an artist?'[2]

Style, technique, expressing personality, giving pleasure: are these all that is needed to constitute art? Not unless we are content with a definition of art so loose as to be meaningless. As R. G. Collingwood put it: 'The terms "art", "artist" and "artistic" and so forth are much used as courtesy titles: the thing which most constantly demands and receives the courtesy title of art is the thing whose real name is amusement or entertainment. The vast majority of our literature in prose and verse, our painting and drawing and sculpture, our music and dancing and acting and so forth, is quite plainly and often quite explicably designed to amuse, but is called art. Yet we know there is a distinction.'[3]

Cardus deserves special attention, not only because of the reverence accorded his writings, but because his use of artistic courtesy titles has distinct social overtones. For one thing in cricket he was apt to confuse style with pedigree. For another, despite all the rhetorical flourishes, he gives the distinct impression that he is merely using cricket as a vehicle for his own loftier purposes. His autobiographies suggest that he may even have felt he was slumming, culturally speaking, when he was at Old Trafford rather than at Hallé concerts or the theatre. So he needed to elevate cricket by high-brow comparisons with the world of art.

An interesting comparison with the kind of vibrant prose Cardus was writing in the 1920s can be found in an essay from a more substantial contemporary. J. B. Priestley has no very lofty notions about cricket: he suggests 'that after all there are other things than games, and England is not ruined just because sinewy brown men from a distant colony sometimes hit a ball oftener than our men do.' However, in the same spirit, he defends the claims of Herbert Sutcliffe to the same artistic status as himself. Priestley purports to admonish friends who believe that 'a man should not play a game for money though they do not object to my method of earning a living. They do not seem to see,' he continues, 'that if it is ridiculous that a man should play cricket for money, it is still more ridiculous that a man should air his feelings for money, that a professional batsman is less absurd than a professional sonneteer.'[4]

Priestley promises more than he actually delivers in this diverting essay. 'The fact is,' he writes, 'that these friends of mine are unjust to Sutcliffe and his fellow professionals because they have not grasped the simple fact that sport and art are similar activities.' But the point he goes on to make, though fair enough, is a side-issue: 'that none of us, whether we are batsmen or poets, bowlers or essayists, work away in our fields or our studies for the money itself. We bat or write because we have a passion for batting or writing and only take the money so that the butcher and baker may be paid while we are so happily engaged.' And again, having got under the ball, as it were, he drops the catch. Priestley tells us that compared with himself Sutcliffe is 'the better performer. Not for long years, if ever at all, shall I achieve in this prose the grace, the lovely ease, that shines through innings after innings of his.' But he offers no exploration of the tension between function and beauty. All he is saying, in effect, is that both writers and batsmen have something we call style.

In Cardus, of course, the cricketer's style is part of something at once more mystical aesthetically and more significant socially. As a result, for all his repeated and conscious efforts, he takes us no further than Priestley, who in his one brief look at cricket was not even trying to go further, in developing the implicit notion that cricket is a performing art. This is unfortunate, for that is what cricket seems to be if it is art at all. Cardus obscures the issue by his descents into vague generalised aestheticisms, spiced with cultural name-dropping. At one point he asks provocatively: 'Why do we deny the art of a cricketer and rank it lower than a vocalist's or a fiddler's?' But in the context of the preceding sentence – 'And Spooner's cricket in spirit was kin with sweet music, and the wind that makes long grasses wave, and the singing of Elizabeth Schumann in Johan Strauss, and the poetry of Herrick'[5] – the thrust of the question is lost.

In his well-known comparisons of cricket with music Cardus seems more concerned with what the neighbours might think than with the actual music. In itself the comparison with music seems to fit cricket better than comparison with literature: unlike the writer the cricketer has no artefact at the end of his innings. This is true of the musician, though not of the composer. It seems unlikely that Cardus had any such distinction in mind when he wrote: 'You will find on every pavilion in the country today men who speak of Gunn's batting as musicians speak of Mozart.'[6] Was he writing metaphorically, meaning 'as musicians speak of a great performance of Mozart's music'? In any event the comparison does not tell the whole story. The cricketer is less than a composer because there is no artefact, but more than an interpreter of someone else's artistic creation. In fact he is more like a jazz soloist than either Mozart or his interpreter because he is creating, improvising, as well as performing, and his art is as ephemeral as that of Louis Armstrong.

Ronald Mason, though contrasting the cricketer with those who create artefacts, aligns him with the actor, which unless he is an actor who makes up his own lines seems not quite a true parallel: 'The writer and the painter and the composer live as long as their works are allowed to live. Wren lives in St Paul's, Shakespeare at the Old Vic, Rembrandt at the National Gallery, Mozart at Sadler's Wells. The actor and the games player, every bit as popular and accomplished in their lifetimes, have no personal power of survival.'[7]

The actor and the games player have indeed much in common. For one thing they are both, if successful, likely to find themselves the subject of adulation. Elsewhere Ronald Mason reminds us of the 'formidable army of middle-aged men in whom the memory of Jack Hobbs is ineffaceable by time. I was one of them; in the words of Whitman, I was the man, I suffered, I was there; I took part in this intense and prolonged relationship between a public and its hero.'[8] Here the actor and the games player share a kind of relationship with the public that writers, painters and composers do not usually have.

But the element of originality and improvisation of the jazz musician is lacking. The dancer may be nearer the mark, in this respect, than the actor. C. B. Fry thought the dance was the basis of all worthwhile games: 'The Greeks knew the secret. A game was not worth the trouble it put you to unless it was first and last a physical fine art. Cricket was a dance with a bat in your hand, or with the encumbrance of a ball. What was exquisite and memorable was the lyric movement of the artist in action. What was incidental was the score that came about from his handling of the ball.'[9] However, the very exposition shows the weakness of this and all other comparisons outside games. Fry may give a very good reason for taking up dancing or a very good description of what he got from cricket. The dance may be a sort of game, but it is not the same sort as cricket. Cricket with nobody caring about runs or wickets may be a good dance, but is no longer a game and, surely, no longer cricket.

An obvious point of contrast is in the significance of the rules in games and in art forms. There are rules and conventions in the performing arts, for the benefit of performer and public, but these are acknowledged to be of lesser importance than the style of the performance: innovation and challenge to the accepted order is often the hallmark of talent. In games it is different: there can be innovations in technique or equipment but they must be within the rules. However well he bowls, the bowler will achieve nothing unless he keeps his foot behind a certain white line. Though rules may need to be changed – for instance to accommodate new techniques or equipment – it is essential that they be observed while they do exist and that the star performer does not set them aside or think himself above them. He has to try to win legally. In cricket he also has to remember that he is a member of a team.

Neville Cardus, some years after his earlier and contentious description, gave a different opinion about early cricket. Presumably he had read Nyren in the meantime: at any rate he came nearer historical accuracy: 'Hambledon cricket was as satisfying to the aesthetic senses as it was stimulating to the combative instincts. In the pages of Nyren we can find as many allusions to the gracefulness of Hambledon cricket as to its skill.'[10] This is the display element that was once greatly admired in cricket and other team games but nowadays tends to be subordinated to competition and excitement. J. M. Kilburn shows how the two elements can coexist for the spectator in this description of Hammond's 240 at Lord's in 1938: 'The mind's eye captured and the heart treasured pictures of drives from the front foot, drives from the back foot scorching through the covers to be greeted with "Oo-oh" and "Aa-ah" of wonder before acknowledgement by crackle of clapping. The clapping applauded the effectiveness of the stroke, its product in runs; the spontaneous cries of wonderment were tribute to the magic in the stroke's creation. Such response is the accolade of the cricket spectator and is rarely given because it is drawn from a quality of batting rarely presented.'[11]

Cardus misses out, of course, the other element in Hambledon cricket: that usually a great deal of money was at stake. This must have given another dimension to the emotions of those involved and an extra edge to the combative element. It is true that many with an eye for beauty have found things to admire in the game, but that does not necessarily mean that it is an art form. Many men with an eye for beauty devote their attention to pretty girls but to think of girls as an art form is, most people would think, to miss the point. With cricket, as with girls, there is more to it than that; and furthermore that something more is what determines what the cricket-lover or the girl-lover thinks is beautiful.

So far as spectators are concerned we must allow for the fact that individuals may take from the game whatever they are seeking from it. But it seems unlikely that Robert Lynd spoke for the majority when he wrote about Bradman: 'Secure conscious mastery of this kind is the crown of genius. By the time he had scored fifty I am sure that even the most ardent pro-English spectator in the ground would have been bitterly disappointed if he had gone out.'[12] The 1977 Test series between England and Australia was chiefly notable for English victories built upon long, patient, disciplined innings by Geoffrey Boycott received in rapture by the crowds. Australia's defeat was assisted by the low scores of their captain Greg Chappell, a much more stylish player (and also a faster scorer) than Boycott. But very few English people would have preferred flamboyance to victory.

Nor can style, in itself, be the most important thing to the cricketer. We can hardly follow Cardus up the garden path in this eulogy of MacLaren. 'I always think of him today as I saw him once playing forward to Blythe beautifully, a majestic rhythm governing the slightest movement. He was clean bowled on the occasion I have in mind for none, but nobody other than a giant of the game could have made a duck so immaculately.'[13] If we are to take this literally MacLaren must have been one of the very few cricketers who ever succeeded in looking and feeling anything other than pretty foolish when bowled through the forward defensive stroke. But even on its own fanciful level this is hard to take: making ducks beautifully is not what cricket is about and if MacLaren had made many of them the selectors would have preferred somebody who could make a few runs, in however ungainly a fashion. His magnificent centuries were fortunately more frequent than his immaculate ducks.

It is no criticism of Tom Richardson, who was one of the great bowlers by any standards, to suggest that his marvellous style was an optional extra. 'His action moved one like music because it was so rhythmical,' writes Cardus.[14] On the other hand Sammy Woods tells us of the Demon Spofforth: 'He delivered every ball with the same action, and as he looked all legs, arms, and nose, it was very hard to distinguish what ball was coming along next.'[15]

For the player the best style is that which achieves its objective most effectively, and the objective must usually be winning. We can leave out of account exhibition games, virtuoso performances when nothing is at stake, because they are not typical and would not exist without the staple of the normal competitive basis of the game, and (also) because even in a festival match the star performer, if he is to make his 50 entertaining runs before adjourning to the bar, must keep the ball out of his stumps.

A batsman's style may be like Sutcliffe's or Bradman's, highly functional but not elegant; and an elegant style may be none the less functional. A. G. Gardiner, in asserting the supremacy of Ranji's technique, writes of his refinement of style, 'which seems to have reduced action to its barest terms . . . It is not jugglery or magic; it is simply the perfect economy of means to end.'[16] Now this is of course a widely held tenet of design theory, that reduction to essentials is the basis of good style, but it is not the only view. C. B. Fry, on Victor Trumper, puts it slightly differently: 'He had no style, yet he was all style. He had no fixed economical method of play, he defied all the orthodox rules, yet every stroke he played satisfied the ultimate criterion of style – the minimum of effort, the maximum of effect.'[17]

But not all genius is effortless. If Fry had written 'apparent minimum of effort' he would have made allowance for the perspiration as well as the inspiration that is also a legitimate part of building up a style. Many apparently brilliant impromptu speeches have been carefully learned and polished. Furthermore in human movement the apparently simple and logical may not actually be so. The early time-and-motion study experts who produced rationalised movement charts found that the theoretically best system was not necessarily the best for everyone. The individual has a natural rhythm which may require peculiarities of movement, and unless these are allowed for the result may be quicker fatigue, or muscle strain, and lower production. A cricketer's style, as any good coach will tell you, is unlikely to stand up to crisis pressures or tests of endurance unless it is based on natural tendencies.

Whether it looks good is a matter of taste, often depending on the fashion of the day. 'I don't like thy writing, Mester Cardus,' the dour Yorkshire batsman Arthur Mitchell is reported to have said. 'It's too fancy.' 'Well, that's more than anybody could say about thy batting, Arthur,' said Maurice Leyland, putting the matter into perspective. There is more than one good style.

There is also, to return to an earlier point, more to art than style. To refer to the contemporary debate in the groves of academe about aesthetics and sport is to risk entering a morass. But we need to tiptoe around its edges. Style is one thing that may often be thought important to both art and games. But it is not the only thing in either, and if a performer possesses a good style that does not make him, in either sphere, an artist. Professor L. A. Reid, in a thoroughly sensible contribution to a somewhat mixed collection of *Readings in the Aesthetics of Sport*, points out that even if the terms used to describe the many ingredients of art and of sport were used precisely there are many hazards in the path of those who want to link the two. 'Because strategy, design, feeling, skill, grace, beauty, sometimes ritual, are common to both art and games, it does not follow that games are art or works of art . . . To argue from some resemblances between art and games to the affirmation that games are *art* is to commit the formal logical fallacy of the undistributed middle.'[18] Even more illogical, we might add, to argue from one pet resemblance, style.

Reid reminds us that when people talk about a great footballer or tennis-player as 'artists' it may well be their craft that is meant. It may be significant that in cricket the mythology evokes loftier associations. C. L. R. James, in the same collection of *Readings*, identifies style as the essential artistic element in cricket. 'Another name for the perfect flow of motion is style, or, if you will, significant form,' he tells us; and again, 'Significant form at its most unadulterated is permanently present. It is known, expected, recognised and enjoyed by tens of thousands of spectators. Cricketers call it style.'

Whether James is being profound or merely pretentious, cricket seems to attract such statements as a honey-pot attracts bees. In part this may be because a greater element of display is intrinsic to cricket than to other games. But there also seem to be social connotations. In the English tradition gentlemen have been considered as a category more stylish than players. And the notion is bound up with reverence for the past.

R. C. Robertson-Glasgow, one of the best of cricket writers, puts it well: 'It is the joy of the critics, when appraising a great player, to say why he is not quite to be compared with this or that hero of the past. When all else fails, they bring up the question of style. "Wonderful," they cry, "yes, very wonderful, but not so beautiful as so-and-so." So-and-so, in his day, of course had the same thing said about him. Thus, elusive perfection is chased ever back. Maybe Adam had an off-drive that made the Serpent weep for very delight.'

His description of Bradman is worth any amount of rhapsody: 'At the wicket, Bradman saw what needed to be done sooner than the others, and did it with more precision. He may or may not have equalled Trumper, Ranji, Macartney, Hobbs, Woolley, in sheer artistry. Such things are arguable. He was not Jovian, like Doctor Grace. He had not the splendour, the mien, of Hammond, who came from the pavilion like the *Victory* sailing to destroy Napoleon. But Bradman went on. He had one eye, as it were, on the heavens and the other on the ledger-book. In the whole game, he was the greatest capitalist of skill. Poetry and murder lived in him together. He would slice the bowling to ribbons, then dance without pity on the corpse. It has been objected that Bradman was fallible on a damaged pitch. He was. This is like saying that a man may slip when walking on ice. But the critics condemn him on one act of rashness against Verity. Verity himself knew better, and told me how Bradman, for over after over at Sheffield in 1938, played his sharpest spinners on a sticky pitch in the middle of the bat.'[19]

Robertson-Glasgow offers an interesting comparison with his near-contemporary, Cardus. He shares with him the rejection of cricket as a powerful moral force. 'I have never regarded cricket as a branch of religion. I have met, and somehow survived, many of its blindest worshippers. I have staggered, pale and woozily, from the company of those who reject the two-eyed stance as Plymouth Brethren reject all forms of pleasure except money-making. I have never believed that cricket can hold Empires together, or that cricketers chosen to represent their country in distant parts should be told, year after year, that they are Ambassadors. If they are, I can think of some damned odd ones.'

On the other hand Robertson-Glasgow extended his scepticism to fine writing, too: 'The air of holy pomp started from the main temple at Lord's, and it breathed over the press like a miasma. "Procul, O Procul Este, Profani!" We are not as other men. Sometimes I look back at reports of games in which I took part, and I have thought: "And are these arid periphrases, these formal droolings, these desiccated shibboleths really supposed to represent what was done and how it was done? What has become of that earthy striving, that comic, tragic thing which was our match of cricket?"'[20]

Cardus, by contrast, though never desiccated or arid could periphrase and drool with the best of them. In this mood he is a blatant purveyor of debased romantic imagery. He is capable of shameless, if sometimes skilful, assemblages of emotive language. Often it dissolves on analysis: 'That day we had watched Woolley in all his glory, batting his way through a hundred felicitous runs . . . Whenever I am in love with cricket's beauty and sentiment I always think of the game as I saw it go to an end that day, in Kent, as though to the strain of a summer's cadence.'[21] And, with more cadences: 'Some of Woolley's innings stay with us until they become like poetry which can be told over and over again . . .

Lovely are the curves of the white owl sweeping
Wavy in the dusk lit by one large star.

I admit, O reader, that an innings by Woolley has nothing to do with owls and dusk and starlight. I am trying to talk of an experience of the fancy; I am talking of cadences, of dying falls common to all the beauty of the world.'[22]

In the real world, according to Arthur Mailey, Woolley moved rather awkwardly because he was slightly knock-kneed. This apart, Robertson-Glasgow approached the task of writing about him somewhat differently from Cardus: 'Frank Woolley was easy to watch, difficult to bowl to, and impossible to write about. When you bowled to him there weren't enough fielders; when you wrote about him there weren't enough words. In describing a great innings by Woolley, and few of them were not great in artistry, you had to go carefully with your adjectives and stack them in little rows, like pats of butter or razor-blades. In the first over of his innings, perhaps, there had been an exquisite off-drive, followed by a perfect cut, then an effortless leg glide. In the second over the same sort of thing happened, and your superlatives had already gone. The best thing to do was to assume that your readers knew how Frank Woolley batted and use no adjectives at all.'[23]

Perhaps to readers of the *Manchester Guardian* in 1938 the daring imagery of their cricket correspondent seemed comparable to the striking juxtapositions of Donne, Andrew Marvell or other metaphysical poets of the seventeenth century. Perhaps it was possible to thrill to this description of Hammond: 'The wrists were supple as the fencer's steel; the light, effortless, yet thrilling movements of his bat suggested that he had now reached the cadenze of his full-toned and full-sized concerto with orchestra.'[24] To the irreverent 1970s it may, on the other hand, seem merely bogus. At its worst Cardus's writing is like advertising copy. He exploits the nostalgic, white-on-green, rustic bliss, dreaming spires and village inn images that can be relied upon to evoke deep and satisfying emotions in cricket-lovers, just as a television commercial exploits sex or greed.

There were other sides to Cardus, of course. In terms of our theme, however, which is to compare cricket's mythology with its reality, this aspect has a special importance. The grandiose in all its forms has found a spiritual home in cricket. This hankering after aesthetic significance is, compared with other archetypal attitudes, harmless and often enjoyable. Any connection with cricket though, is often, as cautious fiction writers used to say, purely coincidental. Consider A. G. Gardiner rhapsodising over the art of Ranjitsinhji – 'It is the great etcher who with a line finds infinity. It is the art of the great dramatist who with a significant word shakes the soul'[25] – or Francis Thompson on Vernon Royle fielding at cover: 'Slender and symmetrical, he moved with the lightness of a young roe, the flexuous elegance of a leopard.'[26]

It is only fair to point out that though it is the English who have most freely conferred the courtesy title of art on cricket they have not been entirely alone in this. C. L. R. James we have already observed bestowing the accolade. Another most distinguished art buff was the late Sir Robert Menzies, the delightful former Prime Minister of Australia and self-confessed cricket addict. He was not only sure that cricket was an art but one that compared favourably with the more conventional sort: 'Indeed, the art of cricket,' he wrote in the Centenary *Wisden*, 'unlike some others, retains its hold upon the art-lover of all generations because its basic elements do not go out of fashion. He does not suffer the puzzlement and frustration of the man who has learned to love and to live with the great works of the Impressionist painters and is then called upon to bow (for fashion's sake) before the abstractionists of the modern school.'

This marvellously question-begging claim illustrates well two points touched on earlier. The first is that when cricket-lovers confer the courtesy-title of art it is usually style to which they are referring. The second is that Robertson-Glasgow was right in suggesting that such references are usually part of an argument about the good old days, evocations of Hornby and Barlow long ago, part of the dream-world. It is a process that, in self-fulfilling prophecy, eliminates from consideration all aspects that do not fit the chosen image. Thus Sir Robert Menzies chides certain of the growing number of cricket-writers for missing the point of it all: 'They include far too many who live for sensation and, if possible, scandal; to whom cricket is a sort of warfare to be conducted on, and, principally perhaps, off the field; who are incapable of understanding art; who think in headlines.'[27]

We shall turn, in the next chapter, to the warfare and consider whether or not it is an invention of the media. Here the question is rather whether Sir Robert's somewhat arbitrary encapsulation of art is good enough. Without labouring the point unduly it seems reasonable to suggest that if we are to bestow the courtesy-title at all, it must be as a performing art and that we must leave the Impressionists and their modern supplanters out of it. Further, the art must be seen as the chance by-product of the contest.

One thing the aesthetic school tends to forget is that the artistic is not to be equated with the beautiful. The vivid, the dramatic, the comic or the epic may be anything but beautiful, but they are all part of art. And they are very much part of cricket. There was nothing beautiful – unless you were an Australian – about the way Lindwall in 1953 with the darkness of the Headingley stand behind him shattered Hutton's stumps with the second ball of the match, but it was dramatic all right, from the hushed expectancy of the crowd as the bowler began his run to their stunned silence afterwards. For many it seemed like the end of the match.

Nor was there anything beautiful about the sight of Cyril Washbrook's jutting backside when in the corresponding match in 1956, with three England wickets swept away for a handful of runs, the veteran recalled to the colours marched out to face the music. But that was dramatic, too, and it stayed so throughout the whole of the day until that marvellous stand was finally broken when May was caught at long leg by a great catch by Lindwall.

Robertson-Glasgow's spectrum – 'that earthy striving, that comic, tragic thing' – is more convincing than cadences or great etchers. The comic in particular must have its due (as of course Cardus and Menzies were both, in less exalted moments, fully aware). We should not want to forget some of the memorable moments recalled by Robertson-Glasgow himself: the festival match in 1923 when the umpires announced that they were going to be very generous about l.b.w. decisions, and George Gunn sidled up from mid-on and said to one of the umpires: 'And I suppose, if anyone's bowled [rhyming with 'scowled'] it's just a nasty accident?' Or the time he bowled Maurice Tate and followed through so far that he nearly stood on the batsman's huge feet: 'Why,' said Maurice afterwards, 'you came down the pitch like Abraham.'[28]

Jack Fingleton's story of the old Lancashire spectator might be apocryphal but it could be true; the Lancastrian saw 'a well clad batsman impeccable in his approach and technique to and at the crease survive a loud appeal for leg-before the first ball and another loud appeal for caught behind off the second; with the third he had his stumps spreadeagled. 'Ee, lad,' said the gaffer as the downfallen one passed him on the pavilion steps, 'thou wert lucky to get a dook.'[29] Even more probable is the Yorkshire variant in which Emmott Robinson, reluctantly playing and even more reluctantly bowling against one of the older universities, trundled up and turned his arm over to clean-bowl the resplendent youth first ball. On his way out the young man graciously commends Emmott. 'Jolly good ball, Robinson.' 'Aye,' said Emmott, 'it were wasted on thee.'

Nor should the quest for the aesthetic ignore that memorable occasion when Crossland, the Lancashire bowler whom Lord Harris refused to play against, bowled out the Rev. J. R. Napier and shouted 'Over goes yon pulpit' or words to that effect. Or Sir Timothy O'Brien given out caught off his shoulder and saying to the umpire 'You must be either a rogue or a fool' and the umpire saying merely 'I guess I'm a bit of both, Sir.' Or Ted Wainwright, getting underneath one of Albert Trott's biggest hits, as high as Blackpool Tower, and then thinking better of trying to catch it, and Lord Hawke on to him with 'Ted, why didn't you try to catch it', and Wainwright replying 'Well your Lordship, it were a bit 'igh weren't it?' Or any one of a hundred other stories that reflect the game's history and its true nature.

Perhaps in the end, though, it is the earthy and the physical that remind us best what cricket is really like. Sammy Woods's description of an incident in a Yorkshire match may not be elegant prose but it is the real thing: 'Yorkshire were in trouble, Tunnicliffe split a finger and J. T. Brown put his shoulder out bowling. I took off my boot and tried to put it [the shoulder] in at once, but couldn't manage it, although I had someone to sit on his head and others to hold him down. He was very sweaty from bowling, I couldn't get a firm grip of his arm, so he had to go to hospital and have it done. I am certain to this day that had he kept still it would have saved a lot of trouble. Poor fellow, I don't think he ever bowled again.'[30]

FOURTEEN

BRUTE FORCE

T HE PHYSICAL SIDE IS very much part of cricket's mythology as well as its reality. It is here that the lofty claims to superior morality are at their most vulnerable. For Neville Cardus, making no such claims, there was no problem. Indeed he was a consistent apologist for violence, an outlook sustained by his social attitudes. Cardus greatly admired the patrician Jardine, writing of him in 1934: 'His influence on modern cricket has been sanitary: he has cleared away cant,' and 'To the Australians he has returned tit-for-tat; it is a pity his chief opponent was not Warwick Armstrong.'[1]

He was in fact a sort of armchair Jardine. Three years later he poured scorn on cricketers who wore protective clothing: 'heavily padded, large leg-guards, and their bodies encased in circular wadding until they look like advertisements for Michelin tyres.'[2] It was the eighteenth-century virility cult, the Old-Etonian Lord Harris attitude of 'what's the bat for', uttered from the safety of the press box.

The gentlemanly attitude to facing fast bowlers and the scorn for protective clothing appeared very early, in a class-conscious limerick made up about Gilbert Jessop when he was hurling them down in his Cambridge days:

> *There was a young fresher called Jessop,*
> *Who was pitching 'em less up and less up,*
> *Till one of the pros*
> *Got a blow on the nose*
> *And said 'In a helmet I'll dress up.'* [3]

Even bodyline produced no headgear. Patsy Hendren invented a sort of helmet like a cap with three peaks after being hit on the head, but he does not appear ever to have worn it. It was not until 1977 that an England player sought protection in this way, when Mike Brearley wore a lattice-work affair that extended from under his cap over his temples. Orthodox opinion tended to the view that this was an odd thing to do, and M. C. Cowdrey and F. S. Trueman in a radio broadcast, commenting on a letter from a lady whose husband had been maimed by a blow on the head in a club match, thought the use of helmets would encourage bowlers to aim at them. It took the ultra-professionalism of the Packer circus to alter things.

The traditional view is one of scorn for such trappings. The professional Richard Daft was mocked for taking what seemed an elementary precaution in 1870. George Summers of Nottingham had been hit on the head, and Daft was next man in: 'We were playing Notts v MCC at Lord's and Platts was bowling a terrific pace that season. Summers . . . before he had scored was struck by a rising ball from Platts on the cheekbone and was carried off the field insensible. The blow caused concussion and the poor fellow died three days afterwards.'[4] Daft wrapped a towel round his head, which seemed so ludicrous to some of his opponents that they laughed at him. The very next ball from Platts went clean over the batsman's head, towel and all. Lord Harris clearly thought Daft was inclined to get ideas above his station when on another occasion a ball hit Daft on the foot and hurt him considerably, 'and he turned to me and said in his most superior way, "This is not cricket, my lord, this is not cricket"'.[5]

The surprising thing is that apart from poor Summers so few people have actually been killed as a result of being struck by the ball, especially as the roll-call began early with a very illustrious name. Frederick Louis, Prince of Wales, was hit on the side of the head by a cricket ball in 1751, an internal abscess formed, and he later died while dancing. In 1800 we learn of John 'Little Joey' Ring who was hit in the nose by one that reared up (from his brother George) and eventually died. In 1870 came Summers. But David Frith in his study of fast bowling records only two other instances where hits have proved fatal: Albert Luty of Yeadon, killed in a local derby in 1883, and, ironically, the fast bowler Jeff Thomson's own flatmate, hit over the heart in a local game in Australia in 1975. However he quotes Robin Marlar as saying, after James Langridge had been hit on the head by the Cambridge University bowler Cuan McCarthy in 1952, 'Jim Langridge was killed by that blow on the temple, but it took him fourteen years to die.' And he lists some of the many appalling head injuries there have been.[6]

The fearful fascination of speed has been part of cricket since the beginning. Even the under-arm bowlers could whip them down, and on bumpy pitches in the days when part of the game was to pick a bit of the meadow for a pitch that suited your own trajectory this cannot have been funny. 'Lumpy' Stevens, one of Nyren's characters, liked to bowl over the brow of a hill, for instance. Another of Nyren's men, David Harris, flicked them at speed from under his armpit. And, a little later, George Brown of Brighton is reputed to have killed a dog through a coat held by a long-stop in a practice game. With round-arm came Alfred Mynn, who whipped them across the batsman's body from round the wicket. It must have been fearsome stuff, and it began to bring out the kind of ferocious humour that Lord Harris was later to think appropriate to his schoolmate Wenlock's affliction. It was one Fellowes who provoked the first version of what can in retrospect be seen as a basic cricket joke. It was said of old Lillywhite who was on the list to go in number eleven that he went to the scorer and said: 'No, put down Lillywhite absent.' The great John Jackson also featured as the hero of a story that was later told of various other speed merchants: he hits a batsman on the pads and the man walks away; the umpire says 'That wasn't out' but the batsman says: 'No, but I'm going.'

It was Jackson who was the subject of the first classic *Punch* joke about cricket: 'I 'ad a hover of Jackson: the first ball 'it me on the 'and; the second 'ad me in the knee; the third was in my eye. And the fourth bowled me out! Jolly game!' When asked by *Old Ebor* whether he had ever taken ten wickets in one innings Jackson said: 'No, but I once did something as good. It was in North versus South at Nottingham. I got nine wickets and lamed Johnny Wisden so that he couldn't bat. That was as good as ten, eh?'[7]

The brutality has been played down in other ways. One is the belief that it is possible, and valid, to distinguish between intentional and unintentional injury. Jackson seems to have been unusual in admitting what he was doing: later the code came to require not only protestations of innocence but apologies to the batsman. Colonel French's post-war exposition of 'it's not cricket' commends 'such generous gestures as bowling one or two balls on the off-side after a batsman has been hit in order to give him time to recover'.[8] But this has often been the merest hypocrisy, and latterly bowlers have begun to say so: as cricketers' autobiographies have become more outspoken and sensationalist there have been admissions – perhaps claims is the right word – that what has always seemed to be happening in such circumstances was in fact taking place.

Bowlers sometimes try to hit batsmen. Poor Peter Lever was unlucky enough to achieve his objective and Chatfield almost died. There is a bizarre kind of etiquette about it. Dennis Lillee suggests that it's quite all right as long as you miss the head: 'I try to hit a batsman in the rib-cage when I bowl a purposeful bouncer and I want it to hurt so much that the batsman doesn't want to face me any more . . . I don't want to hit a batsman on the head because I appreciate what damage that can do.'[9] (Another point is, of course, that head-high bouncers are less likely to take wickets.) But he makes no bones about what he is attempting, and as he says, he is merely uttering what many others have been afraid to admit.

Merely missing the head is not much of a consolation for batsmen. To be hit over the heart can be just as lethal. Arthur Gilligan, an England captain and all-rounder, was not killed by the blow he received in Gentlemen v. Players in 1924, but he could never bowl fast again. Jim Laker tells a terrible story. Peter Heine of South Africa was irritated by Trevor Bailey's defensive play in a Test match: 'Halfway between a sneer and a growl, Heine said: "I want to hit you, Bailey . . . I want to hit you over the heart." He meant every word of it,' continued Laker. 'It was one hundred per cent pure malice.'[10] There is little reason to doubt that Heine and many others would be happy to see the batsman hit anywhere where it hurt and would be reconciled to the possibility of inflicting injury.

Larwood sought after his retirement to draw a distinction between 'making the ball rear' and trying to hit and hurt the batsman. 'I never bowled to injure a man in my life,' he wrote. 'Frighten them, intimidate them, yes.'[11] This does not quite accord with some accounts. According to David Frith, 'Against an Indian touring team he and Voce bet a packet of smokes as to who would hit a particular batsman's turban first. Film exists of the wretched Sikh's assisted exit from the field, forehead garnished with a bump the size of a pigeon's egg.'[12] In any case, with all respect to Larwood and his 'ghost', the claim is nonsensical. Jardine and all the other defenders of bodyline made great play with the fact that Larwood was extremely accurate and therefore could control what happened, but nobody could be so accurate as to guarantee to miss narrowly a man's head or his heart, even if he were to stand as still as a knife-thrower's assistant.

Nor does the question of intent have very much meaning. There does not need to be cold-blooded intimidation: anger or desire for revenge can turn even the most gentlemanly of fast bowlers into marksmen. In a friendly game at the end of the Australians' 1921 tour, in which Gregory and McDonald had inflicted quite a bit of punishment (Ernest Tyldesley twice being struck in the face by Gregory) and there had been some retaliation (Warwick Armstrong being cut over the eye by a ball from Durston), there was the sort of exchange that the Badminton book would have deplored. 'As Arthur Gilligan was about to throw the ball to the wicket-keeper to run out Andrews, his arm was struck by Armstrong's bat as the captain bustled in at the bowler's end. Warwick said: "You don't think I did that on purpose, do you?" Gilligan's next ball to Armstrong knocked his cap off.'[13]

It was this kind of behaviour by Warwick Armstrong that led Cardus to advocate tit-for-tat and to regret only that Jardine could not confront Armstrong directly. There had been blow and counter-blow in matches between England and Australia ever since that memorable moment in 1869 when Ernest Jones, Australia's fast bowler, whipped one down that went through W.G.'s beard. There was W.G. stepping down the pitch and calling out 'What, what, what' in his high-pitched voice and Harry Trott, the Australian captain, saying 'Steady, Jonah' and Ernest Jones apologising: 'Sorry, Doc, she slipped.' F. S. Jackson was less lucky than Grace: he sustained a cracked rib that kept him out of the game for weeks. 'Tibby' Cotter, who once hit a batsman in the back and left a dent the ball could fit into, also bowled what C. B. Fry called rib-ticklers in 1905 and 1909, but it was after the First World War, when Armstrong had Gregory and McDonald at his disposal and England had no one remotely as fast, that the retaliatory process began in earnest.

Gregory first impressed himself on the 1920–21 tourists when playing for New South Wales against MCC. An Australian report said: 'Gregory was bowling very fast and making the ball bump a good deal. He hit Russell on the shoulder and caused him to drop his bat in pain. When he came on again he was greeted with applause. His second ball hit Hobbs on the thigh, but he managed to limp a single. The next ball hit Hendren who was momentarily hurt. Shortly after Gregory knocked Hobbs' bat out of his hand and struck him on the wrist, causing him to dance about for some seconds, leaving his bat where it fell. The next three balls, rising to over six feet, made Hobbs duck to avoid them. In trying to hit them to leg, Makepeace was struck in the chest by a rising ball.'[14]

The crowd may have applauded, but there was nothing artistic about the batsmen hopping around. Nor was there much applause from English crowds or players in 1921 when, under Armstrong's leadership, Gregory consolidated his lethal partnership with McDonald. No doubt one or two vows of revenge were taken. Apart from the Tyldesley episode mentioned earlier some of the casualties were Vallance Jupp (broken thumb), P. R. Johnson and Hubert Ashton (badly bruised hands), J. R. Burns (hit on the head), Percy Perrin (hit in the stomach), Lionel Tennyson (hit over the heart).

It was not only international rivalry that led to bodyline and its repercussions but also the deeply-felt conviction amongst bowlers that they were discriminated against. Between the wars over-prepared pitches (to ensure the game lasted its full distance and so attracted maximum attendance) and bare outfields meant that in normal weather conditions batsmen had things all their own way. In 1927 the ball was reduced in size and in 1931 the size of the wickets was increased to redress the balance a little, but these were mere palliatives. The heart of the matter was that, as R. C. Robertson-Glasgow once suggested, 'the bowler is the slave of the game. Not often for him the spectators' appreciation, the headlines. Crowds came to see batsmen and it was they who got the glory and also, from the umpires, despite dead pitches, the crippling l.b.w. laws, the benefit of the doubt.'[15] Bowlers felt they were entitled to try everything they knew to make a breakthrough.

So to bodyline and the aftermath: Bradman seeking revenge. Whether or not Australia did comb the bush as James Agate hoped they would, they certainly tried hard to find bowlers as quick as Larwood. Until the 1939–45 war they were largely baulked by the placid wickets. Neither Tim Wall, who lacked the last yard of pace, nor Ernie McCormick of the 31-pace run, who had back trouble and insufficient skill, quite filled the bill. But as soon as the war was over there were Lindwall and Miller wreaking havoc under Bradman's calculated captaincy, dealing out retribution with the greatest possible satisfaction. They were aided by a foolish law which gave them a new ball every 55 overs. Most of England took a different view in 1948 from the one that prevailed in 1932–33. Neville Cardus may well have returned from his wartime sojourn in Australia to reflect upon his 1937 complaint that 'Fast bowling is dying out' and his enthusiasm for tit-for-tat.

Now the wheel had spun again. Compton was hit on the head, Washbrook's cap was knocked off, Jack Robertson was hit on the jaw, and the Nottinghamshire members, still feeling thwarted by what had happened to Larwood and Voce, protested bitterly and loudly about Lindwall and Miller's tactics in poor light. Bradman, when they were making them fly around Edrich's head, apologised and said the boys were hard to control in certain moods. Hutton, as we have seen, was foolishly dropped, temporarily, from the England side. He returned to play better than any in the disastrous final Test but the iron had entered his soul. He developed a deep longing for revenge and revenge by speed. When he became captain the search for fast bowlers was given high priority.

Another factor was indicated by Walter Hammond, who wrote prophetically in 1952: 'For many years after Larwood went out of the game it could be said that no young fast bowler was permitted to bounce the ball at all, without earning a reprimand. The result was that most English batsmen ceased to be able to play the fast bouncer at all. During 1951 a few up-and-coming bowlers realised this, and the news ran through that strange "grapevine" of rumour that stretches from pavilion to pavilion that all sorts of famous scalps could be collected cheaply by bouncing a few fast ones . . . A great deal more of them will be seen in 1952 and 1953.'[16]

Though the young Trueman was effective against lesser sides he was not yet dominant against the Australians, but Hutton eventually found what he wanted in 1954–55 when Tyson came in to the side. Lindwall, still in contention, hit Tyson on the back of the head, raising a bump that could be seen from the boundary edge. Tyson recovered sufficiently to bowl Australia out, but the team contest was obviously only part of what was going on. 'Why did you do that, Ray?' Denis Compton asked. 'I wanted to show him how fast I was,' said Lindwall.

Apart from the tit-for-tat contest with Australia, England now found other countries coming into the reckoning, notably South Africa and the West Indies. In the early 1950s the lethal pair of Heine and Adcock were at their peak, hitting nearly as many people as wickets. The West Indians produced a string of fast men, including Hall and Griffith, who made their mark on more than one opponent in the later 1950s and 60s. Trueman, when he was not at odds with the selectors, was England's spearhead; and the bouncer was one of 'Fiery Fred's' favourite weapons. Crowds enjoyed it, but the courtesy of combat diminished. The West Indian Gilchrist was too much for his own Board of Control, who sent him home from India in 1958–59 for bowling beamers. The search for speed also produced illegal bowling actions, and the chuckers were rife for a period from the late 1950s. Australia had Meckiff, South Africa Griffin, the West Indies Griffith and England Harold Rhodes, all with suspect actions.

With or without bent arms the contest has continued. David Frith provides a terrifying catalogue of incidents from 1953, when Bert Sutcliffe of New Zealand had his ear split by Adcock at Johannesburg. Sparling was felled by Trueman in 1958. Loader hit Australia's Burke on the head. Nari Contractor of India got a fractured skull and nearly lost his life when hit by a ball from Charlie Griffith in 1962. Wesley Hall broke Colin Cowdrey's arm at Lord's in 1963 and Brian Close's bruises from Hall and Griffith were front-page news. Jackie Hendriks of the West Indies needed brain surgery when struck by Graham McKenzie of Australia in 1965. Sutcliffe was again hit on the head by Trueman in that year.

John Edrich was put in hospital when a ball from Peter Pollock of South Africa hit him on the head. In 1967 Jeff Jones hit Rohan Kanhai over the heart, knocking his cap off in the process, and caused Terry Jarvis to have fourteen stitches in his face. In 1970 Graham McKenzie had to leave the field with blood streaming from his face after being hit by John Snow, and in the next Test Snow hit Terry Jenner on the head. (The bowler and the England captain Illingworth took exception to the umpire's rebuke, and when the crowd threw beer-cans on the field the team walked off.) In 1972 Tony Greig hit Graeme Watson of Australia on the bridge of the nose and Watson was in the intensive care unit for several days. Duleep Mendis of Sri Lanka was but one of Thomson's victims in 1975.

And so it has gone on, culminating in the 1974–75 Australian tour but not being restricted in any way even after the Chatfield incident: indeed, the opposite. During the second Test of 1977–78 the New Zealanders seemed to be operating according to the principles of total war. 'Richard Hadlee,' wrote Henry Blofeld in the *Guardian*, 'behaved all the time as if he had a personal grudge against the batsmen.' John Woodcock in *The Times*, criticising the stream of bouncers he produced, described his behaviour as 'comparable with Lillee's in its churlishness'. He had apparently not only encouraged the crowd to behave boorishly but conducted them in their exultant chants.

Why this kind of thing is tolerated and where it will end can only be a matter of speculation. The West Indies, as the balance of cricket power shifts, seem capable of producing an infinite succession of dangerous bowlers. Roberts and Holding seem faster than Hall, and Wayne Daniel more likely to cause injury than Charlie Griffith. No doubt Australia, inside or outside the Packer circus, will produce successors to Lillee and Thomson : with even less regard for the values of P. F. Warner and 'it's not cricket'. And if New Zealand is to adopt the same approach to cricket as she has to rugby, then Hadlee will not be her last truculent exponent of force.

Leaving aside the actual damage inflicted there are many things to be said against unrestricted fast bowling. People grow lyrical about the glorious spectacle of a fast bowler's long accelerating run-up to the wicket and the tension of the opening overs. But is that tension only related to the prospect of speed? Can we in any case condone the underlying savagery of what Lillee and the like intend and what their supporters hope will happen? An eye-witness at the 1974–75 Test matches thought there was no doubt that the comment in Lillee's book played its part in provoking the exultant chants of 'Lil-lee, Lil-lee' from the jam-packed Hill that accompanied him along the 30-yard walk to his mark and up the first half of his run-up, to be followed by an expectant hush as he neared the bowling crease.[17] The young Pakistani batsman Haroon Rashid heard the cry two years later when he first faced Lillee as 'Kill, kill, kill.' It is a case of tribal chants during the boring part and silent expectation of mayhem at the climax.

This book has perhaps sufficiently demonstrated that there is no morality in all this except that of an-eye-for-an-eye. On the tour after the Chatfield episode New Zealand spectators were gleefully chanting 'Had-lee, Had-lee, Had-lee' as their hero attempted revenge. It would require considerable mental agility to relate it to art either. It can scarcely be argued that people watching executions or cock-fights were enjoying an aesthetic experience worthy of the name. Whether it should even be within the rules of any modern game is open to question: it seems uncomfortably near the great game of war. All this apart, does this kind of thing in the end add more to the spectators' enjoyment than it takes away (to say nothing of players')?

A long run-up takes time and the slow walk back takes even longer. Without the blood-lust what would be more tedious in fact than the opening overs of contemporary Tests? It is easy to see why Madame Defarge took along her knitting to while away the intervals between the guillotine's intermittent moments of joy. And what of batsmanship, which is a large part of most spectators' enjoyment of cricket? Defending his person, added to defending his wicket, inevitably takes up so much of a batsman's attention that scoring runs is usually the last thing he can think about. With modern accurate field-placing and high standards of fielding the chances of anybody scoring a hundred before lunch ever again seem to have receded to vanishing point. And what has happened to the subtle and entertaining art of slow bowling whilst this tit-for-tat gladiatorial contest has been going on?

Indeed what has happened to first-class cricket has begun to inflict pain even on advocates of its ancient virtues. The summer of 1978 produced dozens of cricketers, even in the county game, wearing huge globular helmets of a kind that made Brearley's innovation seem like earmuffs, and this outraged the aesthetic if not the moral sense of staunch establishment supporters. Had the game come to this, they asked? What was the Test and County Cricket Board going to do about it?

The new trend followed hard upon the first season of Packer super-cricket. The logic of show-business appeared to demand it. Tony Greig had declared that the Americans might eventually take to cricket if the excitement could be heightened by providing a lot of bouncers. 'The truth is,' wrote Tony Lewis, a former England captain in the

Sunday Telegraph of 11 June, with a blinding flash of insight, 'that too many bouncers are being bowled.'

Equally true is that the TCCB, MCC and the like have contributed as much as anyone to this state of affairs. The underlying philosophy of the virility cult has contracted a marriage of convenience with commercialism, largely for social reasons. It is a continuation of a process that allowed bodyline to be absorbed into the code, relying on 'it's not cricket' with a minimum of supporting legislation, ambiguous at best, to keep it in check.

Perhaps when someone is actually killed on the field in a first-class match a halt will be called. Perhaps not. Probably some excuse would be made to the effect that cricket is safer than air travel or home carpentry. Certainly despite Jardine's sanitary influence there has been no subsequent shortage of cant. Whether we believe that civilisation collapsed in 1929 and 'it's not cricket' with it, or whether we point to the rise in nationalism or show-business to explain the decline in cricket, is immaterial. Despite those who breezily advocate the hook shot – mostly from the pavilion bar – it is hard to resist the conclusion that cricket would be better off without intimidatory bowling, and that the laws should be altered to stamp it out altogether.

There have been plenty of suggestions as to how to do it. E. W. Swanton thinks it would be worth experimenting with a horizontal line across the pitch ('repugnant though its introduction would be')[18] beyond which the ball would have to pitch. Or there could be a ten-run penalty for infringing a more strictly enforced version of the present law with the bowler being sent off the field for repetition. The case for limiting run-ups is a strong one, for other reasons, and this might have some marginal effect on speed. Another interesting idea came from a Mr Don Fair who, in a letter to *The Times* on 15 July 1976, advocated lengthening the pitch to 23½ yards, on the grounds that the average height of a man was 5ft. 4¾ inches in 1700 and had now become 5ft. 9 inches. This would give the batsman longer to see the ball.

To compensate the bowler for this reduction in fire-power it would be worth increasing the size of the wickets. Better still, several birds could be killed with the same stone if there were a rational reform of the l.b.w. rule, making the batsman out if a ball which he intercepted with any part of his body would in the umpire's opinion have otherwise hit the wicket regardless of where it pitched. This could provide a logical law that would eliminate deliberate and tedious pad play, would more than compensate for the lengthening of the pitch, and would also encourage more use of spin bowling. Robertson-Glasgow's analysis of the bowler's situation still holds good: consider the comment of John Thicknesse in his highly critical account of the lethal stuff being flung at batsmen by the speed merchants. He found the decisions of umpires Brooks and Bailhache very hard to understand: 'Batsmen sometimes appeared to be immune unless they were right back on the stumps with the ball keeping low.'[19]

These matters have never been discussed fully and rationally by any truly representative gathering of cricketing interests. Ingrained attitudes persist. Traditionalists recoil in horror at such faint-hearted talk. Lord Harris's spirit dies hard. But the problem of the bouncer, like other contemporary problems, will not be solved by resort to traditional attitudes. 'It's not cricket' was never sufficient even in its heyday. The cricket establishment by now have to answer the accusation that other sports, perhaps even football, have solved their problems better than the MCC and its heirs and assigns. Golf in particular maintains an exemplary moral code.

Perhaps the time has come for the saying to be adjusted to 'it's not golf'. It should not be too difficult to demonstrate that golf originated in Kent; indeed it may well have been one of the games that Prince Edward played with Piers Gaveston at Newenden.

FIFTEEN

FUN AND GAMES

WILLIAM TEMPLE ONCE DESCRIBED cricket as 'organised loafing'. Somewhat surprisingly in view of this remark he subsequently became an Archbishop. His is an opinion unlikely to be shared by anyone who is prepared to read a book on the subject – still less by anyone who is prepared to write one. I have been bold enough, it is true, to examine critically some of the grandiose and misleading claims that have been made for cricket and to suggest that they do not accord with reality. But heresy can be firmly denied.

Doubtless certain subjective judgements or even prejudices have crept in. It could be that Lord Hawke's vanity and crudity have been exaggerated. It is conceivable that Lord Harris – declaring that 'Cricket is not only a game but a school of the greatest social importance' or that MCC is 'perhaps the most venerated institution in the British Empire' – has been treated with insufficient respect. Perhaps there is a more liberal, progressive spirit in the Long Room than has been suggested.

If there are such distortions, they arise not from lack of appreciation of the game itself, but on the contrary from concern about its present state and future prospects. The cause of this concern is the way cricket has been controlled in the past at the highest level. (It is not enough to suggest that there are other, better forms of cricket uncorrupted by MCC or Kerry Packer: these variants, however splendid, depend in the last analysis on the standing and quality of the first-class game.)

The controllers of cricket appear to have lived, or tried to live, almost entirely in the past. Those who, like John Arlott for instance, contend that the changes in the game over the years have been reflections of changes in society as a whole are expressing what is at best an over-simplification. If first-class cricket had reflected social changes it might not now be under such threat. Its predicament is that its leaders have, consciously or unconsciously, used eighteenth-century feudal models as their ideal. English cricket-writers have, almost to a man, shared this outlook, and cricketers themselves, players as well as gentlemen, have acquiesced.

To question the underlying values of cricket mythology is not necessarily merely sacrilegious, therefore. If cricket survives it will need, and perhaps may get, a new and more astringent literature. The sensational autobiographies of contemporary cricketers are not enough, though they may be helpful if they show that a cricketer's confessing to something less than saintliness does not inevitably bring about the collapse of civilisation. On the other hand if they are used to support arguments that things aren't what they were then these recollections could delay the honest self-analysis cricket needs. Things have never been what they were said to be.

However, the case against the elevated claims made for cricket is not simply that they were untrue but also – and more important – that in emphasising quasi-religious, social or aesthetic virtues they have undersold cricket as a game. Indeed they appear to have been based on a misunderstanding of the nature, and on underestimation of the significance, of games in general. Games are increasingly being recognised as themselves playing a valuable part in human development. To get this recognition they have had to fight their way, in modern Western society, through clouds of religious, social, political and aesthetic traditions embodying a narrow view of what is serious and respectable. Cricket, for reasons this book has been exploring, has been thought to have greater claims to conventional seriousness and respectability than other games, and this has prevented its being considered, stripped of the humbug, a serious activity in its own right.

Games are not religions, nor stylised versions of social or political philosophy, nor art forms, but they can properly be regarded as of that order of activity. Some would go further. Perhaps the strongest case for games was made by the historian Johan Huizinga who argued that 'The spirit of playful competition is, as a social impulse, older than culture itself and pervades all life like a veritable ferment. Ritual grew up in sacred play; poetry was born in play and nourished on play; music and dancing were pure play.' Indeed, according to Huizinga: 'Wisdom and philosophy found expression in words and forms derived from religious contests. The rules of warfare, the conventions of noble living were built up on play patterns. We have to conclude, therefore, that civilisation is, in its earliest phases, played. It does not come from play like a babe detaching itself from the womb: it arises in and as play, and never leaves it.'[1]

Huizinga presents his arguments extravagantly; and we do not need to go the whole way with him. It is enough to note that the spirit of playful competition pre-dates civilisation and that it can be put in the same category as religion, art and music as external expression of psychological need. That 'play' is part of religion is not to suggest that religion is a game, nor that any game should be a religion. Similarly, though games have things in common with art – they can both be described as structured play – art lacks the element of competition that is a fundamental feature of games.

The common element, play, is not only older than civilisation, it is older than man. To elaborate on this would be a digression: the animal origin of play is relevant only as an indicator of how fundamental it is in the lives of human beings. Human infants engage in play from their earliest days and it comes naturally to them. Unlike the archetypal Yorkshire cricketer, children play 'for fun', that is for its own sake, so by definition play has no immediate function. Nevertheless it appears to have evolutionary value (at any rate the higher the species, the more the play) and it needs no fanciful speculation to suggest why. Play allows the vulnerable young individual to show mastery over external phenomena in a way that is of his or her own choosing and in safety – in a way that is only possible because the phenomena are not real but in the mind. It has psychological value: as rehearsal, as training, and as solace.

Games are a later development in evolutionary terms. They are a form of play but play that is structured, systematic and capable of repetition. In games the exercise of mastery is channelled towards a specific objective. Games require a player to pit himself against obstacles that are devised or that arise by chance. There is competition, either with another person or with another side of oneself.

This 'competition' may not always be simply a matter of notching up points by direct action against an opponent, though that is the usual pattern of modern team games. But there are games like 'Ring-a-Ring-a-Roses' or 'Here We Go Round the Mulberry Bush' in which the competition takes a different form: small children mastering their own bodies to perform the prescribed actions. This is the shady no-man's-land between games and dance.

Another obscure borderline is that with religious ritual. Many rites of primitive societies have incorporated activities akin to games: both can be seen as substitutes for harsher realities. For instance, folklorists have 'explained' counting-out games as harmless versions of choosing victims by lot, 'Nuts and May' as a relic of marriage by capture, and 'London Bridge' as a playful enactment of the charming old custom of burying children alive in the foundations of new buildings. 'Ring-a-Ring-a-Roses' is often referred to as a re-creation of the plague which leaves rosy spots on the victim's cheeks and ends by knocking everybody down.

If we strip the ritual element in games of this kind of significance, however, we are left with a feature that might be called display. This plays a part in all games. So far as team games are concerned it figured more prominently in the past than it does today. Nowadays it tends to be an essential element only in individual activities such as diving, gymnastics and ice-skating, where the skill of the performance, judged according to assessment of an amalgam of technique and artistry, is what counts. Cricket was, in the earliest days, a team game in which display was highly important. It remains still: that is what is recognised by the cricket spectator's cry of delight as distinct from his applause for runs and wickets. But the history of cricket is one of diminishing emphasis on display and growing regard for the excitement of combat.

Changing values of this kind are, however, psychological, not social or ethical. In social and ethical terms games cannot change their values because they do not have any. They may, of course, embody them: thus the Victorians invested cricket with qualities relating to producing leaders of society and of the Empire. But games are commonly put to very different uses today: in education, in military strategy and tactics, or in business, for example. The common element is their usefulness as training.

The association within the Christian tradition of games with frivolity and therefore with sin helped create the Victorian myth that cricket had superior ethical qualities. Muscular Christianity was a new thing and cricket just happened to be one of the vehicles through which it was expressed. The older tradition is that of St Augustine, who as a child was punished for wasting time on games (and who complained that the grown-ups who punished him were themselves addicted to a game that they called business).[2] The Rev. Mr Pycroft's panegyric reflects the need he felt to purge the guilt inbred in him by this tradition. By that time the tradition tolerated games, at the right time and place, in children, but regarded them as evidence of frivolity in adults and therefore suspect. Cricket to him, nevertheless, was at least preferable to the grosser alternatives practised by the ungodly.

The current search, in our post-Freudian society, is for psychological health rather than ethical purity, so that games can be judged by their capacity for doing people good, not making them good. In our relatively guilt-free times it seems justification of frivolity enough to know that there is an impulsion in the species to play and that this often finds an outlet in games.

Not all societies in history have played games but most have done so, and usually the more advanced and sophisticated the society the greater the amount and complexity of its games. Those involving intellectual strategy are only found in advanced societies. So there seems little reason to apologise for cricket considered purely as a game. It is one of the most advanced and sophisticated of the games based on physical skills and it also requires some mental effort. Its extensive literature shows that cricket generates other intellectual play material apart from what happens on the field. It is capable of capturing the imagination.

Cricket to Mr Pycroft also seemed socially desirable because it brought together those of high and low estate. But games are not only ethically but also socially neutral. They can be a form of social cement, as has been claimed for cricket in the past, but they can be the opposite. That the nobility played cricket with their servants may have staved off a revolution, but the Victorians, by elevating this accident into a strategy, opened a Pandora's box when they promoted games as an outlet and training ground for the middle-class virtues. When they did so the second of Britain's two nations got involved as well, and, more spectacularly perhaps in soccer, but also in cricket, asserted its influence on the nation's values. The interaction between the working classes and their commercial exploiters, in show-business and the mass-media, has eroded, if not destroyed, traditional middle-class values, including those grafted on to cricket.

So, though socially neutral, games can be socially important. Many nations, politically as well as socially emergent, have discovered a special significance in games in recent years. The post-war explosion in national competitive games seems to come from an unconscious awareness amongst ordinary people that games can somehow do us good, whether we play them or merely watch or even just talk about them. In this sense they may be a substitute for the old religious observances. Huizinga's book is an eloquent rationalisation and extension of this awareness.

Since publication of this work, drawing on the findings and specu-lations of anthropologists, folklorists and other pioneers, more scientific theories of games have been developed. In the modern manner these theories tend to concentrate on analysis and documen-tation rather than broad principles, on how rather than why. And, as is always likely to happen when something very familiar and ordinary, like a game, is subjected to close analysis the results may seem fanciful or absurd. But they are at least evidence of general acceptance amongst scholars that games are a very serious business.

The two poles of the contemporary approach are the psychogenic and the sociogenic. The first explains games in terms of the individ-ual's state of mind before he plays them, primarily in relation to psychological, but also to physiological or genetic factors. It is con-cerned with such things as the way games can relieve tension, reduce anxiety or sublimate aggression. There is a family resemblance in such thinking to Aristotle's theory of drama as catharsis, or relief of tension.*

Since Freud such interpretations have been influenced by psycho-analytic theory. These in particular are not always easy to take entirely seriously. P. W. Pickford, for instance, compares Rugby football, in

---

*In a tragedy the events on stage are said to purge the soul of pity and terror by inducing them artificially and in situations where they are not disadvantageous to daily living.

which you can legally pick up the ball, and Association, in which you cannot. 'It might be said,' he writes, 'that in Association football the ball is symbolically a dirty and dangerous object, or that it is so powerful in unconscious meaning that it must not be touched by the hand under penalty of foul play. In Rugby football the ball might be regarded as a lovable object that every player tries to caress and hold as if it were a valued possession. In psychoanalytic terms these attitudes suggest that to Rugby enthusiasts the ball is a symbol of loved maternal images while to the Association football enthusiast it is a symbol of paternal potency which is somewhat feared and requires special forms of taboo or control.'[3] (All footballers will at once recognise this as brilliant analysis of their underlying motivation, though they might wish Mr Pickford had said a word or two about goal-keepers: schizophrenics, presumably.)

The sociogenic approach, in contrast to the emphasis on the individual's needs, lays great stress on games as preparation for social roles, conditioning the novitiate to the importance and satisfaction of public approbation, concepts of honour, group loyalties and so on. The Victorians discovered the value of team games as character training, and the public schools, consciously or otherwise, used the discovery for particular social purposes. But the choice of games was accidental. If Newbolt's 'Vitaï Lampada' ('Play up, play up and play the game') was based on cricket, that was because cricket had taken on board the social values of the establishment. Conversely it is no criticism of cricket if the philosophy Newbolt was expressing was that of feudalism and virility transmuted into jingoism.

The Newbolt ethos presents cricket as a preparation for war, not as a substitute for it. But cricket surely does not deserve – despite A. C. MacLaren and his followers – to be thought better training for killing than other games. It is instructive to compare Newbolt's view with that of a perceptive South Sea Island native. Arthur Grimble has recorded how an elder of the Sun Clan once told him: 'We old men take joy in watching the kirikiti of our grandsons, because it is a fighting between factions which makes the fighters love each other.'[4]

Latter-day scholarship has supported the primitive perception. A sophisticated and instructed modern counterpart of the Sun Clan elder might point out that games have psychogenic and sociogenic functions as mock-versions, enacted in comparative safety, of power-struggles in which individuals and groups, notably when they are young, can try out their prowess without doing themselves or anyone else too much damage and in the process can achieve psychological and social satisfactions valuable to their maturation.

But in any language the Sun Clan seem to be in the right of it. Lessons from 'primitive' communities may be increasingly valuable as societies grow more complex. With complexity comes specialisation and the tendency to pay other people, directly or indirectly, to play our games for us. We get our kicks from watching the experts. This specialisation also encourages our tendency to identify with, or hero-worship, superior performers. As societies grow bigger people feel an increasing need to identify with smaller, less overwhelming groups. (This may explain the modern support of convenient 'local' teams, whether local in their membership or not.) And games seem to have more and more to offer us. As the demands of daily life become more intricate or repetitive and performing them more difficult or tedious, people are likely to turn increasingly to those activities that seem to restore to life the essential dramatic combative simplicities.

But it is of the essence of play that it should involve only as much risk as the participant chooses. In modern society the spectator's role clearly becomes more attractive as the amount of risk from actually playing games increases. Also in modern industrial society the value of games which offer, either directly or vicariously, the chance of escape from the ruck has grown in importance. The spiral of high standards and rewards leading to a select and possibly corrupt professionalism, apart from its own obvious inherent defects, may also drive more and more people into spectatorship.

Watching is a lesser form of participation, and watching games is nowadays, even more than in the past, likely to subject the individual to submersion in debasing crowd behaviour. Aristotle's notion that drama purges us of undesirable emotions is not entirely proven so far as sports crowds are concerned; it could be that a more active, physical participation is required in order to release, or sublimate, all the pent-up energy. In any event, it is a matter of commonsense that if games are valuable it is better to have millions playing them than to have a few playing and millions watching. It seems to follow, therefore, that desirably games should not be too physically daunting. Even more important, they should be accessible to everyone from an early age, not so that children can be used, through games, for some specific social purpose, nor so that they can become hostages to commercial exploiters, but out of a true appreciation by society that playing games is good for you.

Games can be measured according to the satisfactions they offer individuals, or according to how they help individuals cope with life. They can be evaluated in the same way socially, but games are likely to suffer – as it has been suggested cricket has suffered – if a society chooses them to achieve specific social or political purposes. Nor is the society itself likely to benefit for long. The true hierarchy of games relates to their complexity, use of strategy and so forth, not to any moral or social values that may be attributed to them.

If games are ethically, socially and politically neutral, then any real or imagined threats to them have to be considered in this light. One threat to the mythology of cricket that seemed important for many years was 'professionalism'. There are, of course, strong arguments against professionalism in sport, and these arguments grow no less. But, in fact, professionalism in cricket was never attacked for these reasons.

Indeed the cricket establishment invented professionalism and proved most reluctant to end the distinction between gentlemen and players which they could have done at a stroke many years ago. When they discarded the distinctions it was to make everyone who played at the highest level a 'professional' in the sense of being free to take payment for playing. Their concern was not to preserve first-class cricket for amateurs – that is, people who wanted to play it 'for fun' – as did, for example, the Rugby Union. They wanted to protect the domain of a privileged class, as players, spectators and administrators. MCC, who, though not solely to blame, must exemplify the attitude they espoused, preferred to sell their souls and denature the game itself rather than alter its social structure so as to make it possible for cricket to be played as an amateur sport at all levels.

The threats first-class cricket faces in the future stem from this paradox. First, the specialisation that has affected all aspects of our increasingly complex society has hit cricket. Second, the values of show-business have been introduced and are likely to encroach more and more on sporting values. Third, the traditions of the virility cult, modulating into the attitudes of show-business, have elevated physical danger in cricket to a point where it dominates the game.

There are other threats, no doubt. But these are enough to be going on with. If they can be disposed of, then those who write about cricket in the future can be assured, as Nyren and Cowden-Clarke, Pycroft, Andrew Lang, 'A Country Vicar', Herbert Farjeon, Cardus, Robertson-Glasgow, H. S. Altham and the rest were assured, that they are writing about something important and alive. If not, then the anthropologists and archaeologists will have to move in.

AFTERWORD, 1989

IT SEEMS A CENTURY ago, not a mere decade. Jimmy Carter was in the White House and Jim Callaghan at Number Ten: a certain Leonid Brezhnev called the shots around the Kremlin. Zimbabwe was still called Rhodesia; no one debated what to call the Falkland Islands, Prince Charles was an eligible bachelor and Bob Geldof a Boomtown Rat. Perhaps the most startling contrast with today leaps out from the pages of *Wisden*, whose Editor, an optimist if ever there was one, headed his review of the 1978 season ENGLAND RICH IN YOUNG TALENT.

Even *Wisden*'s rose-coloured spectacles, however, picked out a couple of specks on the horizon, or blots on the landscape. One was the Packer affair, a cloud no bigger than a man's wallet, and the other an internal feud – a sinister plot by the Test and County Cricket Board to undermine the authority of the Premier Club which drew the sub-head 'MCC under Fire'. Both, we can now see, were emblematic of the upheavals Britain was to experience in the years ahead. These were ushered in by what sciolistic media persons liked to call a winter of discontent, a prolonged and chilblained festival of collective bloody-mindedness that is still painful to recall.

There are personal as well as professional and idealistic reasons for the lingering pain. It was particularly galling, at a time when the smart move would have been to hibernate, to be stricken with insomnia. Fortunately, as the selectors tell successive candidates to the England captaincy, 'adversity doth best discover virtue'. There was great virtue here, not so much in completing *The Willow Wand* (which as well as being a votive offering was fun), as in doggedly and

devotedly compiling a report to the government on a much less entertaining topic. It was doubly wounding, therefore, when this report,
though manifestly embodying all manner of unassailable truths, somehow got shelved. I am not clear about the details – by then I was
sleeping rather better – but as I understand it that particular administration soon collapsed.

There are different opinions about the upwardly mobile forces that
have governed our lives since then. All I can say is that if John Arlott
is right in maintaining that changes in cricket reflect changes in society
then our recent social blessings have been mixed. This does not imply
that the cricket authorities should be allowed to shuffle off their moral
responsibility for the game's predicament, as their soccer counterparts
try to do in the matter of hooliganism, by blaming some general
malaise that is said to flourish in present conditions, whether these are
good or bad. Indeed the cricketing establishment, having for so long,
in the teeth of the evidence, asserted the game's superiority in character formation, Empire-building, creation of team spirit and so forth,
ought seriously to be contemplating whether the top end of it actually
does more harm than good.

Most of the theories expounded in *The Willow Wand* are, fortunately, of the kind that do not get any righter or wronger in a mere ten
years. (Was it Chairman Mao who, asked what he thought were the
principal effects of the French Revolution, replied 'It's too early to tell
yet'?) Some of them do impinge, however, on cricket's recent sharp
decline; notably this question of leadership. Ten years ago it still
seemed sufficient to rely on the concept of cricket as a dream-world
which bestowed on its inhabitants almost total immunity from social
change and which required little more from its leaders than thick skins
and tunnel vision. The successors to the egregious Beauclerk, the
imperious Harris and the protean Warner seemed well-enough
equipped in this respect: indeed the Long Room and associated corridors of power were fertile sources of evidence for students of the
theory of transmigration of souls. True, there were sharp challenges
ahead. But labelling them – violence, show-business, nationalism and
so on – seemed somehow to reduce them to manageable proportions.

This was a snare and a delusion, the cock-eyed optimism of the aca-
demic theorist. I have no new theories, only the deepest melancholy.
Perhaps if I still played cricket, or got my own back umpiring, it would
all seem different, but I confess that I nowadays much prefer to read

about what cricket used to be like or to listen to the BBC radio team talk about their own fantasy version of the game than to watch it as it actually is.

Coarser-fibred friends (a regrettably high proportion of my acquaintance) have suggested that, just as H. M. Hyndman became a revolutionary socialist out of spite because he missed getting a Blue, I have turned against cricket solely, and I quote, 'because Yorkshire get screwed every year in the County Championship'. I refute this entirely: it is only one reason. Ten more years without success may have marginally increased the Yorkshire soul erosion noted in Chapter Ten, but critics should try to see further than their nose ends. After all, many years in the wilderness, with no-one listening, did not affect the reputation of the prophet Isaiah in the long run. Likewise Yorkshire's efforts to preserve true values ('Our Holy Grail' as separatists put it) against the venality of their rivals should be seen in perspective. Over the last ten years even the most insensitive to spiritual considerations cannot deny that the other counties' get-rich-quick policies (of which importing stars is part) have led to the further enfeeblement of the England team because of the domination of the domestic game by chaps nurtured in warmer climes and thus eligible to play for this country only through desperate selectorial manipulation of the regulations.

I am not, let us be clear, blaming overseas players for seeking to exploit their talents in the best way they can, nor suggesting that they should not be welcomed, with open arms and purses, as fine cricketers and entertainers, into the popular show-business versions of the game that now abound. I am simply arguing that the TCCB ought not to have thrust themselves greedily into proprietorship of the emergent commercial circus in the 1970s. Morality obviously didn't remotely concern them, and in this they can perhaps claim to be upholding tradition. Even so they ran a grave risk. The Olympic Games clearly demonstrates what can happen when self-appointed guardians of tradition think they can safely sup with the devil without the customary precaution of a very long spoon.

The TCCB and their international counterparts had, of course, their own Faustian ordeal, and all in their various ways failed the test ignominiously. The British, chauvinistic, version of events, tends to lay most blame (as in related matters such as the *Spycatcher* affair or the decline in British newspaper standards) on vengeful outsiders and particularly Australians. At the end of the 1970s the twin monsters of cricket were Kerry Packer and the Australian Board of Control. Of the two, if one were seeking to blame outsiders, the Board of Control would make the more convincing villains for selling out on their pals. Packer, though tiresome enough in all conscience, seems a bit of a light-weight demon.

(I am struggling to retain some degree of objectivity and to put out of my mind the mingled horror and rage that comes over me whenever I see one of those televised pyjama parties, and especially that appalling sub-Disney steaming and resentful emblematic duck. A score of nought, of which in my time I amassed a better-than-average collection, is, I suggest, a matter between a cricketer and his or her Maker and the experience ought not to be cheapened in such a fashion.)

Whether Packer is, or was, a creep is not the issue. My point is that, at a time when the commercialisation of cricket, worldwide, and the release of player power were powerful inter-acting forces, he seems in retrospect less convincing as an exemplar of mainstream devilry than as a two-dimensional Mephistophelean derivative, supplying not the sin but only the temptation. The sin itself, surely, stemmed from the determination of the cricket establishment to cling to power. Their baffled reaction, after losing in court and having no moral highground to retreat to, was to try to fight fire with fire. Bringing in sponsorship and official one-day internationals to fend off Packerism reflected a belief, as naive as it was nasty, that there is such a thing as a free lunch. Hence what started as an argument over television rights became a struggle for cricket's soul. The TCCB and their associates kept it, but they shrivelled it up in the process.

What else has become clearer after ten years? I stand by my criticisms of Warner, which aroused some Blimpish reaction at the time. He may well have been as charming as his friends made out, but there is further evidence in a recent carefully researched biography of the hypocrisy that was my main target. I was wrong, though, about Boycott. At the time I still hoped he would do something to establish the concept of modern leadership gathering strength from true professionalism. Instead he seems to have wandered off, head in clouds of self-regard, into a Yorkshire jungle denizened with hard-faced reactionaries, badmen turned sheriffs, media persons and toadies.

The less said about Boycott the better, but whether in the process of over-rating him I was unfair to Brearley is another, more complex question. Brearley certainly seems a nicer chap than I implied, and more to the point can justly take pride in his status as England's last successful captain, a position for which there are currently few challengers. Carping critics may say that the success was achieved against weakish opposition, but you can only beat the opponents available. It could be argued that the case of choosing a captain regardless of batting or bowling skill has not really been fully made until it has been tested against the strongest opponents. Brearley was undoubtedly more fortunate in this respect than, say, the junior Cowdrey, pitted briefly against the rampant West Indies in 1988. But who shall say who might better have ordained the arrangement of deck chairs on the *Titanic*?

What Brearley did unequivocally demonstrate is the value in a captain – indeed the scarcity value – of intelligence, especially when native wit has been shaped by lengthy and expensive processes of higher education. (This last point has nothing whatever to do with my life-long professional commitment to prolonging and increasing the costs of these processes.) I say nothing of the specialist knowledge of psychology Brearley is said to have acquired, except that if this is regarded as an unfair advantage he surely needed something special to be able to cope, as he did, with the talented but undisciplined Ian Botham. Perhaps he could be called in as a special consultant for the England team manager, a recent device designed to make captains of all kinds redundant.

Botham, aged 21 and one of the Five Cricketers of the Year in 1978, was described in *Wisden*'s profile as a 'determined, straightforward, pleasant character, who knows where he is aiming, and who, in the best old-fashioned sense, has a good conceit of himself'. Two years later he was England's captain. Readers will have their own views about what went wrong, but it can hardly be denied that it went appallingly wrong, nor that the reason has something to do with the neo-Darwinian enterprise culture into which the TCCB so enthusiastically entered. It is no use relying, as some people seem to hope might happen, on Botham and the like suddenly realising the error of their ways. They will only do so when they are past hell-raising and trouble-making and want to make easy money as consultants, television show performers and so forth. Administrators, selectors, captains and fellow team-members must in future ask themselves, early enough for it to make some difference, whether or not the proclaimed values of cricket really matter or whether they want to condone, go along with or even encourage, for materialistic or other short-term selfish reasons, the attitudes of showbiz.

As to the captaincy it has come in recent years to be passed around like a parcel in a Christmas party game. Endurance and pachydermous qualities are clearly valuable attributes in the modern publicity-conscious era but whatever the explanation it was hard to bear the recent sight and sound of an England captain exchanging obscenities with a Pakistan umpire. The subsequent debate, in which tour manager and full-time side-kick looked for support from Lord's with as much moral right as Jardine and Warner had had on the bodyline tour, was if possible even less edifying. Gatting's subsequent dismissal, for something else entirely and something much less central to the question of cricket's decline, merely confirmed the ambivalent standards of those who control the game's destiny.

The same ambivalence is to be found in their attitude to South Africa and to overseas tours, havering and wavering as they do, in relation to political pressures; to grossly over-crowded tour programmes; to the foolish and self-defeating proliferation of one-day games; to umpiring – in short with regard to anything where money is involved or their own hegemony is threatened. Most serious of all, because it is entirely within the cricket establishment's own control, this ambivalence is applied to the question of violence, or if you prefer euphemisms, fast bowling. Dangerous play is condoned in part because of adherence to an ancient virility cult, sustained by a modern belief that it attracts crowds, and in part because its best exponents, match winners and crowd-pleasers of recent years, the West Indies, will not brook any curtailment of their mastery of so powerful a weapon. The current masters of the game are also resistant to attempts to counteract attendant evils that threaten the game's future, notably slow over-rates.

The end result, after years of compromise, new rules and new rule evasion, is that the quintessential error, acceptance of sustained dangerous attacks on the person as part of the game, has been absorbed and built in to all subsequent calculations. What all the committees and working parties continue to preside over, as annual protests in *Wisden* and the like grow more and more ritualistic and unreal, is institutionalised mayhem. In a year or two, perhaps, there will be a section of *Wisden's* records devoted to spectacular injuries. This can be extended in future to include deaths and the amounts of compensation paid to sufferers and dependants. Then, perhaps, it will be clear that the cricket authorities themselves, not some vague outside influence, are responsible for reducing the game to its present state.

Moral issues apart, can it be claimed that cricket has gained, aesthetically or in any other way from intimidatory bowling, with its Michelin-type batsmen and helmeted and shin-padded close-in fielders, a subject of slightly startled comment ten years ago, but now the norm? Are English cricket lovers pleased and proud that their Test batsmen, even if they have survived injury or shell shock, cannot score runs at the highest level? Do they look merely for the emergence of new and even more violent English storm troopers to extract revenge? Are they happy with the impact of the money-spinning one-day game on the values and the standards of English cricket? Are they content with competitions in which taking wickets is unimportant? Do they like a situation in which the best English spin bowlers are both long in the tooth and negative, and in which English batsmen can no longer play genuine spin? Do they really enjoy souped-up encounters in which slogan-chanting crowds applaud snicks through the slips? Surely not. Surely that's not cricket.

EXCULPATORY NOTE
BY THE AUTHOR, 2000

The Willow Wand, my first cricket book, was published in 1979. The world, back then in the last millennium, was a more sedate and dignified place than it is today; and the traditions of the world of English cricket were conservative in the extreme. Ancestor-worship was its sustaining creed and the life-blood of much of its admired literature. *The Willow Wand* broke new ground in seeking to explore 'the gap between myth and reality in this most English of games.' The audacity of this undertaking was not lessened by my acknowledgement that it was presented 'with an eye to its comic side rather than as evidence of the imminent collapse of civilisation.' It is unlikely that many defenders of the true faith were mollified by my assurance that the book, though perhaps not always reverential to the pundits, by no means sought to devalue cricket itself. On the contrary, it was 'written in deep affection for and appreciation of a great game that has survived despite the efforts of its leaders'.

In spite of this deplorably irreverent outlook, *The Willow Wand* had its admirers. Not all were dangerous radicals, either. Most were simply fellow cricket-lovers interested in exploring unfamiliar facets of their complex addiction. I myself, whilst naturally encouraged by the book's reception amongst liberal-minded reviewers, nevertheless did not wish to be cast in the role of moral crusader for the soul of cricket. My position, as I had implied throughout the book and spelled out in the final chapter 'Fun and Games', was that although playing games, or even watching them (even from the cheaper seats), can be 'good for you', in themselves games are ethically neutral, and best left so. Attempts to invest cricket with some superior morality and to make playing it a quasi-Christian experience were doomed to failure. As we have been sharply reminded by the disclosures that began in early April 2000, with match-fixing allegations against the South African captain, it is no mean feat, when money is at stake, to be able to put on a game that is contested honestly, with everyone trying to win. To seek higher standards of morality, as in the 'It's not cricket' myth, is asking for superhuman standards. To claim to have achieved them, as the cricket establishment were wont to do, is asking for trouble, and risks the charge of hypocrisy, which has been a prime target of English humour since Chaucer's *Canterbury Tales*.

Of course *The Willow Wand* had no pretensions to Chaucerian stature, nor even to be a pale prose shadow thereof. It arose simply out of my love of cricket and my concern about what was happening to it.

I had for many years been interested in the social history of Britain and particularly the sports that had helped to shape the nation and the empire. There were a host of them, and cricket was neither the oldest nor the most popular, but simply my own favourite.

Looking back now at *The Willow Wand*, after more than twenty years, is rather like watching a loved offspring perform in public for the second time, after a long interval when its youthful charms may no longer seem so evident as they did the first time. The temptation to 'improve' it for publication in this new edition was strong.

On reflection, however, it seemed better to present it, warts and all, in its original form, as a product of its time and a pioneering venture. This seemed the best way to re-capture at least something of that first fine careless rapture without the artificial aid of cosmetics or plastic surgery – the resorts of the ageing. Whatever its faults, it was written with a love for the game that may excuse, and with a certain panache that may help to compensate for, its gaucheries.

The 'Afterword' to the 1989 edition is a different matter, however. Written as the Thatcherite era was coming to its acrimonious end, it is not surprising if its tone is rather less cheerful than that of the book itself, and also more moralistic. This may have been the result of the political and economic crisis that enveloped us, or conceivably, of the deeper private anguish that Yorkshire had not won the Championship for over twenty years. (Mercifully I was spared foreknowledge of how much more of this evidence of divine displeasure was yet to come.)

All was not pain and grief. Perhaps after ten years I was able to see some of the controversies of the time through the glass a little less darkly. So, for instance, I took the opportunity to try to make amends to Mike Brearley for what had come to seem imperceptive treatment in Chapter Ten. Alas, after twenty years the amends seem some way short of what was needed. I ought, for example, to have warmly commended Brearley's fine book *The Art of Captaincy*, which had been published in 1985. Reading it again recently I start wondering what Brearley thinks of the present state of English cricket and of the re-organisation being undertaken by the ECB. Mulling over his final paragraph I am particularly intrigued by his concluding sentence. 'One who finds a career that fits in with some of his earliest dreams, and finds that career immensely fulfilling, is indeed fortunate.' I fall to thinking what a splendid thing it would be for cricket, if Mike Brearley could be persuaded back into the game for a few years to put his own stamp on the re-organisation. What it would take to lure him from his distinguished work in the 'real' world I have no idea, but it would be a public service if his seduction were to be undertaken, or at least essayed, by one of the leading head-hunters. Would he be tempted, I wonder, by the post of Cricket Czar? Or perhaps Watchdog? There is no such post at the moment, I know, but it can only be a matter of time. There seems to be one for almost every other object of social concern.

Coming back to the rather sombre 1989 Afterword, I see that Ian Botham is presented only in scapegrace mode. There is no mention of the most important – and perhaps the only relevant – thing about him: that he was a great English cricketer; probably the greatest since Denis Compton, and possibly, as some have suggested, since W. G. Grace. He was, at any rate, a true cricketing hero and his youthful off-the field peccadilloes, even as recounted, more in sorrow than in anger, by his 'uncompromising' biographer, Don Mosey, now seem little more than examples of the admired current fashion of laddishness. It can, of course, be argued that higher standards of conduct are required of English cricket captains (who are, willy-nilly, role models for the young). A similar argument has been used recently with regard to political leaders and other public figures on both sides of the Atlantic. It won some support, but eventually crumbled under the weight of public opinion, which sets more store by efficiency and integrity in carrying out the professional aspects of jobs in the public domain than by private morality. Standards today are more tolerant, not least in recognition of ever-increasing media pressure.

But let us turn to the less sophisticated but sweeter pleasures of the past when the world was newer and fresher, when we were very young, and our dreams were more vivid than Technicolor and suffused with love. And not just any old love, either – no mere earthly thing of passion, what Yeats called 'the fury and the mire of human veins', but a more sublime order of experience – that with which *The Willow Wand* began. There are numerous references in Chapter One to the reverence accorded to cricket in the upbringing of literary celebrities in the early twentieth century. Of the various writers quoted perhaps two will suffice. First Bernard Hollowood, editor of *Punch* in its palmier days and a Staffordshire county cricketer: 'I was brought up to believe that cricket is the most important activity in men's lives.'

And second, R.L. Hodgson, who wrote under the name of 'A Country Vicar': 'I was brought up to believe that the finest county in England (not only in size) is Yorkshire; that cricket is the greatest game in the world; and that the cricketers who play it best come from Yorkshire.'

In *The Willow Wand* I quoted all these writers playfully and often with an eye for the funny side of things. But I treasured these little snippets as characteristic of their time and conceived a great affection for their authors, for they evoke the delicious innocence of childhood. Their irrational belief in the invincibility of a chosen team is of the same order of credence as Santa Claus – a wish rather than a calculated assessment – and often a defiant hope against the odds. The Yorkshire myth had more basis in reality than most, as the record books will show – before 1968, that is. By the same token, though, their subsequent disillusionment and deprivation has been all the greater. This may at first enlist one's sympathies, for the loss of childhood innocence is palpable. But after constant repetition the result can be either pitied or excused, but scarcely warrants warmer and more affectionate feelings amongst outsiders.

Their many years of success in the county championship – when that honour really meant something – had bred in Yorkshire a belief that their way of playing cricket was the true orthodoxy: breeding a sort of Puritanism that led to the exclusion of players not born in the county, a blind faith that true loyalists clung to even when the team were being regularly thrashed by once-weaker counties now buttressed by overseas stars. Similarly Yorkshire's initial lack of enthusiasm for the one-day game involved a convoluted argument about the ill-effects of over-limit competition on young players in the leagues, Yorkshire's traditional recruiting grounds. This further accelerated the downward spiral of results and low morale, and stimulated the latent paranoid attitude to southern-based authority which grew stronger when Leicester and Somerset were able to spirit away two archetypal figures like Illingworth and Close, who both achieved great success despite abandoning the white rose.

Behind all this turmoil and apparently unfocussed bloody-mindedness was a pattern of misplaced and distorted idealism based on the belief that Yorkshire were the rightful keepers of the Holy Grail, envied and resented by 'foreigners.'

A few traces of this may be found in the final paragraph of the Afterword, along with some justified concern about the abiding but temporarily less-publicised problem of dangerous play. That I now seek to disown this misplaced and distorted idealism may indicate that my rational self is now in better control of my emotions with the passing of the years. Be that as it may, the evidence of events suggests that much of the 1989 gloom was unwarranted. The growing sophistication and consequent improvement in the over-limit game is plain to see. To take two simple examples: taking wickets is almost always valuable and often of critical importance; and spin bowling has an honoured place in the strategy of most successful teams. Techniques apart, there is nothing more exciting than a well-contested over-limit game. The Australia v. South Africa clashes in the late stages of the 1999 World Cup were simply unforgettable. And the great and continuing advance in its popularity suggest that the biggest danger to the one-day game now is that of staleness through over-exposure.

In general the concluding paragraphs of the Afterword are somewhat too rhetorical for my liking today, and the final sentence is more explicable as a wisecrack than as a wise remark. But even Chaucer might have taken his eye off the ball occasionally if his subject had been cricket.

NOTES AND REFERENCES

Chapter One: The Mythology of Cricket

1. Though Yorkshire had been playing county cricket since the end of the eighteenth century it does not seem safe to date the tradition of high seriousness earlier than Louis Hall, who was in his prime in the 1880s. Lord Hawke was very glad of him when he became captain in 1883, not least because of his sobriety (see Chapter 2). Tom Emmett, Hawke's predecessor, appears to have had a somewhat happy-go-lucky outlook. As a bowler he took plenty of wickets but also sent down an unusual number of wides. Once after Lord Hawke had taken over as captain, he asked him: 'Tom, do you know how many wides you have bowled this season?' 'Not the ghost of an idea, my Lord. How many?' 'Forty-five.' 'Then give me the ball, my Lord, and I'll soon earn talent money.' (See *Recollections and Reminiscences* by Lord Hawke, Williams and Norgate, 1924.)

2. Quoted in *The English Game* (ed. Gerald Brodribb), Hollis and Carter, 1948.

3. Quoted in *The English Game*.

4. Ronald Mason in *Sing All A Green Willow* (Epworth Press, 1967) includes detailed criticism of the poem.

5. *Cricket on the Brain*, Bernard Hollowood, Eyre and Spottiswoode, 1970.

6. *The Happy Cricketer*, 'A Country Vicar', Frederick Muller, 1947.

7. 'Memories of Fifteen,' an essay in *Herbert Farjeon's Cricket Bag*, Macdonald, 1946.

8. 'When Cricket Was Cricket' in the same book.

9. From *Strangers' Gallery* (ed. Allen Synge), Lemon Tree Press, 1974.

10. *Cricket: A history of its growth and development throughout the world*, Rowland Bowen, Eyre and Spottiswoode, 1970. See also *A History of Cricket*, Volume I, H. S. Altham, Allen and Unwin, 1962; *The History of Cricket*, Eric Parker, Seeley Services, 1950. For the early stages of cricket history all are indebted to the researches of H. P. T. (P. F. Thomas) and F. S. Ashley-Cooper.

11. *The Hambledon Cricket Chronicle* (ed. F. S. Ashley-Cooper), Herbert Jenkins, 1923.

See also John Arlott's Introduction to *The Young Cricketer's Tutor* by John Nyren (first published 1833), new edition Davis-Poynter, 1974.

12. *Felix on the Bat*, Baily Brothers, Cornhill, 1845. Later edition includes memoir by G. Brodribb, Eyre and Spottiswoode, 1962.

13. *Brightly Fades the Don*, Jack Fingleton, Collins, 1949.

14. *A Cricketer's Book*, Neville Cardus, Grant Richards, 1922.

15. *10 for 66 and All That*, Arthur Mailey, Phoenix House, 1958.

16. *All on a Summer's Day*, Margaret Hughes, Stanley Paul, 1953.

17. *Cricket*, John Arlott, Burke, 1953.

18. *Beyond a Boundary*, C. L. R. James, Hutchinson, 1963.

19. *The Field is Full of Shades*, G. D. Martineau, Sporting Handbooks, 1946.

20. *Autobiography*, Neville Cardus, Collins, 1947.

21. *English Cricket*, Neville Cardus, Collins, 1945.

22. *Cricket*, Neville Cardus, Longmans, Green, 1931.

23. Introduction by Andrew Lang to *Kings of Cricket*, Richard Daft, Arrowsmith, Bristol, 1893.

24. *The Cricket Field*, 1851 (1922 edition, St. James's Press, ed. F. S. Ashley-Cooper). Pycroft adds, to clinch the matter: 'Cricket can hardly be said to be naturalised in Ireland.' As Chapter 11 shows, a High Church dignitary in Ireland agreed with this and exuded reciprocal contempt. However, Rowland Bowen, in the most recent history of the game, casts serious doubt on Pycroft's view and even suggests that the emergence of the game in England in the seventeenth century may have resulted from Elizabeth I's troops in Ireland encountering the game there. His researches suggest that the early game was widely played in non-English-speaking countries.

25. From a letter quoted in *The English Game*, op. cit.

26. *Cricket* (ed. P. F. Warner), Longmans, Green, 1920. The chapter 'Playing the Game' is by John Shuter.

27. *A Few Short Runs*, Lord Harris, John Murray, 1921.

28. *It's Not Cricket*, Col. E. G. French, William Maclellan, Glasgow, 1960.

29. *Wickets In The West; Or The Twelve in America*, R. A. Fitzgerald, Tinsley, 1873.

30. *Jubilee Book of Cricket*, K. S. Ranjitsinhji, Blackwood, 1897.

31. Quoted in *The Charm of Cricket Past and Present*, C. H. B. Pridham, Herbert Jenkins, 1949.

32. *The Charm of Cricket Past and Present*, C. H. B. Pridham.

33. *Plum Warner's Last Season*, Ronald Mason, Epworth Press, 1970.

Chapter Two: The Warner Spirit

1. *Next Man In*, Gerald Brodribb, Putnam, 1952.

2. *Second Innings* by 'A Country Vicar', Hutchinson, 1933.

3. *Life Worth Living*, C. B. Fry, Eyre and Spottiswoode, 1939.

4. See *Cricket With The Lid Off*, A. W. Carr, Hutchinson, 1935; *Over to Me*, Jim Laker, Frederick Muller, 1960; *My Dear Victorious Stod*, David Frith, privately published by the author; *Wisden*, 1977 (on W. G. Grace). *46 Not Out*, R. C. Robertson-Glasgow, Hollis and Carter, 1948, also gives an account of W.G.'s prowess.

5. *The Young Cricketer's Tutor*, John Nyren. See also *The Laws of Cricket*, R. S. Rait-Kerr, Longmans, Green, 1950; *The Duke Who Was Cricket*, John Marshall, Frederick Muller, 1967; *Next Man In* by Gerald Brodribb; and the standard histories of H. S. Altham, Rowland Bowen and Eric Parker for the various references in this chapter to the changes in the laws. Gerald Brodribb is the chief source for breaches of the laws.

On the question of the width of the bat Nyren tells us that 'an iron frame, of the statute width' was made for Hambledon. Other clubs had these gauges, too, though there seems to have been little need to use them. Inevitably, however, W. G. Grace, a great stickler for his rights, is reported to have called for the instrument to be applied in 1884 to the bats of the Australians A. C. Bannerman and P. S. McDonnell. Characteristically, though McDonnell's bat was a little too wide, so also was Grace's found to be when the tables were turned.

6. *The Cricket Field*, Rev. James Pycroft.

7. See *Sort of a Cricket Person*, E. W. Swanton, Collins, 1972.

8. *Cricket With The Lid Off*. It did not rain and next day the Nottinghamshire players fielded in their ordinary clothes, hats and overcoats, while Hampshire made the required run.

9. *In Quest of the Ashes*, D. R. Jardine, Hutchinson, 1933.

10. Introduction by J. C. Squire to *Cricket*, Neville Cardus, 1931.

11. *The Young Cricketer's Tutor*. In the 1780s Tom Walker of Hambledon – he of the 'hard, ungain, scrag-of-mutton frame; wilted, apple-john face and long-spider legs without calves' – had tried round-arm. A gentleman of Kent, John Willes, had also tried it, inspired, according to legend, by the sight of his sister Christina giving him batting practice while she was wearing a hooped crinoline skirt which prevented her bowling under-arm. Edward Budd, another amateur, and the professional Lambert also tried it out. However, William Ward, who rescued Lord's cricket ground from debt, persuaded MCC to resist the change.

12. *A History Of Cricket*, H. S. Altham.

13. See *Life Worth Living* where Fry pokes patronising fun at Phillips' heavy-handed approach. Fry's hostility may have had something to do with the fact that Phillips was one of the umpires who no-balled Fry himself for throwing.

Chapter Three: W.G. – Too Clever to Cheat?

1. *A Few Short Runs*, Lord Harris.

2. The Australians, so the argument goes, had only three experienced players in 1946, so Bradman's presence as batsman and captain was vital. He was 38 years old and out

of practice and had been in poor health. He played in the first Test against medical advice and it was in the nature of a trial. Had he gone cheaply he might have retired, but his long innings changed everything. He not only played throughout the series but went on to take the Australian team to crushing victories in England in 1948. See E. W. Swanton's *Sort of a Cricket Person*.

3. *Farewell to Cricket*, Sir Donald Bradman, Hodder and Stoughton, 1950.

4. *History of Cricket*, Roy Webber, Phoenix Sports, 1960.

5. *Willow Patterns*, Richie Benaud, Hodder and Stoughton, 1969.

6. *Arlott and Trueman on Cricket* (ed. Gilbert Phelps), BBC Publications, 1977. Trueman adds: 'Oh, yes, he was a great Australian.'

7. *From the Boundary*, Ray Robinson, Collins, 1951.

8. *Scores and Biographies*, A. Haygarth, Volume I, 1862. The reputation of Lord Frederick Beauclerk, who was playing for England, suggests that honour might have been a minor consideration. However, he may have been temporarily incommoded. Haygarth tells us that Lord Frederick had his finger broken and nearly got lockjaw when Sherman, whom he had rebuked for slackness in the field, hurled the ball back at him.

9. *Test Tussles On And Off The Field*, D. K. Darling, published privately in 1970.

10. See *Next Man In*, Gerald Brodribb, for these and other examples.

11. *Cricket*, Neville Cardus.

12. Quoted in *The Graces* by A. G. Powell and S. Canynge Caple, Cricket Book Society, 1948.

13. *My Dear Victorious Stod*, David Frith.

14. Clement Attlee, quoted in *Beyond a Boundary* by C. L. R. James.

15. *Raffles, The Amateur Cracksman*, 1899.

16. 'The Deserted Parks,' Lewis Carroll: from *Collected Works*, Spring Books.

Chapter Four: The Feudal Ideal

1. *The Odyssey*, translated by E. V. Rieu, Penguin 1946. H. S. Altham jocularly refers to this episode as 'fielding practice'.

2. Altham writes that 'the Northern branch of the Nordic family preferred football to the French game tennis, but that . . . most of all did our forefathers enjoy hitting a ball with . . . a staff or club' and goes on to mention games like 'stool-ball, cat-and-dog, trap-ball and rounders'.

3. The full text is printed in *A History of Cricket*, H. S. Altham's history. It refers to two sets of payments, one at Westminster and one at Newenden. It is not clear whether the playing or the paying took place in those places. The historians assume it is the playing, and they tend to concentrate on Newenden, on the borders of Kent and Surrey, as part of the legend of Wealden origin.

Rowland Bowen, in one of the less convincing sections of his book, argues for the Weald as the birthplace of cricket in England because it was a wild area. He does not mention Westminster. Later on Bowen points out the popularity of churchyards for playing cricket, but he does not raise the question of whether Edward on the first occasion was playing in the Abbey yard.

4. *Cricket* by Rowland Bowen. Bowen elaborates on the theory that the name is derived, through 'criquet', from 'krickstoel', Flemish for a low stool, and not 'crycce', Anglo-Saxon for a staff. The point is hotly debated by serious scholars. As in his Wealden references Bowen is anxious to establish a Celtic origin for cricket. (Regardless of whether it is true or not, this seems a commendable way of challenging the claims of purists.)

5. The Book of Court of Guildford in 1598 includes the testimony of John Derrick that he 'with Diverse of his fellowes did runne and play at crecket' on 'a parcell of land near the Free Schoole of Guldeford' c. 1550.

6. In 1622 at Boxgrove in Sussex six parishioners were prosecuted for playing cricket in the churchyard on Sunday.

7. *English Social History*, G. M. Trevelyan, Longmans, 1944.

8. See *England in the Seventeenth Century*, Maurice Ashley, Penguin, 1967, and G. M. Trevelyan, as well as the histories of Bowen and Altham.

9. See *England in the Age of Hogarth*, Derek Jarrett, Paladin, 1976.

10. Trevelyan's reference to 'women . . . come to see the fun' is a reminder that amongst its other social attitudes cricket includes a firm belief in male superiority. Though women have been associated with cricket from its earliest days they usually appear in the role of helpmate – whether, like Christina Willes, bowling to their brothers or making tea and sandwiches at village matches. They also come in useful as mothers. W. G. Grace, one of five cricketing brothers, wrote: 'Though my mother did not lay claim to being considered a player, I am inclined to believe, judging by the light of later years, that she knew how to play as well as any of them; she was certainly most enthusiastic, and ever ready with sound counsel or cheering words.' (*Cricket*, J. W. Arrowsmith, Bristol, 1891).

The working-class version emerges in H. V. Morton's description (in *A London Year*, Methuen, 1926) of a family game in Hyde Park: 'Mother is twenty-eight and looks thirty-eight because like half the women on earth she is immolated on the altar of the next generation. However, today she is radiantly happy, for she has father and family together in an atmosphere of gaiety. She has forgotten the man with the rent-book, the gas-meter, the eternal problem of food, and a thousand things which to her mean married life . . . Mother hits them all over Hyde Park and looks like making a century' when she has to stop to feed the baby.

In middle-class circles it is usually as sisters that girls appear. Thus we find Alison Uttley, the children's story-writer, recalling (in *Carts and Candlesticks*, Faber and Faber, 1948) that 'Cricket has been the centre of our lives ever since I remember' and

'Cricket and church alike were holy.' This is the public-school tradition in which girls were modelled on boys to the extent of their own lesser capabilities and needs. It is this second tradition that has produced, eventually, a women's equivalent to the men's game, Test matches and all.

Fortunately, nothing seems to have come of an earlier type of women's involvement. The urban equivalent of Trevelyan's rustic bliss included such things as 'a singular performance between the Hampshire and the Surrey Heroines', a match made by two noblemen in 1811 for 500 guineas a side. 'The performers in this contest, we are told, were of all ages and sizes, from fourteen to sixty; the young had shawls and the old long cloaks.' One Ann Baker, despite her long cloak, was said to be, at sixty, the best runner and bowler on the Surrey side. Afterwards both teams of Heroines 'marched in triumph to the Angel, at Islington, where a handsome entertainment had been provided for them by the noblemen that had made the match.' (*Pierce Egan's Book of Sports and Mirror of Life*, 1832.)

11. *The Duke Who Was Cricket*. See also H. S. Altham for details of the Duke of Dorset's kept men.

12. Introduction by John Arlott to new edition of John Nyren's *The Young Cricketer's Tutor*, Davis-Poynter, 1974.

13. *The Making of the English Working Class*, E. P. Thompson, Gollancz, 1963.

14. *The Cricket Field*, James Pycroft.

15. *Celebrities I have Known*, Lord William Lennox, 1876–77, cited by Sir Pelham Warner, *Lord's 1787–1945*, Harrap, 1946.

16. *Scores and Biographies*, Arthur Haycraft.

17. *Lord's 1787–1945*, P. F. Warner.

18. *A History of Cricket*, H. S. Altham.

19. *Lord's and the MCC*, Lord Harris and F. S. Ashley-Cooper, London and Counties Press, 1914.

Chapter Five: Two Nations

1. *The English Game of Cricket*, Charles Box ('Bat'), The Field, 1877.

2. Andrew Lang's Introduction to *Kings of Cricket* by Richard Daft.

3. *The Fast Men*, David Frith, Corgi Books, 1977.

4. *England in the Age of Hogarth*, Derek Jarrett.

5. Ibid.

6. *Many Furrows*, Alpha of the Plough (A. G. Gardiner), Dent, 1924.

7. *The Charm of Cricket Past and Present*, C. H. B. Pridham.

8. The story is told by Jim Laker in *Over to Me*. Laker does not emerge as one of Brown's greatest admirers in this book. He tells the story of 'Bomber' Wells of

Gloucestershire, in one of his very earliest county games, bowling his first ball to F. R. Brown, then a power in the land. 'Nearly had you, there, Fred, straight off,' said Wells, rather like Lamborn to the Duke of Dorset. Brown was not best pleased. 'Even members of Brown's own team would have hesitated to become more familiar with him than "Skipper". Usually it was "Mr Brown".'

9. *Echoes from Old Cricket Fields*, F. Gale, 1871.

10. *The Valiant Stumper*, G. D. Martineau, Stanley Paul, 1957. Martineau underestimates the part played by gentlemen, London as well as country-based, in setting the standards.

11. *Jubilee Book of Cricket*, K. S. Ranjitsinhji.

12. *Test Tussles On and Off the Field*, D. K. Darling.

13. *The Complete Cricketer*, A. E. Knight, Methuen, 1906.

14. A point raised by Peter Walker, the former Glamorgan professional, in a television interview with T. N. Pearce, the (amateur) organiser of the Festival for many years.

15. *History of Cricket*, Roy Webber.

16. 'Cricket and Australian Nationalism in the Nineteenth Century' by W. Mandle in *Sport in Australia*, McGraw-Hill, 1976. Dr Mandle, in a paper reprinted from the *Journal of the Royal Australian Historical Society*, 1973, is chiefly concerned to explore changing Australian attitudes towards the mother country's cricketers (see Chapter Six) but makes interesting points also about Australian and English 'shamateurism.'

17. *The Graces*, A. G. Powell and S. Canynge Caple.

18. *Arlott and Trueman on Cricket*. Dr Mandle in the paper quoted above refers to the money-grabbing behaviour of the 1863–64 tourists who had brought equipment to sell, greedily sought gifts or cheap purchases of gold and jewellery, and liked the high-life, preferably free. The amateur E. M. Grace got £500 expenses. Shamateurism did not end with the golden age: it merely became taken more for granted. By the time the distinction was removed it was often hard to tell the difference. But it was increasingly resented by the more socially-conscious professionals. Jim Laker in his splendidly truculent book tells how on the 1958–59 tour the 'amateurs' were paid broken time. That was one thing, but when the idea spread abroad that this might be regarded as compensation and become tax-free, Laker says he began to think seriously of reverting to amateur status. 'I might have been better off.' He is particularly scathing about amateur captains masquerading as county club secretaries. M. J. K. Smith gets special mention.

19. *Follow On*, E. W. Swanton, Collins, 1977.

Chapter Six: Imperialism and the Great Game

1. *A Few Short Runs*, Lord Harris.

2. *Wickets in the West*, R. A. Fitzgerald.

3. *The Crisis of Imperialism*, Richard Shannon, Hart-Davis, MacGibbon, 1974.

4. Quoted in *Cricket* by Rowland Bowen.

5. *Poems Old and New*, Sir Henry Newbolt, 1912.

6. *Character and Sportsmanship*, Sir Theodore Cook, Williams and Norgate, 1927.

7. *They Made Cricket*, G. B. Martineau, Museum Press, 1956.

8. *The Cricket Field*, Rev. James Pycroft.

9. *England Versus Australia*, David Frith, Lutterworth Press, 1977.

10. The source of this and much of the other information about Australian attitudes incorporated in this chapter is the fascinating paper by the Australian historian Dr W. Mandle noted in Chapter Five ('Cricket and Australian Nationalism in the Nineteenth Century', reprinted in *Sport in Australia*). Mandle's account of the Sydney riot of 1879 illustrates, *inter alia*, the very real sensitivity amongst Australians about the possible effects of the criminal origins of some early settlers – and the lack of sensitivity to their feelings by some English visitors, perhaps. Though gambling, inter-colonial rivalry causing suspicion of the umpires, and fervour to win may have been partly to blame, it seems that physical violence only started when one of the two English profession-als called the mob 'nothing but sons of convicts'. He quotes widely from the contemporary periodical literature to demonstrate the changes that took place in Australian minds and hearts in the second half of the nineteenth century and the part cricket played in the process. Mandle also explains the apparent paradox that amateurs were more expensive tourists than professionals. He cites reports from 1864 to 1873 dealing with the negotiations over amateurs' expenses.

11. *On Top Down Under*, Ray Robinson, Cassell, Australia, 1976.

12. *Cricket With The Lid Off*, A. W. Carr.

13. *On Top Down Under*, Ray Robinson.

14. *Bradman*, Philip Lindsay, Phoenix House, 1951.

15. *Cricket Crisis*, Jack Fingleton, Collins, 1946.

Chapter Seven: Bodyline and the Premier Club

1. *Second Innings*, Neville Cardus. Some cricket legends are so powerful that they are attributed to the heroes of successive generations. Thus F. S. Trueman has been cred-ited with exploits and sayings of distinguished predecessors, such as John Jackson. Here Cardus is telling an elaborate and more socially-conscious version of an anecdote recounted of the Duke of Dorset in his time. When hemmed in by close fielders, we learn, 'His Grace gently expostulated with them on this unfair move and pointed out their danger, which having no effect, he, with proper spirit, made full play at a ball and in doing so brought one of the gentlemen to the ground.' (Quoted by John Clark in *Cricket*, David and Charles, 1972.) The Duke's response, it is worth noting, is in the classical tradition.

2. *In Quest of the Ashes*, D. R. Jardine; *Cricket Crisis*, Jack Fingleton.

3. *Cricket Between Two Wars*, P. F. Warner, Chatto and Windus, 1944.

4. *On Top Down Under*, Ray Robinson. Robinson returned to the subject later in *The Wildest Tests*, Pelham, 1972. His account confirms the point that Warner, for all his subsequent judicious journalism, fell short of his duties as manager. 'From later talks with Woodfull,' writes Robinson, 'I gathered that he felt his words might bring home to the team managers the necessity for them to do something about tactics that threatened to ruin the game. In this his utterance was ineffective.' (Incidentally Robinson also makes clear that it was the leaking of this exchange to the press that turned Warner against Jack Fingleton, a journalist, whom he mistakenly supposed to have been responsible, leading to the episode referred to in Chapter Nine in which the manager offered Larwood a pound to dispose of Fingleton quickly.)

Robinson's account of the actual events on the field in the bodyline tests is full and frank without being in any way sensational. He tells vividly the story of how in the second Test at Adelaide on 14 February Jardine went completely beyond the pale. The fifth ball of Larwood's second over was inches from Woodfull's head. The sixth hit him over the heart and he doubled up in pain. Then, as Larwood's own account had told, Jardine said 'Well bowled, Harold,' a remark, Robinson says, intended to convince the other batsman Bradman that they were deliberately aiming to hit the batsmen. Then, as Larwood ran up to deliver the next ball, Jardine stopped him and ostentatiously moved the slip-fielders over into the leg-trap.

5. *Bodyguard of Lies*, Anthony Cave-Brown, W. H. Allen, 1976.

6. *Farewell to Cricket*, Sir Donald Bradman, Hodder and Stoughton, 1950.

7. *Bodyline?*, Harold Larwood, E. Mathews and Marrot, 1933.

8. *Cricket With The Lid Off*, A. W. Carr.

9. *History of Indian Cricket*, Edward Docker, Macmillan Co. of India, 1976.

10. *Cricket Between Two Wars*, P. F. Warner.

11. *History of Indian Cricket*, Edward Docker.

12. Ibid.

13. *Sort of a Cricket Person*, E. W. Swanton.

14. *Lord's 1787–1945*, Sir Pelham Warner.

15. *Cricket Between Two Wars*, P. F. Warner.

16. *Cricket With The Lid Off*, A. W. Carr.

17. *Express Deliveries*, W. E. Bowes, Stanley Paul, 1953.

Chapter Eight: Born Leaders: Lord Harris and Lord Hawke

1. *A Few Short Runs*, Lord Harris.

2. Article in *Wisden*, 1974, by C. T. Bennett.

3. *Lord's*, P. F. Warner.

4. *Cricket With The Lid Off*, A. W. Carr.

5. *Lord's*, P. F. Warner.

6. *Cricket Highways and Byways*, F. S. Ashley-Cooper, Allen and Unwin, 1927.

7. *W. G. Grace*, Bernard Darwin, Duckworth, 1934.

8. *Brightly Fades the Don*, Jack Fingleton.

9. *Headingley*, John Marshall, Pelham Books, 1970.

10. *Express Deliveries*, W. E. Bowes.

11. *Headingley*, John Marshall.

12. *Arlott and Trueman on Cricket*, ed. Gilbert Phelps, BBC Publications, 1977.

13. *Cricket's Secret History*, Walter Hammond, Stanley Paul, 1952.

Chapter Nine: The Magic Circle

1. *M.C.C.*, Colin Cowdrey, Hodder and Stoughton, 1976.

2. *Pro: An English Tragedy*, Bruce Hamilton, Cresset Press, 1946.

3. *Cricket's Secret History*, Walter Hammond.

4. *Autobiography*, Neville Cardus.

5. *Cricket*, Neville Cardus.

6. *Autobiography*, Neville Cardus.

7. *The Complete Cricketer*, Albert E. Knight.

8. *Bernard Shaw*, Hesketh Pearson, Macdonald and Jane's, 1976.

9. *Cricket Gallery* (ed. David Frith), Lutterworth Press, 1976.

10. *Sort of a Cricket Person*, E. W. Swanton.

Chapter Ten: Loyalties and Modern Values

1. *Cricket*, Rowland Bowen.

2. Richie Benaud in *Wisden*, 1973. Benaud later became one of the chief associates of Kerry Packer.

3. Article in *The Cricketer* quoted in *The English Game* (ed. Gerald Brodribb).

4. *Autobiography*, Neville Cardus.

5. Article by John Armitage in *The Cricketer*, quoted in *The English Game*.

6. We should notice that Yorkshire's policy is nothing to do with racialism, as such. In February 1978 it was announced that Steven Gurphal Singh, born of Indian parents in Ilkley sixteen years earlier, was being regarded as a future county player. They have traditionally been scornful of Lancashire's exotic imports, from E. A. McDonald, a Tasmanian, to Sonny Ramadhin and Clive Lloyd of the West Indies and Farokh Engineer of India, but this is because they were not born and bred in Lancashire. It is a fundamentalist concept of the county as a source of pride.

7. 'Brearley Provides Room at the Top for Boycott', *The Times*, 7 August, 1978.

8. 'Boycott Back in Ring', *Guardian*, 7 August, 1978.

9. When Brearley, coming in at 301 for 3, struggled to 50 on the second day, having been subjected to slow hand-clapping and other derisive noises by the Trent Bridge crowd, the selectors' sighs of relief could be heard for miles around.

10. 'Hampshire Should Not be Tempted by Overseas Market', *The Times*, 8 August, 1978.

11. Reported in *The Times*, 12 August, 1978. Amiss was eventually re-engaged.

Chapter Eleven: Beyond the Boundary in the West Indies

1. *Cricket*, John Arlott.

2. Quoted in *Football*, Nicholas Mason.

3. The nearest approach to disorder in a Test match in England was in 1921 at Old Trafford when about 6,000 people waited through a Saturday of recurring showers only to be told at 4.30 p.m. that play was to be abandoned. Several hundred invaded the pitch but were ushered away by the constabulary and placated by offers of tickets for the Monday. This was the day when the Hon. L. H. Tennyson tried to declare at 5.40 p.m. on what had become the first day of a two-day match, which turned out to be illegal and to save the Australians from 20 minutes in the field. The baffled crowd hooted the Australians, and in particular Warwick Armstrong, chiefly, it seems, on principle.

In 1884 there had been an ugly scene in a representative game when the Players of England, on the brink of defeat by W. L. Murdoch's Australians, wanted to get it over with before lunch but were prevented by the tourists themselves, who wanted to prolong the game until after lunch in order to avoid heavy losses by the caterers. A section of the crowd took exception to this and marched to the middle and grabbed the stumps. (See Ray Robinson, *The Wildest Tests*.)

4. Article by Clive Taylor, *Wisden*, 1974.

5. *Cricket*, Rowland Bowen.

6. Article by Sir Learie (later Lord) Constantine, *Wisden*, 1966.

7. *Phoenix History of Cricket*, Roy Webber.

8. *The Wildest Tests*, Ray Robinson.

9. *Island Cricketers*, Clyde Walcott, Hodder and Stoughton, 1958.

10. *Through the Caribbean*, Alan Ross, Hamish Hamilton, 1960. Alan Ross is by any standards one of the best of cricket writers. On cricket itself he is shrewd and perceptive, vivid rather than lyrical. And his tour books show an awareness that is well-nigh unique of the lands that house the cricket-fields: they are amongst the best of trade books. He is witty and colourful, and he can convey in a single adjective what lesser writers fumble to say in several lines.

Sometimes, indeed, his adjectives refer to things of which cricket writers seem dimly, if at all, aware. Nationalism and colonialism are two such. In two pages towards the end of his book he reveals a more sympathetic understanding of the West Indian situation, as it then was, than had crept into cricket literature. His account of the Port of Spain riot and what followed has the distinct advantage of appearing to be about real people.

11. *M.C.C.*, Colin Cowdrey. Cowdrey's account differs slightly from that of Ray Robinson who writes: 'The decision was a formality, because Butcher, turning with the shot, saw the ball settle in Parks' red-palmed glove and walked without looking to see how Sang Hue was answering the Englishmen's appeal. As he turned away, however, some of the crowd took a shake of his head for disagreement rather than a sign of his feelings about having to bat on so execrable a pitch.'

12. Many people may never have taken them very seriously in the first place. Those beamed by Gilchrist would be unlikely to do so. Nor would those who remembered Charlie Griffith rearing them up at the young Derek Underwood, a frail-looking tail-end batsman. The Editor of *Wisden* severely criticised Roberts and Holding for hurling bouncers at the veterans John Edrich and Brian Close at Old Trafford in 1976. But only the myth of 'more than a game' would lead anyone to expect any different. That racial characteristics exist – except insofar as they reflect cultural and environmental differences – has yet to be demonstrated. Games-players cannot shed their cultural backgrounds altogether, but games come as near as anything can to pitting man against man. And essentially men of all countries and all ages have more in common than they have differences.

Chapter Twelve: The South African Connection

1. *Pavilioned in Splendour*, A. A. Thomson, Museum Press, 1956.
2. *Cricket*, Rowland Bowen.
3. *M.C.C.*, Colin Cowdrey.
4. *Sort of a Cricket Person*, E. W. Swanton; *M.C.C.*, Colin Cowdrey.
5. Quoted in 'The South African Tour Dispute: A record of conflict' by Irving Rosenwater (*Wisden*, 1971) – a factual account from which the summary of events in this chapter is drawn.

Chapter Thirteen: Cardus and the Aesthetic Fallacy

1. *Days In The Sun*, Neville Cardus, Jonathan Cape, 1929.
2. 'Artists and Cricketers', Neville Cardus, from *The Summer Game*, Jonathan Cape, 1929.

3. *The Principles of Art*, R. G. Collingwood, Oxford, 1938.

4. 'Sutcliffe and I', J. B. Priestley, from *Open House*, Heinemann, 1927.

5. *Good Days*, Neville Cardus, Jonathan Cape, 1934.

6. *A Cricketer's Book*, Neville Cardus.

7. *Plum Warner's Last Season*, Ronald Mason.

8. *Jack Hobbs*, Ronald Mason, Hollis and Carter, 1960.

9. *C. B. Fry*, Denzil Batchelor, Phoenix House, 1951.

10. *Cricket*, Neville Cardus.

11. *Overthrows*, J. M. Kilburn, Stanley Paul, 1975.

12. *Both Sides of the Road*, Robert Lynd, Methuen, 1934.

13. *A Cricketer's Book*, Neville Cardus.

14. *Days In The Sun*, Neville Cardus.

15. *My Reminiscences*, S. M. J. Woods, Chapman and Hall, 1925.

16. 'The Jam Sahib of Nawanagar' from *Pillars of Society*, A. G. Gardiner, Nesbit, 1913.

17. *Life Worth Living*, C. B. Fry.

18. *Readings in the Aesthetics of Sport* (ed. H. T. A. Whiting and D. W. Masterson), Lepus Books, 1974.

19. *46 Not Out*, R. C. Robertson-Glasgow, Hollis and Carter, 1945. Robertson-Glasgow's description of Sammy Woods is too long to quote in full and does not readily lend itself to selection but it is as fine a short essay as there is in cricket literature.

20. Ibid. Lord's is unquestionably a holy place. Compare J. M. Kilburn: 'I once recommended an Australian visitor to go to Lord's and immediately he referred to it as the place where you take your hat off as you go in! No gesture could be more appropriate, for Lord's does command respect and in return it has to offer the most delightful prospect cricketers can know.' (*In Search of Cricket*, Arthur Barker, 1937.)

21. *Cricket*, Neville Cardus.

22. *Good Days*, Neville Cardus.

23. *Cricket Prints*, R. C. Robertson-Glasgow, Laurie, 1943. Some writers saw no reason to change their adjectives as fastidiously as Robertson-Glasgow. G. J. V. Weitzall, for instance, a Woolley enthusiast and assiduous correspondent of *The Cricketer*, gave his editor, P. F. Warner, quite a bit of trouble: 'The vocabulary of cricket is doubtless limited, but Gerry often used the same adjectives five times in three lines . . . I suggested that he should do a course of Macaulay during the winter and the following conversation took place.

G.J.V.W. 'What, the Yorkshire bowler?'

P.F.W. 'No, you d . . . fool, the historian.'

G.J.V.W. 'Well, anyway, you're lucky to have me, for every word I write is golden, and you know it, Pelham.' (*Cricket Between Two Wars*, P. F. Warner.)

24. Article in the *Manchester Guardian*, 1938. Reprinted in *Cardus on Cricket*, Souvenir Press, 1977.

25. *Pillars of Society*, A. G. Gardiner.

26. *A Prince of India on the Prince of Games*, Francis Thompson, quoted in *The English Game*.

27. *Cricket – An Enduring Art*, Sir Robert Menzies, *Wisden*, 1963.

28. *46 Not Out*, R. C. Robertson-Glasgow.

29. *The Ashes Crown The Year*, Jack Fingleton, Collins, 1954.

30. *Between The Wickets* (ed. E. Parker), Philip Allan and Co., 1926.

Chapter Fourteen: Brute Force

1. *Good Days*, Neville Cardus. Bodyline would have been a heavy price to pay for the elimination of cant, even if it had actually done so.

2. *Australian Summer*, Neville Cardus, Jonathan Cape, 1939.

3. *The Croucher*, Gerald Brodribb, London Magazine Editions, 1975.

4. *Kings of Cricket*, Richard Daft.

5. *A Few Short Runs*, Lord Harris.

6. *The Fast Men*, David Frith.

7. *Cricket All His Life*, E. V. Lucas, Rupert Hart-Davis, 1951.

8. *It's Not Cricket*, E. G. French.

9. *Back To The Mark*, Dennis Lillee (as told to Ian Brayshaw), Hutchinson, 1974.

10. *Over to Me*, Jim Laker.

11. *The Larwood Story*, Harold Larwood (with Kevin Perkins), W. H. Allen, 1965.

12. *The Fast Men*, David Frith.

13. *On Top Down Under*, Ray Robinson.

14. Quoted in *Next Man In*, Gerald Brodribb.

15. *Bowling and the Bowler*, R. C. Robertson-Glasgow.

16. *Cricket's Secret History*, Walter Hammond.

17. Article in *Wisden*, 1976 by John Thicknesse.

18. *Follow On*, E. W. Swanton.

19. *Wisden*, 1976.

Chapter Fifteen: Fun and Games

1. *Homo Ludens*, J. H. Huizinga, Paladin Books, 1970.

2. *Confessions 1:10*, St Augustine. This and other references to the theory of games in this chapter are taken from *The Study of Games* by Elliott M. Aveden and Brian Sutton-Smith, John Wiley and Sons, 1971. Reference has also been made to the article by John Armitage in the *Encyclopaedia Britannica*, 15th edition.

3. 'The Psychology of the History and Organisation of Association Football,' *British Journal of Psychology* 31, 1940. Quoted in *The Study of Games*.

4. *A Pattern of Islands*, Arthur Grimble, John Murray, 1952.